The Collected Works of

Langston Hughes

Volume 12

Works for Children and
Young Adults: Biographies

Projected Volumes in the Collected Works

The Poems: 1921–1940

The Poems: 1941–1950

The Poems: 1951–1967

The Novels: *Not without Laughter*
 and *Tambourines to Glory*

The Plays to 1942: *Mulatto* to *The Sun Do Move*

The Gospel Plays, Operas, and Other
 Late Dramatic Work

The Early Simple Stories

The Later Simple Stories

The Essays

Fight for Freedom and Other Writings on Civil Rights

Works for Children and Young Adults: Poetry,
 Fiction, and Other Writing

Works for Children and Young Adults: Biographies

Autobiography: *The Big Sea*

Autobiography: *I Wonder as I Wander*

The Short Stories

The Translations

The Sweet Flypaper of Life

An Annotated Bibliography of the
 Works of Langston Hughes

The Collected Works of

Langston Hughes

Volume 12

Works for Children and
Young Adults: Biographies

Edited with an Introduction
by Steven C. Tracy

University of Missouri Press
Columbia and London

Copyright © 2001 by Ramona Bass and Arnold Rampersad, Administrators
   of the Estate of Langston Hughes
Introduction copyright © 2001 by Steven C. Tracy
Chronology copyright © 2001 by Arnold Rampersad
University of Missouri Press, Columbia, Missouri 65201
Printed and bound in the United States of America
All rights reserved
5 4 3 2 1   05 04 03 02 01

Library of Congress Cataloging-in-Publication Data

Hughes, Langston, 1902–1967
   [Works. 2001]
   The collected works of Langston Hughes / edited with an introduction by
Steven C. Tracy
      p. cm.
   Includes bibliographical references and indexes.
   ISBN 0–8262-1372–3 (v. 12 : alk. paper)
   1. African Americans—Literary collections.   I. Tracy, Steven C.   II. Title.
PS3515.U274   2001
818'.5209—dc21   00066601

⊗™This paper meets the requirements of the
American National Standard for Permanence of Paper
for Printed Library Materials, Z39.48, 1984.

Designer: Kristie Lee
Typesetter: BOOKCOMP, Inc.
Printer and binder: Thomson-Shore, Inc.
Typefaces: Galliard and Optima

Contents

Acknowledgments

The University of Missouri Press is grateful for assistance from the following individuals and institutions in locating and making available copies of the original editions used in the preparation of this edition: Anne Barker and June DeWeese, Ellis Library, University of Missouri–Columbia; Teresa Gipson, Miller Nichols Library, University of Missouri–Kansas City; Ruth Carruth and Patricia C. Willis, Beinecke Rare Book and Manuscript Library, Yale University; Ann Pathega, Washington University.

The *Collected Works* would not have been possible without the support and assistance of Patricia Powell, Chris Byrne, and Wendy Schmalz of Harold Ober Associates, representing the estate of Langston Hughes, and of Arnold Rampersad and Ramona Bass, co-executors of the estate of Langston Hughes.

Chronology
By Arnold Rampersad

1902 James Langston Hughes is born February 1 in Joplin, Missouri, to James Nathaniel Hughes, a stenographer for a mining company, and Carrie Mercer Langston Hughes, a former government clerk.

1903 After his father immigrates to Mexico, Langston's mother takes him to Lawrence, Kansas, the home of Mary Langston, her twice-widowed mother. Mary Langston's first husband, Lewis Sheridan Leary, died fighting alongside John Brown at Harpers Ferry. Her second, Hughes's grandfather, was Charles Langston, a former abolitionist, Republican politician, and businessman.

1907 After a failed attempt at a reconciliation in Mexico, Langston and his mother return to Lawrence.

1909 Langston starts school in Topeka, Kansas, where he lives for a while with his mother before returning to his grandmother's home in Lawrence.

1915 Following Mary Langston's death, Hughes leaves Lawrence for Lincoln, Illinois, where his mother lives with her second husband, Homer Clark, and Homer Clark's young son by another union, Gwyn "Kit" Clark.

1916 Langston, elected class poet, graduates from the eighth grade. Moves to Cleveland, Ohio, and starts at Central High School there.

1918 Publishes early poems and short stories in his school's monthly magazine.

1919 Spends the summer in Toluca, Mexico, with his father.

1920 Graduates from Central High as class poet and editor of the school annual. Returns to Mexico to live with his father.

1921 In June, Hughes publishes "The Negro Speaks of Rivers" in *Crisis* magazine. In September, sponsored by his father, he enrolls at Columbia University in New York. Meets W. E. B. Du Bois, Jessie Fauset, and Countee Cullen.

1922   Unhappy at Columbia, Hughes withdraws from school and breaks with his father.

1923   Sailing in June to western Africa on the crew of a freighter, he visits Senegal, the Gold Coast, Nigeria, the Congo, and other countries.

1924   Spends several months in Paris working in the kitchen of a nightclub.

1925   Lives in Washington for a year with his mother. His poem "The Weary Blues" wins first prize in a contest sponsored by *Opportunity* magazine, which leads to a book contract with Knopf through Carl Van Vechten. Becomes friends with several other young artists of the Harlem Renaissance, including Zora Neale Hurston, Wallace Thurman, and Arna Bontemps.

1926   In January his first book, *The Weary Blues,* appears. He enrolls at historically black Lincoln University, Pennsylvania. In June, the *Nation* weekly magazine publishes his landmark essay "The Negro Artist and the Racial Mountain."

1927   Knopf publishes his second book of verse, *Fine Clothes to the Jew,* which is condemned in the black press. Hughes meets his powerful patron Mrs. Charlotte Osgood Mason. Travels in the South with Hurston, who is also taken up by Mrs. Mason.

1929   Hughes graduates from Lincoln University.

1930   Publishes his first novel, *Not without Laughter* (Knopf). Visits Cuba and meets fellow poet Nicolás Guillén. Hughes is dismissed by Mrs. Mason in a painful break made worse by false charges of dishonesty leveled by Hurston over their play *Mule Bone.*

1931   Demoralized, he travels to Haiti. Publishes work in the communist magazine *New Masses.* Supported by the Rosenwald Foundation, he tours the South taking his poetry to the people. In Alabama, he visits some of the Scottsboro Boys in prison. His brief collection of poems *Dear Lovely Death* is privately printed in Amenia, New York. Hughes and the illustrator Prentiss Taylor publish a verse pamphlet, *The Negro Mother.*

1932   With Taylor, he publishes *Scottsboro Limited,* a short play and four poems. From Knopf comes *The Dream Keeper,* a book of previously published poems selected for young people. Later, Macmillan brings out *Popo and Fifina,* a children's story about Haiti written with Arna Bontemps, his closest friend. In June, Hughes sails to Russia in a band of twenty-two young African

Americans to make a film about race relations in the United States. After the project collapses, he lives for a year in the Soviet Union. Publishes his most radical verse, including "Good Morning Revolution" and "Goodbye Christ."

1933   Returns home at midyear via China and Japan. Supported by a patron, Noël Sullivan of San Francisco, Hughes spends a year in Carmel writing short stories.

1934   Knopf publishes his first short story collection, *The Ways of White Folks*. After labor unrest in California threatens his safety, he leaves for Mexico following news of his father's death.

1935   Spends several months in Mexico, mainly translating short stories by local leftist writers. Lives for some time with the photographer Henri Cartier-Bresson. Returning almost destitute to the United States, he joins his mother in Oberlin, Ohio. Visits New York for the Broadway production of his play *Mulatto* and clashes with its producer over changes in the script. Unhappy, he writes the poem "Let America Be America Again."

1936   Wins a Guggenheim Foundation fellowship for work on a novel but soon turns mainly to writing plays in association with the Karamu Theater in Cleveland. Karamu stages his farce *Little Ham* and his historical drama about Haiti, *Troubled Island*.

1937   Karamu stages *Joy to My Soul*, another comedy. In July, he visits Paris for the League of American Writers. He then travels to Spain, where he spends the rest of the year reporting on the civil war for the *Baltimore Afro-American*.

1938   In New York, Hughes founds the radical Harlem Suitcase Theater, which stages his agitprop play *Don't You Want to Be Free?* The leftist International Workers Order publishes *A New Song*, a pamphlet of radical verse. Karamu stages his play *Front Porch*. His mother dies.

1939   In Hollywood he writes the script for the movie *Way Down South*, which is criticized for stereotyping black life. Hughes goes for an extended stay in Carmel, California, again as the guest of Noël Sullivan.

1940   His autobiography *The Big Sea* appears (Knopf). He is picketed by a religious group for his poem "Goodbye Christ," which he publicly renounces.

1941   With a Rosenwald Fund fellowship for playwriting, he leaves California for Chicago, where he founds the Skyloft Players. Moves on to New York in December.

1942 Knopf publishes his book of verse *Shakespeare in Harlem*. The Skyloft Players stage his play *The Sun Do Move*. In the summer he resides at the Yaddo writers' and artists' colony, New York. Hughes also works as a writer in support of the war effort. In November he starts "Here to Yonder," a weekly column in the Chicago *Defender* newspaper.

1943 "Here to Yonder" introduces Jesse B. Semple, or Simple, a comic Harlem character who quickly becomes its most popular feature. Hughes publishes *Jim Crow's Last Stand* (Negro Publication Society of America), a pamphlet of verse about the struggle for civil rights.

1944 Comes under surveillance by the FBI because of his former radicalism.

1945 With Mercer Cook, translates and later publishes *Masters of the Dew* (Reynal and Hitchcock), a novel by Jacques Roumain of Haiti.

1947 His work as librettist with Kurt Weill and Elmer Rice on the Broadway musical play *Street Scene* brings Hughes a financial windfall. He vacations in Jamaica. Knopf publishes *Fields of Wonder*, his only book composed mainly of lyric poems on nonracial topics.

1948 Hughes is denounced (erroneously) as a communist in the U.S. Senate. He buys a townhouse in Harlem and moves in with his longtime friends Toy and Emerson Harper.

1949 Doubleday publishes *Poetry of the Negro, 1746–1949*, an anthology edited with Arna Bontemps. Also published are *One-Way Ticket* (Knopf), a book of poems, and *Cuba Libre: Poems of Nicolás Guillén* (Anderson and Ritchie), translated by Hughes and Ben Frederic Carruthers. Hughes teaches for three months at the University of Chicago Lab School for children. His opera about Haiti with William Grant Still, *Troubled Island*, is presented in New York.

1950 Another opera, *The Barrier*, with music by Jan Meyerowitz, is hailed in New York but later fails on Broadway. Simon and Schuster publishes *Simple Speaks His Mind*, the first of five books based on his newspaper columns.

1951 Hughes's book of poems about life in Harlem, *Montage of a Dream Deferred*, appears (Henry Holt).

1952 His second collection of short stories, *Laughing to Keep from Crying*, is published by Henry Holt. In its "First Book" series for children, Franklin Watts publishes Hughes's *The First Book of Negroes.*

1953 In March, forced to testify before Senator Joseph McCarthy's subcommittee on subversive activities, Hughes is exonerated after repudiating his past radicalism. *Simple Takes a Wife* appears.

1954 Mainly for young readers, he publishes *Famous American Negroes* (Dodd, Mead) and *The First Book of Rhythms.*

1955 Publishes *The First Book of Jazz* and finishes *Famous Negro Music Makers* (Dodd, Mead). In November, Simon and Schuster publishes *The Sweet Flypaper of Life,* a narrative of Harlem with photographs by Roy DeCarava.

1956 Hughes's second volume of autobiography, *I Wonder as I Wander* (Rinehart), appears, as well as *A Pictorial History of the Negro* (Crown), coedited with Milton Meltzer, and *The First Book of the West Indies.*

1957 *Esther,* an opera with composer Jan Meyerowitz, has its premiere in Illinois. Rinehart publishes *Simple Stakes a Claim* as a novel. Hughes's musical play *Simply Heavenly,* based on his Simple character, runs for several weeks off and then on Broadway. Hughes translates and publishes *Selected Poems of Gabriela Mistral* (Indiana University Press).

1958 *The Langston Hughes Reader* (George Braziller) appears, as well as *The Book of Negro Folklore* (Dodd, Mead), coedited with Arna Bontemps, and another juvenile, *Famous Negro Heroes of America* (Dodd, Mead). John Day publishes a short novel, *Tambourines to Glory,* based on a Hughes gospel musical play.

1959 Hughes's *Selected Poems* published (Knopf).

1960 *The First Book of Africa* appears, along with *An African Treasury: Articles, Essays, Stories, Poems by Black Africans,* edited by Hughes (Crown).

1961 Inducted into the National Institute of Arts and Letters. Knopf publishes his book-length poem *Ask Your Mama: 12 Moods for Jazz. The Best of Simple,* drawn from the columns, appears (Hill and Wang). Hughes writes his gospel musical plays *Black Nativity* and *The Prodigal Son.* He visits Africa again.

1962 Begins a weekly column for the *New York Post.* Attends a writers' conference in Uganda. Publishes *Fight for Freedom: The Story of the NAACP,* commissioned by the organization.

1963 His third collection of short stories, *Something in Common,* appears from Hill and Wang. Indiana University Press publishes

Five Plays by Langston Hughes, edited by Webster Smalley, as well as Hughes's anthology *Poems from Black Africa, Ethiopia, and Other Countries*.

1964   His musical play *Jericho–Jim Crow*, a tribute to the civil rights movement, is staged in Greenwich Village. Indiana University Press brings out his anthology *New Negro Poets: U.S.A.*, with a foreword by Gwendolyn Brooks.

1965   With novelists Paule Marshall and William Melvin Kelley, Hughes visits Europe for the U.S. State Department. His gospel play *The Prodigal Son* and his cantata with music by David Amram, *Let Us Remember*, are staged.

1966   After twenty-three years, Hughes ends his depiction of Simple in his Chicago *Defender* column. Publishes *The Book of Negro Humor* (Dodd, Mead). In a visit sponsored by the U.S. government, he is honored in Dakar, Senegal, at the First World Festival of Negro Arts.

1967   His *The Best Short Stories by Negro Writers: An Anthology from 1899 to the Present* (Little, Brown) includes the first published story by Alice Walker. On May 22, Hughes dies at New York Polyclinic Hospital in Manhattan from complications following prostate surgery. Later that year, two books appear: *The Panther and the Lash: Poems of Our Times* (Knopf) and, with Milton Meltzer, *Black Magic: A Pictorial History of the Negro in American Entertainment* (Prentice Hall).

The Collected Works of

Langston Hughes

Volume 12

Works for Children and
Young Adults: Biographies

Introduction

By virtue of his facility with language, his appreciation and understanding of the African American vernacular tradition, and his commitment to reaching a large audience through a variety of genres, Langston Hughes bridged the gap between the popular and the literary with a success that few could match. The elements that give Hughes's writing its broad appeal are the same elements that make his works for children so successful. They also may account for the assessment of Hughes's writing by some in the literary establishment as too facile to be taken seriously. Wonder, joy, enthusiasm, and optimism are common in Hughes's work, as is a persistent desire to maintain the audience's interest and understanding. This is not to say that Hughes was unaware of the complex social, political, and intellectual currents of his times. But he understood the need for directness, forthrightness, and immediacy in presenting his portrait of both a decadent American sociopolitical system and the cultural network that helped African Americans survive that system. In the African American vernacular, in spirituals and jazz and blues and gospel, one could find the courageous attempts of entire generations of African Americans to make sense out of a corrupt and hypocritical world. What need was there to obscure that achievement with foreign verbal tricks and gratuitous ingenuity? And why not tell that history in a variety of genres, in a number of ways, across a series of decades, not only to adults needing to know the full history of their country, but also to children who craved its spiritual and intellectual nourishment and its social and political motivation?

Hughes began writing works for children early in his career, alongside the works he produced for adult audiences and for avowedly political purposes. His collection of poems for children, *The Dream Keeper and Other Poems,* and his novelistic collaboration with Arna Bontemps, *Popo and Fifina,* were both published in 1932, the same year Hughes and Prentiss Taylor published the Marxist play *Scottsboro Limited,* which had appeared in the *New Masses* the year before. Hughes's humanistic convictions and social commitment motivated these works equally, though their approaches and tones varied according to audience. Indeed, many of the poems included in *The Dream Keeper* were initially published in volumes directed to the adult market, indicating that Hughes himself did not approach his work in terms of rigid audience "boundaries." It would be another twenty years before Hughes published another volume devoted exclusively to children's literature, and then he concentrated on nonfiction essays and biographies, occasionally with narrative frames or imaginative threads to increase readability for a younger audience. Still, his purpose remained to appreciate and celebrate the contributions of African Americans to the American enterprise and the human spirit while acknowledging the torturous path they had traveled, and continued to travel.

Langston Hughes approached the three books included in this volume as an artist committed to his race and to letting "America be America again" by reaffirming the principles of democracy through his writings. Hughes's earlier works for children and young adults reflected his own remarkable sensitivity to the issues and situations facing young people, as well as his awareness of the aspirations, wonder, and whimsy of childhood and adolescence. Yet, although direct and simple, as befitted his audience, the works were not naive in their portrayal of race and class prejudices. In the case of *Famous American Negroes* (1954), Hughes's tactic was to refocus the lens of history and culture on significant African American contributors to American and world history. Some of the people discussed in Hughes's three books were known more generally to an African American audience for their achievements as reported in the black press. Others might have achieved fame among African Americans through lessons in segregated African American schools. Some might even have been noticed by the white press. In the last category, for instance, Hughes calls attention to the intense scrutiny to which Jackie Robinson was subjected, but it is clear that the fame was generated to a large degree out of controversy, even though Robinson deserved his celebrity. But a more widespread fame was reserved for those who had access to or were accessible to the white-controlled publishing industry, which by and large aimed its books at a "white" popular market.

Famous American Negroes, then, is in one sense a very public missive, directed to a white audience. By describing the achievements of personages known in the African American community, Hughes was asserting that they deserved to be recognized by a broader public. By writing books that would provide future generations with more accurate historical information, he was providing African Americans with a recognition they had lacked.

In 1954, the year of the landmark *Brown v. Board of Education* decision declaring segregation in public schools to be unconstitutional, Hughes produced two children's books, *Famous American Negroes* for Dodd, Mead and *The First Book of Rhythms* for Franklin Watts. *Famous American Negroes* took literary aim at the vestiges of American slavery in the American education system, just as the *Brown v. Board* decision extended the judicial reach of integration. Hughes sought to correct misconceptions about African Americans by emphasizing in his introduction that in addition to learning about the lives of the African Americans who had been enslaved, children could look for inspiration to nonslave blacks and blacks who escaped slavery—Paul Laurence Dunbar's father is mentioned as an example of an escaped slave. However, Hughes was careful to emphasize that those who were not slaves were still affected by the institution because of prevalent attitudes about the nature and capacity of African Americans.

In this way, Hughes demonstrates that despite a diversity of backgrounds, a harmony of commitment was needed among his readers to continue the work of famous African Americans of the past. Furthermore, in spite of the adversity faced by African Americans in America, Hughes affirms that his readers can take pride in the fact that "American democracy has produced the largest group of outstanding Negroes in the world." Hughes is also careful to point out that the main ingredient for the success of his subjects was "great strength or great talent, within the flexibility which democracy possesses." Thus, his is an integrationist message, not a separatist one. But clearly American integration could succeed only if the openness, egalitarianism, and mobility characteristic of a truly democratic system were available to everyone. The book examines "how they did it" and "the circumstances under which they did it" as a way of encouraging children to recognize and be proud of their slave, fugitive, and free heritage. It describes exemplary lives and the circumstances surrounding them in order to encourage young readers to emulate those who made positive contributions to African American, American, and world history and culture.

As he did in his earlier *First Book of Negroes* (1952), in *Famous American Negroes* Hughes advises regularly about the benefits of education, religious organizations, civic responsibility, and hard work. He also calls attention to the beauty of dark skin, describing Phillis Wheatley, for example, as being "dark as chocolate . . . and rather pretty in an exotic African way." Notably, Hughes also mentions young Phillis's appreciation of the kindness of the white Wheatleys. In a poetically written ending, he imaginatively confronts the question of whether Wheatley ever dwelt on her African past, concluding that the style of poetry at the time prevented her from expressing her feelings on the matter. In this way Hughes encourages consideration of the accomplishments of these figures in their proper historical context. He emphasizes that poets like Wheatley were outstanding, even revolutionary, in their time, because they extended themselves, at the risk of ridicule and neglect, into arenas previously closed to African Americans. In this sense the volume can be seen as a commentary on Hughes's own life and art. He was surely aware of the risks that public utterance posed to the African American artist. In his own life he suffered the circumscriptions of patrons, the co-optings of the communists, the censorship of the right wing, and the intimidations of the Klan. He knew that his enemies would dog him determinedly simply because of his being in a place where he was not wanted, or despite his protestations at being misunderstood, or regardless of his repudiation of past publications during the McCarthy era.

There are affinities as well between Hughes and the other poet included in the volume, Paul Laurence Dunbar. Hughes's earnest retelling of the story of the young Dunbar's emergence as a poet while working as an elevator operator mirrors the experience of Hughes himself, who gained a measure of celebrity while earning his living as a busboy at the Wardman Park Hotel in Washington, D.C. Hughes, an early champion of the autonomy of the African American literary artist, also highlights Dunbar's ability to write in both dialect and standard English. He emphasizes the need for an artist to create independently, according to his own aesthetic, rather than kowtowing to the strictures of the intelligentsia or the critics. Dunbar's well-known dissatisfaction with writing what he unfortunately described as "a jingle in a broken tongue" in his dialect poetry demonstrates the ways in which the African American artist's work was proscribed and circumscribed by critical opinion. Significantly, Hughes quotes from Dunbar's "The Cornstalk Fiddle," a dialect poem that champions the beauty of art rooted in humble, even unexpected origins, an aesthetic that imbues much of Hughes's best work. The lines quoted from "Little Brown Baby" must surely have touched a Langston starved for parental love in their joyous evocation of a playful father's nurturing presence in his child's life. The themes the poem treats—the beauty of blackness, the importance of love, and the desire to protect the family from harm—are crucial in the lives and art of African Americans. And Dunbar's publication of his poetry with Dodd, Mead, mentioned specifically by Hughes, makes another connection in a volume itself being published half a century later by that same company.

Famous American Negroes does not contain the narrative thread that tied together *The First Book of Negroes,* opting instead for a straightforward, occasionally dramatically rendered biographical treatment of fourteen men and three women distinguished in the areas of literature, religion, theater, politics, education, science, the visual arts, journalism, music, business, labor, and sports. Twelve of the fourteen had careers that either spanned from the nineteenth century into the twentieth or took place wholly in the twentieth century. A number of these had been mentioned in *The First Book of Negroes,* including Harriet Tubman, Booker T. Washington, George Washington Carver, Ralph Bunche, Marian Anderson, and Jackie Robinson. Indeed, Anderson was also depicted later in *Famous Negro Music Makers.* As was the case in *The First Book of Negroes,* as a result of leftist political leanings Paul Robeson and W. E. B. Du Bois are notable in their absence, despite the fact that a few years earlier, in 1949, Hughes had named Du Bois to *Ebony* magazine as the figure he admired the most in literary race relations. Du Bois's opposition to Booker T. Washington's accommodationist policies as manifested in the Pan African Congresses, Niagara Movement, and NAACP is not mentioned in the Washington biography. Nonetheless, Hughes does recount the arguments of Washington's detractors, putting into others' mouths the criticisms of Washington as an opportunist, compromiser, and Uncle Tom. In this way he highlights the difficulties inherent in characterizing the adopted social and political positions of a man who could, in the introduction to the biography, be connected to Harriet Tubman and Frederick Douglass. Hughes tried to be both frank and fair, but clearly he had limits imposed upon him with regard to some subject matter.

In fact, editors at the press mandated a variety of cuts of material referring to specific instances of racial discrimination, excised the section on the blond-haired, blue-eyed African American Walter White, and removed a picture of Josephine Baker after the first printing as a result of a complaint that she was a communist.[1] Interestingly, although there were cuts amounting to fourteen lines in the essay on A. Philip Randolph, he is included as organizer of the Brotherhood of Sleeping Car Porters, is even admired for his work with the socialist *Messenger* (which

---

1. Arnold Rampersad, *The Life of Langston Hughes,* 2 vols. (New York: Oxford University Press, 1986, 1988), 2:229–30.

is described by Hughes with its slogan, "The Only Radical Negro Magazine in America"), and is cited for attacking American hypocrisy during World War I.

Despite the cuts and omissions, the book remained a successful collection of biographical essays, the rights to which were purchased by the United States Information Agency of the Department of State for translation into a variety of languages, among them Hindi, French, and Arabic. The symbolism and significance of the volume are clear: these were figures of international importance attaining not only a national but an international audience through the efforts of a literary figure whose own international fame in some ways preceded his national recognition.

Simultaneous with the writing and publication of *Famous American Negroes,* Hughes was generating other material for the adult and youth market. The year 1954 also saw the publication of the brilliant *First Book of Rhythms,* a true masterpiece of children's literature that demonstrated Hughes's creative sensitivity to the natural and produced pulses in the world around him. In 1955—the year Marian Anderson became the first African American to appear as a featured singer with the Metropolitan Opera Company, Charlie Parker died, and the folk music boom that grew in part out of the leftist interest in singers like Big Bill Broonzy, Josh White, and Leadbelly was reaching the American mainstream—Hughes published two complimentary music books for children, *The First Book of Jazz* (Franklin Watts) and *Famous Negro Music Makers* (Dodd, Mead).

While *The First Book of Jazz* focused on jazz musicians, *Famous Negro Music Makers* includes the contributions of African Americans in a variety of musical genres. The twelve men and five women profiled, all but two of whom are twentieth-century performers, include six stage and pop stars, four each from the classical and jazz/blues fields, and two involved with sacred performance, with Leadbelly as the sole folk singer. Ever mindful of his vernacular roots, Hughes catalogs a roster of artists in a separate section devoted to the jazz musicians so important to his artistic aesthetic. Throughout, Hughes details the dedication to craft, sense of mission, hard work, and catholic tastes of many of the performers. He describes James Bland as a gentleman of culture, Bert Williams's love of books, William Grant Still's study with W. C. Handy and Edgar Varèse, and Ethel Waters's adoption of orphans. But Hughes does not avoid the unsavory or the unpleasant. He refuses to gloss over Leadbelly's murder charges, the trials of the performance "circuit," and Lena Horne's refusal to appear before segregated audiences. Hughes also takes the time to discuss the money that a number of these performers make as one measure, but certainly not the only one, of their success. The portraits present artists both in arenas normally associated with African Americans and in those not often associated with them as a way of demonstrating talent without artificial limits. In several instances, Hughes specifically mentions how these artists willfully resisted the limitations imposed on them by others, as when the fathers of James Bland and William Grant Still attempted to dissuade them from their chosen artistic endeavors.

These Negro music makers as a whole are portrayed as successful world citizens who attempt in many cases to give back to their communities. Those in nonclassical fields are shown to be serious musicians, at times through their associations with classical musicians or music, suggesting not that jazz is less serious or valuable, but rather that musicians in each genre approach their creative work with a broad knowledge and set of skills. As the varied musicians swap inspiration within and be-tween stories, once again the notion of a world community united by one entity—in this case, music—emerges. The book confidently asserts the strength, pride, and worthiness of the African American artist, yet without any macho swagger. The contributions of these musicians, both artistic and social, as exemplified in the Fisk Jubilee Singers' use of the beauty and power of the spirituals to support the causes of literacy, ed-ucation, and social advancement, demonstrate what the proud and re-sponsible African American artist can do.

Hughes's next work of biographical portraiture, *Famous Negro Heroes of America* (Dodd, Mead, 1958), profiles sixteen explorers, military figures, and freedom fighters. The subjects are divided almost equally among figures of the eighteenth, nineteenth, and twentieth centuries, with one glance backward to Esteban, the sixteenth-century discov-erer of Arizona. Two are women and two, Douglass and Tubman, are also profiled in *Famous American Negroes*. Once again, Hughes calls at-tention to skin color frequently, from Charles Young ("of almost pure African descent") to the black Esteban to the very dark Harriet Tubman to the nut-brown Ida B. Wells to the light-complexioned mulatto Cris-pus Attucks, striving to foster pride in the variety of shades of African Americans.

Freedom—the freedom to explore, to live unfettered, to fight for one's principles, to fight for one's country, to affirm the worthiness of all human beings—is the focus of the book. In the section on Gabriel Prosser, Hughes makes it clear that a subject frequently avoided at the time of publication, the prevalence of slave revolts, was well worth remarking: "Freedom is a mighty word—and a word best understood perhaps by those who do not possess it. . . . Nobody ever enjoyed being anybody else's slave, so means of escape were always being devised." The book itself is one of those means of escape. It fights ignorance and racism and historical gaps with concrete portraits of sixteen authentic African American heroes and references along the way to "all the men and women, white and black, who had contributed to their freedom." Unfortunately, except for crusader Ida B. Wells, whose career straddled the nineteenth and twentieth centuries, none of the twentieth-century figures are political agitators or race leaders. Marcus Garvey does garner a mention in the section on Hugh Mulzac, who captained the S.S. *Yarmouth* in Garvey's Black Star Line. But Garvey, termed a "famous negro leader" in passing, is treated as only incidental to Mulzac's significant contributions to the World War II effort.

Hughes underscores once again in this volume the importance of interracial and intercultural understanding and cooperation to the fulfillment of the American promise of democracy. The aforementioned Mulzac biography notes that Mulzac refused to take command over a ship that restricted his crew to African Americans. Frontiersman James P. Beckwourth lived among the Crow and Blackfoot Indians, married an Indian woman, and died among the Crow. Frederick Douglass learned that not all white people, even white southerners, were bad. And Civil War hero Robert Smalls was celebrated among Lincoln, William Lloyd Garrison, Harriet Tubman, and Frederick Douglass at the termination of the conflict. As if to underscore the importance of cooperation and collaboration, Hughes interpolates a section from the writings of his old friend Arna Bontemps in his biography of Benjamin O. Davis, Jr. It was not, of course, the first collaboration of the two, and it comes, significantly, in a biography that describes how a father, Benjamin O. Davis, Sr., passed on to his son the strength and abilities that allowed that son to serve in a distinguished fashion in the same field the father chose. In the final story of the book, it was indeed fitting to bring together the words of Hughes and Bontemps to discuss how one generation could bestow its strength and pride on the next, since Hughes himself emphasized contributing to the communal legacy in his writing, and since one impetus for his biographies was to keep the stories flowing in ever wider and deeper channels. His writings frequently embodied the articulations of communal collaborators, demonstrating that the heroes of whom he wrote were from, of, and for the people they felt the responsibility to serve.

Langston Hughes devoted a substantial portion of his life to generating his verses of the American song. Like Walt Whitman, Hughes sang America, in a range of voices, moods, and settings. If Hughes attempted to make his poetic voice the amalgamation and culmination of a variety of voices, a one-man multivocal chorus, at least part of the impetus for his biographical writings was to survey the individual inflections that created that chorus. The old verse from the blues song, "If anybody should ask you, mama, who composed this song," recognizes the value of understanding who has created the world in which we live. Langston Hughes's art, whether poetry, fiction, drama, essay, autobiography, or biography, was a calling, and one that established him as among the famous American Negroes, famous Negro music makers, and famous Negro heroes of America he celebrates in his biographical books. Like Whitman in *Song of Myself,* as Hughes celebrates himself, he is celebrating the power and beauty and potential of all, be they farmers or philosophers, prostitutes or presidents, singers or the silent who deserve to be heard. His was a significant and beloved art of which he could be justly proud. So we complete the lyric: "Tell 'em it was Langston, mama, done been here and gone." Hughes has surely been here, leaving his significant mark on the lives of people the world over. And as for gone—well, Hughes may be gone, but the melody lingers on.

A Note on the Text

This edition follows the original books published by Dodd, Mead in 1954, 1955, and 1958. In preparing the text, I have silently corrected typographical and spelling errors. The original punctuation has been retained, except in a few cases where it was clearly wrong and not a matter of style or preference. Stylistic inconsistencies among the three original books have been allowed to stand.

These works reflect the spirit of the times in which they were written and may seem outdated in the light of social, political, and technological changes that have taken place since. While the biographies no longer function as up-to-date discussions of the subjects treated, they nonetheless provide us with valuable reflections on the world at the time in which Hughes was writing, and allow us to reflect on how much— or how little—has changed since then. Although many of those profiled herein were still living at the time Hughes wrote, no effort has been made to update the information provided. In addition, items such as birth dates that are inconsistent with more recent sources have been retained as in the original. Interested readers are directed to consult biographical dictionaries such as the *Dictionary of American National Biography* for more recent information on those profiled by Hughes in these texts.

**Famous
American
Negroes**

(1954)

To Ivan and Dorothy

Contents

Introduction

The history of the American Negro, contrary to common belief, did not begin with slavery. There were many Negroes in the Americas who were never slaves. Some of them came to the Western World as explorers. One of the pilots with Christopher Columbus, Pedro Alonso Niño, was, so some historians believe, a colored man. When Balboa discovered the Pacific Ocean in 1513, his expedition included a number of Negroes who helped to clear the first highway from the Atlantic to the Pacific, across what is now the Isthmus of Panama. And, four hundred years ago, there was an African, Estavanico, connected with the earliest written history of the American Southwest. This dark explorer came to the New World with a group of Spaniards who were shipwrecked on the coast of Florida. All but four of them were drowned. These remaining four, including Estavanico, wandered for eight years among the Indians, and eventually traveled as far South as Mexico City. From there, with Friar Marcos de Niza, in 1539 Estavanico set out on an adventurous trek toward the North in search of the Seven Cities of Cibola. These fabled cities of gold they did not find. But when, near the Rio Grande, the Spaniards tired of the desert heat, they sent the Negro on alone with a few Indian runners to bring back reports of what he found. Estavanico discovered and opened up to European settlers what is now the rich area of Arizona. His discovery occurred eighty years before the first slave ship arrived at Jamestown and the custom of selling human beings was established in North America.

From the earliest days of our history not all slaves remained in bondage. Some ran away to freedom—as did the sailor, Crispus Attucks, who died fighting the British at the beginning of the American Revolution. Some slaves were allowed to hire themselves out for wages and so succeeded in working out their purchase price. Others, like the poet, Phillis Wheatley, were granted freedom by their owners. And many like Sojourner Truth, Harriet Tubman, and Frederick Douglass not only escaped themselves, but devoted their lives to freeing others. Certainly before the War between the North and the South, in one way or another, for nearly two hundred and fifty years the lives of all the Negroes in America, free or slave, were affected by slavery. Just as since the War between the States, the lives of colored citizens have been greatly affected by the problems left in its aftermath. Freed without land, money, or education, since Abraham Lincoln signed the Emancipation Proclamation in 1863, the story of the Negro is one continuous struggle upward toward the status of full citizenship. In some parts of our country this goal has not yet been attained, although progress has been tremendous.

The careers of the famous American Negroes in this book were achieved, not only in the face of the handicaps which any other Americans might have, but *in spite of* the additional difficulties which Negro Americans have known—beginning with slavery when a man did not belong to himself but to someone else, and since continuing with such varied racial discriminations as not being permitted to vote, to go to a state university, to draw a book from a public library, buy or rent a house in some localities, or perform on the stages of concert halls in some sections of our United States. Such difficulties in one form or another are an integral part of the handicaps which each individual in this book had to overcome. Yet, with their great strength or great talent, within the flexibility which democracy possesses, they were able to make themselves into unusual men and women. *How* they did it is one part of their story. The *circumstances* under which they did it is another. The two elements cannot be separated if we are to understand what their careers mean both in terms of personal effort and of democratic possibilities.

American democracy has produced the largest group of outstanding Negroes in the world—from the Colonial poet, Phillis Wheatley, to the contemporary Pulitzer Prize winner in poetry, Gwendolyn Brooks; from the fearless fighter for freedom a hundred years ago, Frederick Douglass, to the recent champion of the world in the prize ring, Joe Louis; from the great Shakespearean actor of the early 1800's, Ira Aldridge, to such stars of the theater, radio, and screen as Ethel Waters or the late Canada Lee; from distinguished ministers of the slave period like Richard Allen, to Howard Thurman, Dean of the Chapel at Boston University. There have been many famous Negro citizens in our country. They have worked in almost all fields of human endeavor from the sciences to politics, the arts to sports, religion to business. It is my privilege now to write about only a few, but their careers are representative of many others of whom our country may well be proud.

L.H.

Phillis Wheatley
Whose Poetry George Washington Praised

About 1753–1784

She was a frail mite of a child, dark as chocolate, cute, shy, and rather pretty in an exotic African way. There was something about her delicate face and bright eyes that appealed to John Wheatley so, soon after the sails were lowered on the ship that brought her from Senegal, he bought her as a servant for his wife and their twin son and daughter. The little girl's eyes were wide at the busy wonders of a strange new world as Mr. Wheatley led her from the dock through the streets of Boston. But the cobble stones were cold to her bare feet, and the child didn't know where she was going, or whether to laugh or cry.

John Wheatley was a well-to-do tailor and he took the youngster to his comfortable home where she was received with kindness. No one knew how old the girl was but, because she was losing the last of her baby teeth, her mistress thought she must be six or seven. Since the child did not know a word of English, and no one in Boston in 1761 could speak Senegalese, not only the young one's background but even her name remained unknown. So the Wheatleys called her Phillis and gave her their last name, Wheatley. Before the girl was twenty-one this name, Phillis Wheatley, had become famous throughout the Colonies and even in England. This little African slave grew up to become one of the best known poets of her time.

It happened that Phillis had a gentle mistress who, seeing that she was a bright child, soon taught her to read and write. In those days in many parts of colonial America it was against the law, and certainly contrary to custom, to teach slaves to read and write. Nevertheless, by some good fortune, a number of slaves did learn. And some of them, even before Phillis had published her poems, became known as poets. A colored woman named Lucy Terry in Deerfield, Massachusetts, in 1746, wrote, among other verses, *Bars Fight,* a vivid rhymed account of an Indian raid on the town where she lived. Another Negro in bondage, Jupiter Hammon, began publishing poems as broadsides in Queens Village, Long Island, in 1760. And eighteen years later he paid tribute to the

Boston slave girl whom he had never met in his *A Poetical Address to Phillis Wheatley.*

When the ship with its cargo of slaves which included the delicate child whose name was to be Phillis dropped anchor in Boston harbor, the Thirteen Colonies were becoming increasingly resentful of English domination. The soldiers of King George III patrolled the streets of Boston. When Phillis was in her early teens, in the street where she lived, a group of rebellious citizens clashed with the British soldiers. Among these angry Bostonians that night was a tall Negro seaman named Crispus Attucks. When the Red Coats fired, Crispus Attucks was the first man to fall, shedding his blood for American freedom. His body lay in state in Faneuil Hall, and today there is a monument to his memory in Boston Common.

Five years later the Revolutionary War began in earnest under the leadership of General George Washington. During the siege of Boston, Phillis wrote a poem about George Washington, terming him "first in peace." Its closing lines are:

> "Proceed, great chief, with virtue on thy side,
> Thy every action let the goddess guide.
> A crown, a mansion, and a throne that shine,
> With gold unfading, *Washington!* be thine."

From his encampment the man who was soon to become "The Father of His Country" wrote the young Negro poet a most gracious letter, thanking her for the poem—"however undeserving I may be of such encomium"—and paying tribute to her unusual poetic talent. He closed his letter by saying:

> "If you should ever come to Cambridge or near headquarters, I shall be happy to see a person so favored by the Muses, and to whom Nature has been so liberal and beneficent in her dispensations.
> I am with great respect,
> Your Obedient Humble Servant,
> George Washington."

When the Revolutionary War was over and our country had achieved its freedom, Phillis Wheatley composed one of her best poems, *Liberty and Peace,* which begins:

> "Lo freedom comes. Th' prescient muse foretold
> All eyes th' accomplish'd prophecy behold:

> Her port describ'd, 'She moves divinely fair,
> Olive and laurel bind her golden hair!' "

And its closing lines are:

> "Auspicious Heaven shall fill with fav'ring gales,
> Where e'er Columbia spreads her swelling sails:
> To every realm shall peace her charms display,
> And heavenly freedom spread her golden ray."

New Englanders after the American Revolution continued to hold slaves, but the Wheatley family, perhaps in recognition of her genius, had already granted the young poet her personal freedom in 1772. Slavery for Phillis had not been harsh. She matured in a cultured home where, although it was most unusual for a slave to have a room alone, Phillis had her own room with heat and light so that she might read and write when her work was done. Certainly she profited by this generous consideration for the chronicles of her time report that she became one of the most cultivated young women in Boston—in a day when it was unusual for women of any race to be well read, to write poems, or to study Latin. Phillis read the Bible as well as Milton, Dryden, and other popular writers. Alexander Pope's translation of Homer was her favorite book, and his formal metres and carefully contrived couplets were the chief influence on her writing, in a day when the style in poetry was not personal, but high-flown and elegiac, with many references to classical gods and goddesses.

This amazing young African poet was received in the homes of many friends of the Wheatleys. She became a member of Old South Church. Some of the leading personages of Boston were her patrons and her poetry was widely discussed. Some people claimed a slave could not possibly have written it, but others wrote letters to the papers saying that they knew for a fact that she did compose her own verses. Since she was not treated as a slave, in her poetry Phillis wrote of bondage hardly at all. But she had known in Boston slaves less fortunate than herself. And, in one passage in a poem dedicated to the Earl of Dartmouth, it is clear that she condemned slavery:

> "I, young in life, by seeming cruel fate
> Was snatch'd from Afric's fancy'd happy seat:
> What pangs excruciating must molest,
> What sorrows labour in my parent's breast?
> Steel'd was the soul and by no misery mov'd

That from a father seiz'd his babe belov'd.
Such, such my case. And can I then but pray
Others may never feel tyrannic sway?"

Phillis was thirteen when she wrote her first verses. She was sixteen when she published *On the Death of the Reverend George Whitefield*. And she was only twenty when, because of her frail health, her mistress permitted her to go on a sea voyage to England. It was in London that arrangements were made for the appearance of her first volume, *Poems on Various Subjects, Religious and Moral*. In England Phillis Wheatley was a guest of the Countess of Huntingdon, who saw to it that she met many of the intellectuals there. The Countess was about to have her meet the King when, in Boston, Mrs. Wheatley became gravely ill, and Phillis sailed for home. Before she left, the Lord Mayor of London presented Phillis with a fine 1770 Glasgow folio edition of Milton's *Paradise Lost*.

Mrs. Wheatley did not live long after Phillis returned to Boston. And a few years later John Wheatley died. Their twins, Mary and Nathaniel, no longer lived in the family homestead for Mary was married and her brother was in Europe. Perhaps in search of a home and security, Phillis married a man, who, it turned out, was a jack-of-all-trades and a master of none. This husband, John Peters, worked sometimes as a baker, sometimes a barber, sometimes a grocery clerk; and sometimes he sported a gold-headed cane and a powdered wig and said that he was a lawyer or a doctor. Maybe John Peters married Phillis because she was famous and he wanted, without too much effort on his part, to "be somebody." They had three children but he did not take care of them well. Two of them died in infancy. After the third child came, John Peters went away, leaving Phillis to work as a drudge in a poor boarding house. Both she and the baby fell ill and, in the cold of winter, at almost the same moment a little before Christmas, they died. They were buried together. The year was 1784. The first American edition of Phillis Wheatley's poems had just appeared in Boston.

In those days, as now, poetry brought in very little money. Phillis died in poverty. Following the funeral, her rare and beautiful edition of *Paradise Lost* was sold to pay the debts her husband had contracted. Now the book is preserved in the Library of Harvard University. Since her death there have been published at least eight editions of the poems of Phillis Wheatley. Today throughout America many schools, women's clubs, and branches of the Y.W.C.A. are named after this poet whose brief life encompassed Africa, Boston, London; the confines of slavery and the hospitality of royalty; fame and poverty; the poetry of Homer, Milton, Pope, and the drudgery of service in a boarding house. Towards the end of her life, Phillis Wheatley, perhaps out of shame and poverty, lost track of most of her friends. They were shocked and surprised to read in the papers a brief notice of her death.

But Phillis was never ungrateful for the good fortune that gave her early in life the kindly guidance of Susannah Wheatley. When Mrs. Wheatley passed away, Phillis wrote to a friend:

"I have lately met with a great trial in the death of my mistress; let us imagine the loss of a parent, a sister or brother; the tenderness of all were united in her. I was a poor little outcast and a stranger when she took me in; not only into her house, but I was treated by her more like her child than her servant. No opportunity was left unimproved of giving me the best of advice; but in terms how tender! how engaging! This I hope ever to keep in remembrance. Her exemplary life was a greater monitor than all her precepts and instructions; thus we may observe of how much greater force example is than instruction."

To a sensitive little African girl, under the circumstances of slavery, fate could hardly have been more generous. The Wheatleys were good people. But in spite of their kindness, as a child, sometimes in the night, Phillis must have wept for her own mother. In the cold New England winters she sometimes must have remembered the sunshine and the palm trees of far away Senegal. In her teens as she read the measured rhythms of Pope by candle light, dim in memory, perhaps the drums of Africa came to mind. Did she try not to recall them because she knew she would never hear them again? Did she maybe cry? Did she sometimes feel lost and lonely like a motherless child? If she did, since it was not the fashion of her times to be personal in poetry, she never wrote about it.

Richard Allen
Founder of the African Methodist Episcopal Church

About 1760–1831

Religion was a comfort that could not be denied even to a slave. In fact some slave owners used Christianity as an excuse for enslaving the African "heathen" in order, so they said, to save his soul. But once saved, they often made it difficult for him to worship God. Richard Allen, one of Negro America's first great ministers, was born a slave about 1760, in Philadelphia. He was sold while still a child to a planter in Delaware. As a young man he became a Methodist preacher and, with his master's permission, held religious services on the farm. His eloquence and sincerity were so great that he converted even his master. During the Revolutionary War Richard Allen earned money as a wagon driver and, by 1777, he had saved enough to purchase his freedom. He was twenty-six when he returned to Philadelphia to live as a free man.

Allen's gifts of pulpit oratory and mass leadership were such that many people were attracted to his prayer meetings. In those days there was no Methodist congregation in Philadelphia composed of Negroes, so young Richard joined the St. George Church, which some free and some slave colored people attended. At times he was even permitted to preach at St. George's. On such occasions Negro attendance at the church increased greatly—in fact, to such an extent that the officials suggested that colored worshippers be segregated. Some of the white members objected strongly to Allen's preaching, and some did not wish any Negroes in their church at all. One Sunday while Richard Allen and two friends, Absolom Jones and William White, were bowed in prayer, they were rudely interrupted by an usher, who literally snatched them from their knees and told them in no uncertain words that their presence was unwelcome. It was then that Allen, with the help of Jones, founded the Free African Society, a religious and civic organization that led to the formation of Bethel Methodist Episcopal Church, dedicated in Philadelphia in 1794 as a place where Negroes might worship in peace.

The year before this church was dedicated, a great epidemic of yellow fever spread with such rapidity throughout the city of Philadelphia that there were not enough doctors or nurses to attend the sick, and the dead were often left unburied. Since white people thought that Negroes did not seem to be dying of the disease in such great numbers as whites, and since many whites fled the city or were afraid to go near the ill or dead, a printed call was issued to the Negro citizens to attend the sick and bury the dead. Those who were slaves, of course, were forced to do this. But free Negroes were angered that such an unusual and dangerous request should be specifically directed to their race. A public meeting was called and Richard Allen and Absolom Jones, both being respected ministers, were appealed to for advice. After prayer and deep consultation, it was agreed that it was the duty of all Christians to help in the emergency as much as they could, so a committee of colored people called upon the mayor to offer their services to the city without reservation.

The Negroes of Philadelphia in large numbers went into white homes as nurses and aids. They tended the dying. They buried neglected corpses. A great physician of that day, Dr. Benjamin Rush, enlisted Allen and Jones as his special assistants. He quickly instructed them how to care for the disease and administer medicines, for many white doctors had died, others were exhausted, and some had taken their families—and themselves—away. There was panic in the city. No well person wanted to go near the sick, for fear of contagion. Without the ministration of the colored citizens, the dreaded plague might have decimated almost the entire population.

Nevertheless, when the siege was over, a white citizen, Mathew Carey, wrote *A Short Account of the Malignant Fever Lately Prevalent in Philadelphia* in which he praised Allen and Jones. But he asserted that on the whole the Negroes should have done much more, and also that some had profited financially by their labors. He singled out only the Negro citizens for such censure. Mathew Carey, it developed, had himself left the city at the height of the epidemic, while Allen, Jones, and most of the members of their churches had remained. During the plague some three hundred Negroes died. In answer to Mathew Carey, Allen and Jones wrote a reply, setting forth the true facts under the title *A Narrative of the Proceeding of the Black People during the late Awful Calamity in Philadelphia,* in which they gave a listing of all monies received which, they said, had been less than enough to pay for the coffins bought and the labor hired. They related in detail their services, and stated how through religion they had "found the freedom to go forth, confiding in Him who can preserve in the midst of a burning furnace" for, they wrote, "The Lord was pleased to strengthen us, and remove all fear from us, and dispose our hearts to be as useful as possible." Certainly the Mayor and the City Council felt that the Negro citizens of Philadelphia had contributed greatly to the alleviation of the common distress during the terrible plague for they drew up a resolution formally thanking them for their services.

Richard Allen's fame as a minister and civic leader spread. And the Negro Methodists, under his leadership, rapidly grew in numbers. Mother Bethel, as his church was known, prospered. By 1820, there were over four thousand colored Methodists in Philadelphia. And churches of that faith under African Methodist Episcopal auspices had been established as far west as Pittsburgh and as far south as Charleston, South Carolina. But the great Denmark Vesey slave rebellion in Charleston in 1822 checked the spread of separate Negro churches in the South. The slave masters feared the unity which such congregations helped to develop among Negroes. Colored ministers were imprisoned and slaves whipped for going to church. And in Virginia, in 1830, after Nat Turner had led another slave uprising there, all Negro preachers were silenced by law. Nevertheless, Christians continued to hold meetings in woods, in cabins, and, sometimes when gatherings of any kind were strictly prohibited, a man or woman would worship alone where, as the spiritual says:

> "Way down yonder by myself,
> I couldn't hear nobody pray."

Slave owners had good reason to fear the rise of a Negro church. They were beginning to realize that the old slave song they heard in the fields:

> "Go down, Moses,
> Way down in Egypt's land
> And tell old Pharaoh
> To let my people go. . . ."

was not just a song about the Israelites, but a cry of freedom born on the weary lips of enslaved men and women in their very midst. Out of the Negro churches then, and ever since, have come many distinguished leaders, ranging from Prince Hall who, about the time of the Boston Tea Party, established a church in Cambridge and became the founder of Freemasonry among Negroes, to Adam Powell, pastor of Abyssinia Baptist Church (the world's largest congregation of that faith) and a member of Congress from New York.

Richard Allen became a bishop of the church he had founded. But his activities extended far beyond his own faith. As the leader of the Free African Society he drew up many petitions calling for the abolition of slavery. He was a contributor to *Freedom's Journal*, America's first Negro newspaper. Under Allen's leadership three thousand Negroes met in Philadelphia in 1817 to register their opposition to the plans of the American Colonization Society to repatriate free colored peoples to Africa as a solution for the race problems of America. When some white proponents of colonization even went so far as to seize free men in the night and lash them until they were willing to say they wanted to go to Africa, out of self-protection the Negroes of New York, Pennsylvania, Delaware, and Maryland began to think in terms of a permanent organization to protect themselves from such indignities. The ever increasing enactment of laws "abridging the liberties and privileges of the Free People of Color" alarmed them, too.

In 1830 a committee which included Bishop Allen met in Philadelphia and constituted itself the first Colored Convention. Allen was elected president. It was agreed that the Convention would "divise and pursue all legal means for the speedy elevation of ourselves and brethren to the scale and standing of men." The Negro people were urged by their leaders to be diligent, buy land, work to achieve unity, and to take advantage of "every opportunity placed within our power by the benevolent efforts of the friends of humanity in elevating our condition to the rank of freemen." It became obvious that these Negroes wanted full citizenship for themselves, freedom for their enslaved brethren, and a place as citizens in America where they were born, *not in Africa*. The constitution of this first Colored Convention was signed by Bishop Richard Allen.

Long before his death, Allen was recognized as one of the most distinguished citizens of the City of Brotherly Love. Today he is remembered chiefly as the founder of the African Methodist Episcopal Church. This denomination has well over a million members. It owns hundreds of beautiful churches, has established a number of accredited colleges, controls a great publishing house, and is a national force for good throughout America, and even abroad where its missionaries have gone as teachers and preachers.

Ira Aldridge
A Star Who Never Came Home

1807–1867

The father of the first great Negro actor to be born in America was a minister, the Reverend Daniel Aldridge, pastor of a Presbyterian chapel in New York. When his son was born in 1807, the child was christened Ira. The records are not clear as to whether Ira Aldridge came into the world in Manhattan or somewhere in Maryland. But at an early age his name appeared on the rolls of the African Free School in New York City. And almost from that time on, his life is a matter of public record. He soon became an actor.

While yet in school, young Ira Aldridge carried a spear in mob scenes or filled in as a member of the crowd in performances at the African Grove on Bleecker Street. There in the early 1800's a company of Negro actors presented Shakespearean plays and other dramas. The director, James Hewlett, starred in "Richard the Third" and "Othello." He also wrote a ballet in which he danced. The theater was not far from the Negro-owned Fraunces' Tavern where George Washington often dined. It was near the African Free School, too, which made it easy for young Ira to find his way there.

When white hoodlums began to make a practice of breaking up performances at the African Grove, the police forced the theater to close. The growing Ira Aldridge then took a job at night at the Chatham Theater where he could at least listen to the actors backstage. He took part in amateur theatricals, as well, and played one of the leading roles in Sheridan's play, "Pizarro." His love for the theater must have perturbed his father, a minister, for in those days playhouses were considered by the devout as dens of iniquity, and the profession of acting did not rate highly. It might have been for this reason that the Reverend Aldridge decided to send his teen-age son abroad to further his education.

The University of Glasgow was known as being receptive to Negro students, and a number of anti-slavery leaders had been educated there. In Scotland Ira applied himself well to his studies, but it is not recorded that he remained long enough to graduate. He soon felt the lure of the stage again and, before he was twenty, he was playing the difficult role of Othello at the Royalty Theater in London. He was an immediate success. From that time on he toured the capitals of Europe regularly. Even in lands that did not understand his language there were long lines outside the theaters where he played. He was written about voluminously in the papers. His career spanned two generations. For forty years Ira Aldridge was a star.

At a theater in Dublin, the great English actor, Edmund Kean, saw Aldridge perform and was so taken with the power of his acting that he suggested they present "Othello" together, with Kean as the villain, Iago. Their production of this Shakespearean classic, which opened in London at Covent Garden in 1833, is reported to have been one of the greatest presentations ever. The two actors became close friends and for several seasons toured the English provinces and the Continent together. As the Moor in one of Shakespeare's most popular plays, Aldridge needed no makeup, being brown, tall, regal, and very handsome. His diction was clear, his voice resonant.

Although it was as Othello that Ira Aldridge received the greatest acclaim, he had mastered many other classical roles. He revived *Titus Andronicus,* which had not been staged in England for almost two centuries. In France the great Alexandre Dumas, author of *The Count of Monte Cristo* and himself a man of color, was one of his admirers. The composer, Richard Wagner, was a follower of his performances. The King of Sweden issued a personal invitation to Aldridge to appear in Stockholm. The medal of the Order of Chevalier was conferred upon him by the King of Prussia, and the Czar of Russia granted him the Cross of Leopold. He was the sensation of Moscow and St. Petersburg during his performances there. Aldridge was often accorded the highest honor the students of Moscow University could bestow. They would unhitch the horses from his *droski* as he left the theater and themselves pull his carriage through the streets to the hotel.

An international star, Ira Aldridge had a long and colorful career as one of the greatest actors of his time. He was feted and lionized everywhere. After he became famous, he never returned to the land of his birth, but married and lived all his adult life in Europe. Still a star at the age of sixty, he died while on a tour of Poland. Today, in the Shakespeare Memorial Theater at Stratford-on-Avon, there is an Ira Aldridge Memorial Chair.

Frederick Douglass
Fighter for Freedom

About 1817–1895

During the period when Ira Aldridge was playing Shakespeare, another American Negro became famous in Europe, too. He had crossed the ocean three times, once fleeing America for his life. But he did not remain abroad. He always came home to battle for the freedom of his people. His name was Frederick Douglass. His father was white but, nevertheless, Frederick was born a slave. His grandmother cared for him, and he never remembered seeing his mother more than a half dozen times in his life. The last time he saw her, she had walked twelve miles after dusk to hold him on her knees until he went to sleep. Then she had to walk twelve miles back to a distant plantation before sunrise to be at work in the fields.

When Frederick was born in the backwoods of Maryland, his name was not Douglass. It was Bailey. About the time when he was shedding his first teeth the boy was taken from his grandmother, and, with a dozen other slave children, put into the care of a mean old hag on the plantation who whipped them often and frequently sent them to sleep on a dirt floor without their suppers. Frederick was ragged, neglected, and sometimes so hungry that he would wait at the kitchen door of the mansion house for the serving girls to shake the bones and crumbs from his master's table cloth. Then he would scramble with the dogs to pick up what fell into the yard. Fortunately, however, while still a young lad, he was sent to work for his master's relatives in Baltimore as errand boy and servant to that family's little son. Seeing that he was an apt boy, his new mistress taught him his A-B-C's. But her husband soon stopped her, saying, "If you teach him how to read, he'll want to know how to write, and this accomplished, he'll be running away with himself." However, white playmates in the streets sometimes lent him their blue-backed spellers and helped him to learn the words. When he was thirteen, with fifty cents earned from shining shoes, he bought a copy of *The Columbian Orator,* which included the speeches of William Pitt and other great men. This was his only book so he read it over and over. Many of the speeches were about liberty and freedom—as applied to white people, of course. But young Frederick took them to heart. "I wish myself a beast, a bird, anything rather than slave," he said.

His whole life eventually became a dedication to freedom. There was an old song he must have heard about "hard trials and deep tribulations." Such trials young Fred knew well. Meanwhile, he found comfort in religion under the guidance of a kindly old Negro named Lawson who could not read very well. Young Frederick taught Lawson "the letter" of the Bible; Lawson in turn taught Frederick "the spirit." Lawson strengthened his hope for freedom by assuring him, "If you want liberty, ask the Lord for it *in faith,* and He will give it to you." Frederick had begun to discover, too, that there were white people in America who did not believe in bondage. These were called *Abolitionists.* The Baltimore papers were always condemning them roundly as anarchists in league with the devil. But Frederick Douglass thought to himself that whatever the Abolitionists might be, they were not unfriendly to the slave, nor sympathetic to the slaveholder.

The more Frederick read the Bible and the newspapers, the more he began to realize that learning opened the way to achievement. As his master had warned, Frederick soon began to want to learn to write. In secret, at night in the loft where he slept, with a flour barrel for a table, his copy books being the Bible and a hymnal, the teen-age boy began to teach himself. When no one was at home, he sometimes borrowed his white master's pen and ink. In time he learned to write. When he was sent to work for another branch of the family in a small town, he found a Sunday school held there in the home of a free Negro. Frederick was asked to be one of the instructors. But on his second Sunday in this Sabbath school, a white mob rushed in armed with sticks and stones and drove everybody away. Young Fred was warned that if he kept on teaching Sunday school, he would be filled with shot. In the small community this sixteen-year-old slave who could read and write had gotten the reputation of being a "dangerous Negro," putting thoughts into other Negroes' heads. Shortly his apprehensive master sent him away to a "Negro breaker" to be made a better slave—that is, to be tamed, humbled, taught to be contented with slavery—in other words, "to be broken."

The man's name was Covey. His plantation was a sort of reformatory work-farm on a sandy, desolate point of Chesapeake Bay. Covey specialized in taking unruly young slaves for a year and "cutting them down to size," so that their masters would have no more trouble with them. Three days after Frederick arrived there, Covey gave him a team of untamed oxen and sent him to the woods for a load of logs. The boy had never driven oxen before, but he dared not object to the job. The oxen ran away, overturned the wagon, and smashed a gate. For this the sixteen-year-old lad had his clothes torn from him by the "slave-breaker," and was flogged on his bare skin with ox-goads. As he described it many years later in his autobiography, under Covey's "heavy blows blood flowed freely, and wales were left on my back as large as my little finger. The sores from this flogging continued for weeks, for they were kept open by the rough and coarse cloth which I wore for shirting . . . during the first six months I was there I was whipped, either with sticks or cow-skins, every week. Aching bones and a sore back were my constant companions." The scars which Covey put on Frederick's shoulders never went away.

Work from before dawn until long after sundown was a part of Covey's system. One day Frederick fainted in the broiling sun of the treading-yard where the wheat was being separated from the straws. He was dizzy. His head ached violently. He was deathly ill. When Covey commanded him to rise, he could not. The slaver gave him a series of savage kicks which finally brought him to his feet. Frederick fell down again, whereupon Covey took a hickory slab and struck him in the head, leaving him bleeding beside the fence. That night Frederick in despair dragged himself seven miles through the woods to his own master's house to beg that he be taken away from the slave-breaker. But his master did no such thing. Instead, he accused the boy of trying to avoid work and sent him back the next day to finish out his year with Covey. Then it was that Frederick made up his mind to defend himself and never to let anyone mistreat him so again. He returned to the plantation but, it being the Lord's Day, Covey waited until Monday morning to flog him. To the slaver's surprise and chagrin, the tall young Negro had resolved to fight it out, man to man. Instead of submitting to a whipping, he flung the slave-breaker on the ground each time he came near. Covey finally gave up. Frederick was not whipped again as long as he was there. But Covey almost worked him to death.

"I was a changed being after that fight," Douglass wrote in his *Life and Times*. "I was *nothing* before; I was a *man* now." On Christmas Day, 1834, his year with the slave-breaker was up. But his spirit, far from being broken, had been strengthened. His hatred of the cruelties of slavery intensified. And his determination to be free grew ever stronger. When the boy was transferred to a new master, even though conditions were much more pleasant, he began to plan a break for freedom. Frederick persuaded five other slaves to run away with him. On the eve of their departure, someone betrayed them. Frederick was bound and dragged off to jail. When he was released, he was not wanted on that plantation any more. (He was a "dangerous Negro.") So he was sent back to Baltimore and put to work in a shipyard where he learned the calker's trade. But the white workers objected to Negroes working with them. One day a number of them ganged up on Frederick (who was certainly there through no fault of his own) and beat him almost to death. In fact, he was beaten so badly that his master, for fear of losing a valuable slave, did not send him back to the shipyards again. Instead, he allowed Frederick to hire himself out, providing that every Saturday night he turned *all* his wages in to his master. Sometimes he might let Frederick keep a quarter for himself. Eventually, Frederick managed to save enough secretly to pay his fare to New York. Though it might mean his life if he were captured, Frederick decided to dare to try to escape from slavery again. Disguised as a sailor, and with borrowed seaman's papers, he leaped on a train just as it was leaving Baltimore. A day later, he reached New York. He was twenty-one years old when he set foot on free soil. A dream had at last come true. *He belonged to himself.*

A new world had opened for him. "I felt as one might feel upon escape from a den of hungry lions," he wrote in his first letter to a friend. But soon his money was gone. In the big city nobody paid any attention to him. He was afraid to approach anyone, since he did not know whom to trust for fear he might be returned to slave territory. As he later described his condition, "I was without home, without acquaintance, without money, without credit, without work, and without any definite knowledge as to what course to take or where to look for succor. In such an extremity, a man has something beside his new-born freedom of which to think. While wandering about the streets of New York, and lodging at least one night among the barrels on one of the wharves, I was indeed free—free from slavery—but free from food and shelter as well."

A sailor who lived near the docks took him in, gave him a place to sleep, and put him in touch with a committee whose work it was to help escaped slaves. While in hiding in New York, Frederick was married to a girl with whom he had fallen in love in Baltimore and who followed him to the big city. Together they set out for Massachusetts on the deck of a steamer, for Negro passengers were not allowed in the cabins. In New Bedford he found employment on the wharves. There he dropped his slave name, Bailey, and took the name of one of the characters in *The Lady of the Lake*—Douglass. From then on he was known as Frederick

Douglass, a name shortly to be in headlines around the world. For the young freeman was not satisfied just to be free himself. He became an Abolitionist.

In 1841, Douglass made his first talk at an Anti-Slavery Society meeting in Nantucket. There, groping for words, since he had never faced an audience before, he told the story of his childhood, his bondage, and his escape. People were deeply moved. William Lloyd Garrison, who followed Douglass as a speaker, cried, "Is he a man or a thing?" And proceeded to point out how, in spite of slave-owners treating Frederick as a *thing,* free people could see that here was a man, worthy of being treated as a man.

Douglass was then twenty-four years old, six feet tall, with hair like a lion, and very handsome. The more speeches he made, the more effective he became. Soon he was persuaded to quit his work on the docks and become an orator for the cause of freedom. In 1845 he made his first trip to England to tell sympathizers there about the plight of America's slave millions. When he returned he began to publish a paper in Rochester, called *The North Star.* From then on, for fifty years, Douglass was a great public figure. He spoke on platforms with many of the distinguished men and women of his times—Wendell Phillips, Harriet Beecher Stowe, Charles Sumner, and Lucretia Mott. He published his life story. He defied the Fugitive Slave Law of 1850 and sheltered runaways in his home. Mobs attacked his meetings. He was sometimes stoned. After John Brown's famous raid on Harpers Ferry, in which he had no part, the newspapers and the slave owners sought to implicate him. Douglass had to flee for his life to Canada, whence he made his second trip to England. When the War between the States broke out, he was back in this country, counselling with President Lincoln and recruiting troops for the Union Army—in which his own sons served. More than two hundred thousand Negroes fought in this War for freedom and the preservation of the Union. Many were inspired to do so by the brilliant speeches of Frederick Douglass.

When the War was over, Douglass became one of the leaders of the Republican Party. He was made a United States Marshall. Later he was appointed the Recorder of Deeds for the District of Columbia. And in 1889 he was confirmed as United States Minister to the Republic of Haiti. Active not just as a leader of the Negro people, at the first convention for women's suffrage Douglass was the *only* man of any color to stand up on the floor and defend the right of women to the ballot equally with men. "Right is of no sex," he stated in the first issue of *The*

North Star. He was active, too, in the national temperance organizations and many other movements for social betterment. After Emancipation, Douglass demanded no special privileges for Negroes. For them he wanted simply the same freedom of action he felt *every* citizen should have. In a famous speech called *What the Black Man Wants,* he said, "The American people have always been anxious to know what to do with us. I have had but one answer from the beginning. Do nothing with us! . . . If the Negro cannot stand on his own legs, let him fall. All I ask is, give him a *chance* to stand on his own legs! Let him alone! If you see him on his way to school, let him alone—don't disturb him. If you see him going to the dinner table at a hotel, let him go! If you see him going to the ballot box, let him alone—don't disturb him! If you see him going into a workshop, just let him alone."

The only school from which Douglass was ever graduated, as he of-ten repeated, was the school of slavery. His diploma was the scars upon his back. But he had about him a wit and wisdom that many a better educated person did not possess. His speeches moved thousands to ac-tion. As a writer he left behind him his *Life and Times,* an autobiography that is an American classic. His simple but effective use of words, tinged sometimes with wry humor, is illustrated in the final paragraph of a letter he wrote to his former master on the tenth anniversary of his escape to freedom. In this letter he listed all the wrongs this man had done him, but closed by stating:

> "There is no roof under which you would be more safe than mine, and there is nothing in my house which you might need for your comfort, which I would not readily grant. Indeed, I should esteem it a privilege to set you an example as to how mankind ought to treat each other.
> "I am your fellow man, but not your slave,
> Frederick Douglass."

Harriet Tubman
The Moses of Her People

About 1823–1913

"Then we saw the lightning, and that was the guns; and then we heard the thunder, and that was the big guns; and then we heard the rain falling, and that was the drops of blood falling; and when we came to get in the crops, it was dead men that we reaped." So the escaped slave, Harriet Tubman, described one of the battles of the War between the North and South in which she took part, for she was in the thick of the fighting. Before the War, like Frederick Douglass, Harriet Tubman devoted her life to the cause of freedom, and after the War to the advancement of her people.

Like Douglass she was born in Maryland a slave, one of eleven sons and daughters. No one kept a record of her birth, so the exact year is not known. But she lived so long and so much was written about her that most of the other facts of her life are accurately recorded. She was a homely child, morose, wilful, wild, and constantly in rebellion against slavery. Unlike Phillis Wheatley or Douglass, Harriet had no teaching of any sort, except the whip. As a little girl, on the very first day that she was sent to work in the Big House, her mistress whipped her four times. Once she ran away and hid in a pig sty for five days, eating the scraps thrown to the pigs. "There were good masters and mistresses, so I've heard tell," she once said, "but I didn't happen to come across any of them."

Harriet never liked to work as a servant in the house, so perhaps because of her rebellious nature, she was soon ordered to the fields. One day when she was in her early teens something happened that affected her whole life. It was evening and a young slave had, without permission, gone to a country store. The overseer followed him to whip him. He ordered Harriet to help tie him up. As Harriet refused, the slave ran. The overseer picked up a heavy iron weight from the scales and threw it. But he did not hit the fellow. He struck Harriet's head, almost crushing her skull, and leaving a deep scar forever. Unconscious, the girl lingered between life and death for days. When at last she was able to work again,

Harriet still suffered fits of unconsciousness. These lasted all her life. They would come upon her at any time, any place, and it would seem as if she had suddenly fallen asleep. Sometimes in the fields, sometimes leaning against a fence, sometimes in church, she would "go to sleep" and no one could wake her until the seizure had passed. When she was awake, this did not affect her thinking. But her master thought the blow had made her half-witted. Harriet continued to let him believe this. Meanwhile, she prayed to God to deliver her from bondage.

When she was about twenty-four years old, she married a jolly, carefree fellow named Tubman, who did not share her concern for leaving the slave country. A few years later, when her old master died, Harriet heard that she and two of her brothers were to be sold, so they decided to run away, together. It was dangerous to tell anyone. Harriet had no chance to let even her mother know directly. But on the evening that she was leaving, she went about the fields and the slave quarters singing:

> "When that old chariot comes
> I'm gwine to leave you.
> I'm bound for the Promised Land . . ."

And the way she sang that song let her friends and kinfolks know that to Harriet the Promised Land right then meant the North, not heaven. That night she left the Brodas Plantation on the Big Buckwater River never to return. Before dawn her brothers became frightened and went back to the slave huts before their absence was discovered. But Harriet went on alone through the woods by night, hiding by day, having no map, unable to read or write, but trusting God, instinct, and the North star to guide her. By some miracle she eventually got to Philadelphia, found work there, and was never again a slave.

But Harriet could not be happy while all her family were slaves. She kept thinking about them. So, some months later, she went back to Maryland, hoping to persuade her husband to come North with her. He said he did not wish to go. She led others Northward, however, and within two years of her own escape, she had secretly returned to the South three times to rescue two brothers, a sister and her children, and a dozen more slaves. The Fugitive Slave Law of 1850 now made it dangerous for runaways to stop anywhere in the United States, so Harriet led her followers to Canada where she spent a winter begging, cooking, and praying for them. Then she returned to Maryland to rescue nine more Negroes.

During the first years of her own freedom, Harriet spent most of her time showing others how to follow in her footsteps. Her fame as a fearless leader of "freedom bands" spread rapidly. Shortly large rewards were offered by the slaveholders for her capture. But she was never captured, and she never lost any of her followers to the slave catchers. One reason for this was that once a slave made up his mind to go with her and started out, Harriet did not permit any turning back. Perhaps her experience with her two brothers when she first ran away accounted for this insistence. Her method of preventing frightened or weak travelers on the freedom road from returning to slavery, and perhaps being whipped into betraying the others, was simple. Harriet Tubman carried a pistol. When anyone said he could not, or would not go on, Harriet pulled her gun from the folds of her dress and said, "You *will* go on—or you'll die." The strength or the courage to continue was always forthcoming when her faltering companions looked into the muzzle of Harriet's gun. Through swamp and thicket, rain and cold, they went on toward the North. Thus everyone who started out with Harriet Tubman lived to thank her for freedom.

Long before the War between the States came, so many slaves were escaping, and so many white people in the North were helping them, that the routes to freedom became known as the "Underground Railroad." Secret "stations" where escaping slaves might be hidden, warmed, and fed were established in homes, barns, and sometimes even churches along the way. The Quakers were especially helpful and active in this regard. And a strong Anti-Slavery Society supported such activities. Slave owners were losing thousands of dollars worth of slaves by escape every year. Harriet Tubman became known as a "conductor" on the Underground Railroad. She was not the only "conductor" but she was the most famous, and one of the most daring. Once she brought as many as twenty-five slaves in a single band to freedom.

Another time she had in her party of runaways a big strong slave worth $1500. His name was Josiah Bailey and the Maryland countryside was plastered with posters offering a reward for his capture. There were ads in the papers for his return. On the way through New York City a friend of freedom recognized Bailey from the description in the papers and said, "I'm glad to meet a man whose head is worth fifteen hundred dollars!" Josiah was so shocked at being recognized and so afraid that he would be captured that a mood of deep despair descended upon him and he would not speak the rest of the trip. When the train was carrying the runaways across the bridge at Buffalo into Canada, Bailey would not even look at the wonder of Niagara Falls. But when they got on free soil and he was finally safe, he burst into song, and nobody could stop him from singing. He cried that at last, thanks to God, he was in Heaven! Harriet Tubman said, "Well, you old fool, you! You might at least have looked at Niagara Falls on the way to Heaven."

Harriet had a great sense of humor. She enjoyed telling the story on herself of how, not being able to read, she once sat down and went to sleep on a park bench right under a sign offering a big reward for her capture. When she began to make speeches to raise money for the cause of freedom, she often told jokes, sang, and sometimes even danced. She might have been a great actress, people said, because without makeup she could hollow out her cheeks and wrinkle her brow to seem like a very old woman. She would make her body shrink and cause her legs to totter when she chose to so disguise herself. Once, making a trip to Maryland to rescue some relatives, she had to pass through a village where she was known. She bought two hens, tied them by their feet and hung their heads down around her neck, then went tottering along. Sure enough, a slave catcher came up the street who might, she thought, recognize her, tottering or not. So she unloosed the squalling chickens in the middle of the street and dived after them, purposely not catching them so she could run down the road in pursuit and out of the slave catcher's sight, while all the passersby laughed.

Sometimes, knowing that her band of fugitives was pursued by angry masters, she would get on a train headed South—because nobody would suspect that runaway slaves would be going South. Sometimes she would disguise the women in her party and herself as men. Babies would be given a sleeping medicine to keep them quiet and then wrapped up like bundles. Sometimes she would wade for hours up a stream to throw the hounds off scent. In the dark of night when there was no North star, she would feel the trunks of trees for the moss that grows on the northern side, and that would serve as a guide toward freedom. Often when all seemed hopeless—although she never told her followers she had such feelings—Harriet would pray. One of her favorite prayers was, "Lord, you've been with me through six troubles. Be with me in the seventh." Some people thought that Harriet Tubman led a charmed life because, within twelve years, she made nineteen dangerous trips into the South rescuing slaves. She herself said, "I never run my train off the track, and I never lost a passenger."

Her father and mother were both over seventy years of age when she rescued them and brought her parents North to a home she had begun to buy in Auburn, New York. At first they stayed in St. Catharines, Canada, where escaped slaves were safe, since, in 1833, Queen Victoria had declared all slavery illegal. But it was too cold for the old folks there. And Harriet's work was not on foreign soil. She herself seemed to have no fear of being captured. She came and went about the United States as she chose. And became so famous that, although she never sought the spotlight, it was hard for her not to be recognized wherever she was. Once at a great woman's suffrage meeting where her old head wound had caused her to go sound asleep in the audience, she was recognized, and awoke to find herself on the platform. Her speech for women's rights was roundly applauded. In those days neither Negroes nor women could vote. Harriet believed both should, so, like Frederick Douglass, she followed the woman's suffrage movement closely.

In appearance "a more ordinary specimen of humanity could hardly be found," but there was no one with a greater capacity for leadership than she had. Among the slaves, where she walked in secret, Harriet began to be known as Moses. And at the great public meetings of the North, as the Negro historian William Wells Brown wrote in 1854, "all who frequented anti-slavery conventions, lectures, picnics, and fairs, could not fail to have seen a black woman of medium size, upper front teeth gone, smiling countenance, attired in coarse but neat apparel, with an old-fashioned reticule or bag suspended by her side, who, on taking her seat, would at once drop off into a sound sleep. . . . No fugitive was ever captured who had Moses for a leader." She was very independent. Between rescue trips or speeches, she would work as a cook or a scrubwoman. She might borrow, but she never begged money for herself. All contributions went toward the cause of freedom in one way or another, as did most of what she earned.

But when the War between the States began and she became a nurse for the Union Armies, and then a military scout and an invaluable intelligence agent behind the Rebel lines, she was promised some compensation. Technically she was not a registered nurse, and being a woman, she could not be a soldier. Yet she carried a Union pass, traveled on government transports, did dangerous missions in Confederate territory, and gave advice to chiefs of staffs. But she never got paid for this, although she had been promised $1800 for certain assignments. To Harriet this made no difference until, after the War, she badly needed money to care for her aged parents. Petitions were sent to the War Department and to Congress to try to get the $1800 due her. But it was never granted.

Harriet Tubman's war activities were amazing. She served under General Stevens at Beaufort, South Carolina. She was sent to Florida to nurse those ill of dysentery, small pox, and yellow fever. She was with Colonel Robert Gould Shaw at Fort Wagner. She organized a group of nine Negro scouts and river pilots and, with Colonel Montgomery, led a Union raiding contingent of three gunboats and about 150 Negro troops up the Combahee River. As reported by the Boston *Commonwealth,* for July 10, 1863, they "under the guidance of a black woman, dashed into the enemy's country, struck a bold and effective blow, destroying millions of dollars worth of commissary stores, cotton and lordly dwellings, and striking terror into the heart of rebeldom, brought off near 800 slaves and thousands of dollars worth of property." Concerning Harriet Tubman, it continued, "Many and many times she has penetrated the enemy's lines and discovered their situation and condition, and escaped without injury, but not without extreme hazard."

One of the songs Harriet sang during the War was:

"Of all the whole creation in the East or in the West
The glorious Yankee nation is the greatest and the best.
Come along! Come along! Don't be alarmed,
Uncle Sam is rich enough to give you all a farm."

But Harriet Tubman never had a farm of her own. Her generous nature caused her to give away almost all the money she ever got her hands on. There were always fugitives, or relatives, or causes, or friends in need. She was over forty years old when Abraham Lincoln signed the Emancipation Proclamation, making legal for all the freedom she had struggled to secure. She lived for almost fifty years after the War was over. Some people thought she was a hundred years old when she died in 1913. Certainly she was over ninety.

A number of books have been written about her. The first one, *Scenes in the Life of Harriet Tubman,* by Sarah H. Bradford, appeared in 1869, and the proceeds from its sale helped Harriet pay for her cottage. She wrote her friend, Frederick Douglass, who had hidden her and her runaway slaves more than once in his home in Rochester, for a letter about her book. In his reply he compared their two careers:

"The difference between us is very marked. Most that I have done and suffered in the service of our cause has been in public, and I have received much encouragement at every step of the way. You, on the other hand, have labored in a private way. I have wrought in the day—you in the night. I have had the applause of the crowd and the satisfaction that comes of being approved by the multitude, while the most that you have done has been witnessed by a few trembling, scared and footsore bondsmen and women, whom you have led out of the house of bondage, and whose heartfelt, *God bless you,* has been your only reward. The midnight sky and the silent stars have been the witnesses of your devotion to freedom and of your heroism."

When years later, in her old age, a reporter for *The New York Herald Tribune* came to interview her one afternoon at her home in Auburn, he wrote that, as he was leaving, Harriet looked toward an orchard nearby and said, "Do you like apples?"

On being assured that the young man liked them, she asked, "Did you ever plant any apples?"

The writer confessed that he had not.

"No," said the old woman, "but somebody else planted them. I liked apples when I was young. And I said, 'Some day I'll plant apples myself for other young folks to eat.' And I guess I did."

Her apples were the apples of freedom. Harriet Tubman lived to see the harvest. Her home in Auburn, New York, is preserved as a memorial to her planting.

Booker T. Washington
Founder of Tuskegee

About 1858–1915

Booker T. Washington was a speaker at the memorial ceremonies for Harriet Tubman in Auburn, New York, the year after her death. He, too, had been born in slavery, but freedom came while he was still young, so Booker T. did not undergo the years of cruelty that Frederick Douglass and Harriet Tubman suffered. His struggle was to center in education, not freedom. And he was to become a teacher.

Like Frederick Douglass, Booker T. Washington's father was white, his mother a Negro slave, the plantation cook, and the cabin in which he was born was the plantation cook-house. It had a dirt floor and no windows. With the fireplace constantly going, it was very hot in summer and very smokey in winter. There was a cat-hole in one wall, so the cat could come in and out at night. And, in the middle of the cabin, there was a plank-covered hole in the earth where sweet potatoes were stored. As a child the boy had only one name, Booker. It never occurred to him that he needed another name until he started to school after the War between the States.

During the War his step-father followed the Union armies. When, at the end of the War, all the slaves were freed, the man sent for his family to join him where he had found work in the salt mines at Malden, West Virginia. Booker was about eight years old when he, with the other slaves, stood in the yard before the porch of the "big house," where his master's family had gathered, and heard the Emancipation Proclamation read. Then the slaves were told that they were free. He heard their wild shouts of rejoicing and saw their happy tears. But the rejoicing lasted only a few days for, as Booker wrote afterwards in his life story, *Up From Slavery*, "The great responsibility of being free, of having charge of themselves, of having to think and plan for themselves and their children, seemed to take possession of them. . . . In a few hours the great questions with which the Anglo-Saxon race had been grappling for centuries had been thrown upon these people to be solved. These were the questions of a home, a living, the rearing of children, education,

45

citizenship, and the establishment and support of churches." They had no money, they had no land, they had nothing—but freedom.

In West Virginia little Booker was put to work at a salt furnace where his day began at four o'clock in the morning. At night he and his mother struggled together to learn the alphabet from an old speller she had somehow gotten for him. They had to learn alone because there was no literate person around who could help them. Then one day a young man who could read came to town, and all the colored people pooled their money and paid him to open a school for them. His pupils were of all ages, for every Negro wanted to learn. The older people wanted, at least, to be able to read the Bible before they died. For those who worked, the teacher held night classes. And folks who could get help at no other time even took their spellers to Sunday school with them. Day-school, night-school, and Sunday school were all crowded. But the greatest disappointment of little Booker's life was that his step-father would not let him go to school. His family needed the money that he earned working all day at the salt furnace. Finally, with his mother's help, a few lessons at night were arranged. Then, at last, his step-father relented and said that if Booker would work from dawn until school time, and then go back to work after classes, he could go to day school when the new term started.

This is what happened on his first day at school. The teacher began by asking each pupil his name so that he could record it on the roll. As he went from row to row, Booker's heart began to thump madly, because every child there had two and sometimes even three names—but he had only one! He grew hot with shame and hung his head, puzzled, because he did not know what to do. Then, suddenly his turn came and he shouted out, "Booker Washington." He never knew how that second name happened to come into his head on the spur of the moment. But it did, so he kept it. Later he added a middle name, Taliaferro. But this was a hard name to pronounce and to spell, so from his youth on, his middle name served mostly to provide him with an initial. People always called him Booker T.

Since he was getting big enough now to work in the salt mines rather than just at the furnace, and his family needed all the money he could earn, he did not remain in school long. And from the salt mines, he went to the coal mines, deep underground, where the labor was not only hard, but dangerous. In the coal mines there was always the chance of being blown to pieces by an explosion, or crushed to death by falling slate. Sometimes Booker's light would go out and he would get lost in the enormous darkness. But it was in the coal mines that the boy first heard men talking about a school called Hampton in Virginia where, they said, one could work for an education. Young Booker T. decided to go there. Gradually he managed to save a little money. The old people in the community, proud of his determination to go away to school, gave him nickels, dimes, quarters, or the gift of a handkerchief or a pair of socks. From somewhere he got a battered old suitcase. Booker T. was fifteen years old. Hampton was five hundred miles away. One day he started out over the mountains in an old-fashioned stage-coach intending to ride as long as his funds lasted.

Late in the evening the stage-coach stopped at a ramshackle inn where the passengers were to take supper and be accommodated for the night. The travellers were all white except Booker T. When he presented himself at the desk, the proprietor rudely turned the Negro lad away, refusing to allow him food, or even to remain inside the building. All night the cold, hungry boy walked up and down the road to keep warm until the stage-coach started off in the morning. "This was my first experience in finding out what the color of my skin meant," he wrote in *Up From Slavery*, but "My whole soul was so bent upon reaching Hampton that I did not have time to cherish any bitterness toward the hotel-keeper."

By the time Booker T. got to Richmond, all his money was gone, so he slept that night under a wooden sidewalk. When passing footsteps overhead woke him up in the morning, he found himself near the river where a vessel was unloading pig iron. The captain gave him work helping to unload the ship, so he remained in Richmond several days. But in order to save for the remainder of his trip, he continued to sleep under the sidewalk. As soon as he had a little money, he went on to Hampton, walking part of the way. He arrived there with exactly fifty cents to commence his education. As he entered the grounds and looked up at a big three-story building, it seemed to him the largest and most beautiful building he had ever seen, and he thought he was in paradise. But the picture changed when he presented himself, covered with the dust of the road, hungry, and tired, to Miss Mary F. Mackie, the head teacher. She thought he was perhaps a tramp and she had very grave doubts about admitting him. Since she did not definitely say, "No," however, he lingered in her office, becoming more and more discouraged as he saw other students being assigned to classes. Finally Miss Mackie said, "The adjoining recitation room needs sweeping. Take the broom and sweep it."

Young Booker T. knew that that was his entrance examination. He not only swept the room once, he swept it three times, moving all the furniture. Then he dusted it four times, putting everything carefully back in place. When he was through, he reported to the head teacher. She took her clean white handkerchief and rubbed it over the woodwork and the furniture, but she could not find a particle of dirt or dust. She looked at the anxious young Negro and said quietly, "I guess you will do to enter this institution." Miss Mackie gave him a job as a janitor and, by working late into the night cleaning the school rooms and getting up early in the morning to build the fires, Booker T. got his education and acquired the trade of bricklayer. He learned to read well, to speak clearly, to bathe every day, and to sleep *between* sheets. He was put into a dormitory room with seven other young men. He did not want them to know that he had never slept in a bed with sheets before, and that he did not know what to do with them. The first night Booker T. slept under both sheets. The second night he slept on top of both of them—until finally he found out that he should sleep *between* them. In 1875 he was graduated with honors from Hampton.

General Armstrong, the founder of Hampton Institute, and all the other white teachers there who had come into the South to help the freed Negroes gain an education, made a great impression on young Booker T. through their hard work, self sacrifice, sympathy, and understanding of the problems of their students, many of whom were older than the teachers. A conscientious New Englander, Miss Mackie herself, when not teaching, cleaned halls and washed windows along with Booker T., who wrote of such teachers years later, "What a rare set of human beings they were! They worked for the students night and day, in season and out of season. . . . Whenever it is written—and I hope it will be—the part that the Yankee teachers played in the education of the Negroes immediately after the War will make one of the most thrilling parts of the history of this country."

When General Armstrong, finding the school over-crowded and not wishing to turn away any new students, put up tents and asked for volunteers willing to sleep in them all winter, almost all the students volunteered, so great was their love for him. Booker T. was one who slept through the bitter cold that year in a tent that sometimes blew away in the night. But every morning the General would come to visit the young men in their tents and "his cheerful, encouraging voice would dispel any feeling of discouragement." Booker T. wanted to be like General Armstrong. So he became a teacher of the lowly, too.

After graduation he went back home to Malden to teach from eight o'clock in the morning until sometimes ten o'clock at night. The young man who had taught him had gone, so Booker T. was the only teacher. His night classes were as large as the day classes, for many working people wanted to learn. On Sundays he conducted two Sunday schools, one in town and one in the country. Meanwhile, he began to give private lessons to several young men that he was preparing to go, as he had done, to Hampton. Booker T. particularly wanted his older brother, who had, up to now, worked hard in the mines, to get an education. So he helped him learn to read and encouraged him to go to Hampton also. In fact, the students that Booker T. sent to Hampton from Malden made such a good record that General Armstrong was convinced they had had a good teacher. This caused him to invite Booker T. to return to Hampton to teach there and to supervise a dormitory for a hundred Indians coming to study. Booker T. and the Indians got along fine together. The Negro students cordially welcomed the "red men," took them as room-mates, and helped them to learn English. For a number of years Hampton was America's leading institution for both Negro and Indian students. Young Booker T. was "house father" to the Indians.

But in 1881 he was called deep into the Black Belt of the South to establish a school at Tuskegee, Alabama. A Negro shoemaker and a white banker had written General Armstrong to send them someone for that job. Armstrong sent Booker T. Washington. In a tumble-down old church with thirty students ranging in age from fifteen to forty, with himself as the only teacher, Tuskegee Institute began. With no equipment, but with "hundreds of hungry, earnest souls who wanted to secure knowledge," Booker T. set to work. At first there were so many holes in the roof of his school that when it rained, one of the students held an umbrella over the teacher while others recited. The Alabama State Legislature voted $2,000 for teachers' salaries, but nothing for buildings or grounds. So Booker T. and his students decided to raise funds, buy land, and build a schoolhouse. They did. They planted the foundation and laid the bricks themselves. From a single room with a leaky roof to dozens of fine buildings, from one teacher to more than a hundred, from thirty students to three thousand, Tuskegee eventually grew until it became the most famous vocational school in the world, and Booker T. Washington gradually became America's most prominent Negro citizen.

The year after Booker T. opened his school, 255 Negroes were lynched in the South. The Ku Klux Klan had begun its terror. The use of the ballot, which an amendment to the Federal Constitution had granted the freedmen, was being taken away by state legislation. Prejudice and poverty, ignorance and despair, hung like a pall over the freedom. What could a lone young teacher in the middle of Alabama do to help in such a situation? First the Negro people must be taught to work well, to keep clean, to be healthy, to be self-respecting, and they must learn how to better conditions right in their own houses, their own yards, and cultivate the soil where they were. That was one reason why Booker T. wanted his students to construct their own school buildings—so that they would learn how to build with their *own* hands and not be dependent on others. That is why he used part of the first land his school purchased for a farm. He soon acquired livestock and taught the students the care of animals. Behind all this was pride in working with the hands, in learning how "to do a common thing in an uncommon manner." He began by trying immediately to fit the school to the needs of the community— a community of poor, unlettered, country people—and to prepare his students to "return to the plantation districts and show the people there how to put new energy and new ideas into farming, as well as into the intellectual and moral and religious life of the people." Tuskegee was the first institution to use farm and home demonstration methods, and to have a "movable school"—a truck carrying books and tools and teachers directly to the remote rural districts.

From the beginning Booker T. was able to get the help and advice of almost all the people of the countryside, both white and Negro. Even the poorest and oldest of the Negroes who had spent most of their days in slavery would bring gifts of coins, sugar and cane, quilts, and cotton to Tuskegee. One day one old woman over seventy, and in rags, hobbled into the principal's office leaning on a cane with a basket on her arm. She said, "Mr. Washington, God knows I spent the best days of my life in slavery. God knows I's ignorant and poor. But I knows you is trying to make better men and better women for de colored race. I ain't got no money, but I want you to take dese six eggs what I's been savin' up, and I want you to put dese six eggs into de eddication of dese boys and gals." Later many large gifts came to Tuskegee from the wealthy and famous. Andrew Carnegie gave the school a lump sum of over a half million dollars. But no gift ever moved Booker T. Washington more than this old woman's gift of her six eggs.

With these people whom he taught and among whom he lived all his life, Booker T. never lost touch, even after he became internationally famous. President McKinley and his Cabinet visited Tuskegee. President Theodore Roosevelt invited Booker T. to luncheon at the White House. He was a guest of Queen Victoria at Windsor Castle when he visited

England. But always when he came back to Tuskegee, whose principal he was until his death, Booker T. would join the farmers when they had a meeting on the campus, talk and joke and eat with them all day, and help them with their problems. Perhaps it was because Washington was as much at home in a black sharecropper's cabin as he was in a white Fifth Avenue mansion, that he became a sort of liaison officer between the white people and the colored people of America. It was as a kind of statesman of the race problem that he grew to be better known even than he was as the educator of Tuskegee. The years of his adult life were some of the most difficult years for race relations in our country. The newly freed Negroes were determined to go forward. But there were some white Americans who were determined that they should not progress. There were white teachers willing to sacrifice their lives at schools for Negroes in the deep South. But there were also Klansmen who would burn down the schools and run the teachers away. The white hoods and robes of the Ku Klux Klan rode through the night terrorizing Negroes, and their white friends, as well.

Booker T. Washington sought a way to make peace between the races in the South. He said, "Any movement for the elevation of the Southern Negro, in order to be successful, must have to a certain extent the cooperation of the Southern whites." To that end, he made his famous speech at the opening of the Cotton States Exposition at Atlanta in 1895. Before an audience of thousands, Washington began by saying, "One third of the population of the South is of the Negro race." He then told his oft repeated story about a ship at sea signalling another ship for fresh water since it had none aboard. The other ship kept signalling back to cast down their buckets. Finally when the buckets were let down, the thirsty ship found that it was in a fresh water zone good for drinking. Washington continued, "To those of my race who . . . underestimate the importance of cultivating friendly relations with the Southern white man, who is their next-door neighbor, I would say, 'Cast down your bucket where you are.' Cast it down in making friends in every manly way of the people of all races by whom we are surrounded. Cast it down in agriculture, mechanics, in commerce, in domestic service, and in the professions. . . . No race can prosper until it learns that there is as much dignity in tilling the field as in writing a poem. . . . To those of the white race . . . I would repeat what I say to my own race, 'Cast down your bucket where you are.' Cast it down among the eight millions of Negroes . . . who have, without strikes and labor wars, tilled your fields, cleared your forests, builded your railroads and cities, and brought forth treasures from the bowels of the earth." Then came his most famous statement, "In all things that are purely social we can be as separate as the fingers, yet one as the hand in all things essential to mutual progress. There is no defense or security for any of us except in the highest intelligence and development of all."

For the next twenty years, from that time on until his death in 1915, Booker T. Washington was always consulted by civic leaders and politicians whenever any problems arose in regard to Negro citizens. He was considered *the* authority on Negro-white relations. And he was called upon to make hundreds of speeches all across the country. For years he was the center of a great controversy between those who agree entirely with his Atlanta speech and its social program, and those who thought he did not stress strongly enough full equal rights for Negroes in every phase of American life. Because he believed in taking advantage of small opportunities, so some people felt, to the exclusion of greater ambitions, he was called an opportunist. Because he thought, so some people declared, that a half loaf was better than none, he was termed a compromiser. Because he did not protest color prejudice vigorously, but stressed rather making the best of things under the circumstances, some labeled him an "Uncle Tom." In later life he became a highly controversial figure.

But controversy did not lessen Booker T.'s fame. His school at Tuskegee grew until it became a little city in itself. On its founder were bestowed many honors. Harvard University awarded him the degree of Master of Arts, and Dartmouth College that of Doctor of Laws. His bust, designed by the distinguished Negro sculptor, Richmond Barthé, stands today in New York University's Hall of Fame. Booker T. Washington is buried on the campus at Tuskegee where boys and girls from the plantation country he loved still come to get an education. His letters and his speeches are in the Library of Congress. *Up From Slavery,* the story of his life, translated into many languages, is in the libraries of the world.

Daniel Hale Williams
A Great Physician

1858–1931

About the time that Booker T. Washington was born in the South, another Negro boy destined to become famous was born in the North. At Hollidaysburg, Pennsylvania, in 1858, Daniel Hale Williams came into the world. His parents were free Negroes. His childhood was a happy one, spent with a brother and five sisters who did not know the trials and tribulations that slave children knew just a few miles farther South in Delaware and Maryland. Daniel went to school regularly and proved himself a bright pupil. But when, after his father's death, his mother moved with the other children to Janesville, Wisconsin, and Daniel was left with friends in Annapolis, he became lonesome for the rest of his family. One day he bundled up his clothes and went down to the railroad station and told the ticket agent how much he wanted to see his mother, but that he had no money to buy a ticket to Wisconsin. The ticket agent took pity on him and gave him a pass on the train. All alone, the boy Daniel headed West.

His mother was so glad to see him that she did not scold him much for running away. But he had left all his school books behind and she did not have any money to buy him new ones. So, when he entered school in Janesville, all the ten-year-old boy had was an old dictionary. This he took to school with him every day and each strange word that came up in class, Daniel would look it up in his dictionary, underline it, and study it. Of course, he often found new words that he had never heard of at all. These, too, he would learn, so he soon had a very large vocabulary. He loved to read, and was particularly fascinated by history and the sciences. After grammar school, his mother encouraged him all the way through Hare's Classical Academy. But when he was graduated there, Daniel did not have the money to go to college, so he entered a law office in Janesville, thinking he would become a lawyer. But he did not enjoy the bitter quarrels and fights around which many law cases evolved, so he soon gave up that ambition.

His interest in the sciences caused him to begin thinking about being a doctor. But with such a large family, his mother could not help him any financially. Fortunately, a family friend, a barber named Mr. Anderson, took an interest in the boy and aided him in every way that he could. Soon young Daniel had the great good luck to be employed by the office of the Surgeon General of the State, Dr. Henry Palmer, where he could both work and study. From Dr. Palmer he learned a great deal about medicine, with the result that two years later he was able to pass the examinations and enter the medical school of Northwestern University, at Evanston, Illinois, where he remained until he was granted his M.D. degree. During the summers he earned his tuition by playing in an orchestra on the excursion boats on Lake Michigan. Because of his outstanding record as a student, Daniel Williams was asked when he was graduated in 1883 to remain on the campus at Northwestern as an instructor in anatomy. At that time it was most unusual for a large university to have a Negro instructor, so this appointment was indeed a real testimonial to his exceptional ability.

Young Dr. Williams began his professional practice as a surgeon at the Southside Dispensary in Chicago. Soon he became one of the doctors at the Protestant Orphan Asylum, too. Within a few years after he started his professional life in the great city on Lake Michigan, his services were so outstanding that he was invited to become a member of the Illinois State Board of Health. At that time, there were many young Negroes in Chicago who wanted to become doctors and Daniel Williams tried to help as many as he could. But none of the Chicago hospitals would accept them as interns, and there were no training schools where Negro women could study to become nurses. Only whites were admitted as nursing students. Dr. Williams decided to do something about this frustrating situation which he discussed at great length with other doctors and with city and state officials. As a result of his efforts, in 1891 Provident Hospital on the South Side of Chicago was established. In connection with it, the first Training School for Negro Nurses in the United States was opened.

While a surgeon at Provident Hospital, one day Dr. Williams performed an operation that was immediately heralded by newspapers and written about in medical journals around the world. It was the first time in history that such an operation had ever been done successfully. One day a man was brought into the emergency ward with a deep stab wound in the chest, bleeding profusely. Dr. Williams was called. He attended to the man. But the next day when he went to his bedside to see him, the man was worse, and still bleeding internally. To find out why this should be, Dr. Williams opened the wound and extended it so that he might discover the source of the trouble. He found that the man had literally been stabbed to the heart, and that there was a puncture in that vital organ. No one expected the man to live, but Dr. Williams decided to try to save him. The walls of the vessel surrounding the heart were cut and, while other doctors with forceps held these walls open, Dr. Williams carefully sewed up the knife wound in the man's heart. Then he replaced the walls of his heart while it continued beating. To do this required great skill, daring, and very steady nerves. The man lived. And the operation became a famous one in medical history.

The President of the United States, Grover Cleveland, invited the young Negro physician to come to see him in Washington. He offered him a position as head of the new Freedman's Hospital, recently established in the District of Columbia. Dr. Williams found in Washington the same needs for the training of student doctors and nurses of color as he had in Chicago. So he established in connection with Freedman's Hospital a nurses' training school. And during his five years there he made the hospital a welcome place for young Negro doctors to practice their internships. He was not only a distinguished surgeon, but a great organizer and administrator. He had many requests to head hospitals or to teach, but he returned to his own private practice in Chicago. However, once a year he held a demonstration clinic in surgery at Meharry Medical College in Nashville, attended by young doctors from many states who came to watch his operations.

In the early 1900's, Dr. Williams became a member of the surgical staff of Cook County Hospital in Illinois and later an associate surgeon at Chicago's famous St. Luke's Hospital. In 1913 he received the exceptional honor of being made a Fellow of the American College of Surgeons. He attended most of the leading medical conventions and clinics of our country for many years. When he died, Daniel Hale Williams had long been considered one of America's greatest physicians.

Henry Ossawa Tanner
Whose Painting Hangs in the Luxembourg

1859–1937

Henry Ossawa Tanner did not leave behind him a dramatic life story, but he left many beautiful paintings in the museums of Europe and America. He wanted to be an artist and he became one. His father was a bishop of the African Methodist Episcopal Church, so as a child, although his family was by no means rich, Henry did not know hunger or the darkness of ignorance. He was born in Pittsburgh, but early in life was taken to Philadelphia where he grew to young manhood. As a boy walking in Fairmont Park one day, he saw an artist painting a view of the park. Then and there he decided he wanted to be an artist.

Henry went home and immediately painted a picture on the back of an old geography, the same scene, as nearly as he could remember it, that the man was painting that afternoon. Soon, the youngster got some clay and began to make models of the animals in the Philadelphia zoo. Later he became impressed with some canvases he saw of the sea, so he made a trip to Atlantic City during his teens especially to paint the ocean. All of this seemed very impractical to his father who thought that art was for vagabonds. Nevertheless, young Tanner enrolled at the Pennsylvania Academy of Fine Arts. And it was not long before he sold a painting for $40.00—a price which astonished him, for if he sold a picture for five or ten or fifteen dollars, he considered himself lucky. Even his very early paintings must have had some appeal, because one that he had sold for $15.00 was later resold at public auction for $250.00.

When young Tanner finished his studies at the Academy, he took a position as a teacher of drawing at Clark University in Atlanta. There, to supplement his meagre salary, he opened a photographic studio. He continued painting in his spare time, too, and sold an oil entitled "A Lion At Home" for $80.00. The venerable Bishop Daniel A. Payne, a colleague of Henry's father and a friend of Frederick Douglass, became interested in his painting and gave him a great deal of help. Young Tanner made a bust of the Bishop, and the Bishop in turn acquired three of the youthful artist's pictures which he presented to Wilberforce

University. In 1891 Tanner had enough paintings for a one-man show, so he organized an exhibition in Cincinnati. But there he did not sell a single picture. Again, however, a generous churchman, learning that the artist wished to go abroad, came to his rescue with the sum of about $300.00 so that Tanner might study in Rome.

On the way to Italy, Tanner stopped in Paris—and it was several years before he got any further! He was entranced, as artists have always been, with the art center of the world, so there he remained, studying first at the Academy Julien and later with various French masters of the era. Constant, Gérôme, Jean Paul Laurens, and Thomas Eakins especially influenced his work. But it was the beauty and artistic freedom of Paris that really caused the young painter to turn out canvas after canvas. And in a few years, one of his oils had received honorable mention, his first official recognition, at the French Salon. Perhaps it was his close family connection with the church, and his childhood familiarity with the great Bible stories, that caused the budding artist to turn toward religious subjects. He traveled a great deal in the Holy Land, studying the people, the architecture, the shrines, and the relics there, and for a long period he confined his canvases almost entirely to Biblical subjects. In 1897 his "The Resurrection of Lazarus" was bought by the French government to hang in the Luxembourg, one of the world's great galleries. Crowds came to view it, critics praised it, and from that time on Tanner's reputation as a painter of merit was solidly established.

At the Paris Exposition of 1900 his work received a medal of honor. That same year he was awarded the Walter Lippincott Prize in Philadelphia, and shortly thereafter he brought a number of his paintings from Europe to the United States for an exhibition in the city where he had grown up. But Tanner did not remain in the land of his birth long. To his friends he confided that, as a Negro, he found life in Europe much less difficult, for there he could travel freely and without segregation. When he wanted to paint rural landscapes, he had no difficulty because of color in finding an inn at which to sleep, or a place to eat. So, like the actor, Ira Aldridge, before him, his career flowered in Europe. He resided abroad until his death in Paris. His beautiful studio attracted many visitors. Some of the great artists of the day were his friends. And he lived to see his paintings bring him a sizable income.

Tanner's fame rests chiefly on his contributions in the field of religious painting. His life-like figures of Biblical characters in dramatic poses, his use of light to symbolize the presence of God, his combination of mysticism and realism, had a wide popular appeal. Richly academic in style and visually naturalistic, his work was never difficult for the layman to understand, yet it possessed the technical excellencies and strength of craftsmanship that also brought him the approval of his fellow artists. Tanner's "Christ Walking on the Water," "The Disciples on the Road to Bethany," "The Flight into Egypt," and "The Miraculous Draft of Fishes" are moving portrayals of familiar scriptural scenes that people love. In Philadelphia's Memorial Hall in Fairmont Park today, not far from the spot where the idea of being an artist came to Tanner, his beautiful painting, "The Annunciation," hangs.

George Washington Carver
Agricultural Chemist

About 1864–1943

One of the most important things that Booker T. Washington ever did was to engage George Washington Carver as a teacher at Tuskegee. Like Washington, Carver had been born in slavery. Shortly after his birth on a farm near Diamond Grove, Missouri, his father was run over by a wagon and killed. And before George was a year old, a band of Night Riders who made a specialty of kidnapping slaves and selling them to other masters far away surrounded his mother's cabin in the night. An older brother escaped capture, but little George and his mother were tied on a horse and taken over the Ozark Mountains into Arkansas. No one knows what became of his mother. But their master, Moses Carver, sent a man looking for them. Having no money, the master offered the man a tract of land if he found the woman, and a horse if he found the child. The baby George contracted whooping cough, so the callous Night Riders abandoned him somewhere on the road, to continue their journey with the mother who was never seen again. But the man found the sick child and brought him back to his master, who gave the promised horse as a reward for the baby.

The Carver family kept little George, and gave him their name. They were kind people, with no other slaves and no children, so they reared the child and his brother almost as if they were their own sons. And, even though slavery had ended with the War between the States, the boys stayed with them. As a child, while his older brother was at work, little George had a great deal of time to roam the woods and the fields nearby. He was always bringing back to Mrs. Carver some strange root or plant that he had found, wanting to know what it was. He seemed to have more than a normal child's curiosity about what made the petals of flowers different colors, why leaves had varying patterns, why bees loved clover, or why dew-drops sparkled. The Carvers were not educated people, but they answered his questions as best they could. And, noting his intelligence, they secured for him a spelling book which he and his brother puzzled over before the fireplace at night. But the days he spent mostly alone out of doors, often trying literally to get at the very roots of growing things, to puzzle out why the acorn made a tree, the sunflower seed a flower. He made himself a secret garden to bring back to life sick plants. He loved the feel of the earth in his little hands. Many years later he said, "People murder a child when they tell it to keep out of the dirt. In dirt is life."

George was about ten years old when his big brother decided to leave the farm to look for work elsewhere. Then the boy was more lonely than ever, except when he was busy helping the Carvers. Mrs. Carver taught George to cook and to clean and even to sew. He tended the fires in winter and learned to save the ashes to make soap. In Spring he cut sassafras bark and searched the woods for herbs and spices for medicines and seasonings. He helped spin flax and wool, tan cowhides for shoes, and boil barks for dye. By now he had learned every word in his old blue-backed speller. And he had heard that there was a school for colored children at Neosho, eight or ten miles away. He begged the Carvers to let him go there, and they did. He walked. A big strong kindly colored woman named Mariah Watkins took him in, and let him work for his board and keep. But she mothered him, too, and loved him, and his months with her became the happiest of all his young life. He was particularly happy because he could sit on a log bench in a log-cabin school with seventy other children and learn from their one teacher.

Being a washerwoman, Mariah Watkins taught young George to wash and iron. For this he was in later years to be deeply grateful. Mariah Watkins gave him a Bible, too, that became his most cherished possession. For seventy years, no matter where he went, he kept that Bible. Because there was no high school in Neosho, when he was about thirteen George hitchhiked a ride in a covered wagon to Kansas. There, at Fort Scott, he entered high school, working meanwhile as a houseboy for the richest family in town. One evening his employers sent him downtown to the drugstore. Near the courthouse he observed a great crowd of white men milling about. And, as he stopped to watch, he saw them storm the jail, break down its doors, drag a poor helpless Negro into the street, and kick and beat him to death. Meanwhile other men and boys were building a bonfire in the town square and, when it was blazing high, they threw the bleeding Negro into it. Young Carver's heart almost stopped beating and he became sick at the stomach. That night the boy packed up his few belongings and left town.

For almost ten years he wandered about the western country, from place to place, town to town, harvesting wheat, cutting wood, working sometimes as a gardener, sometimes as a cook, sleeping on haystacks, in sheds, in stables. Whenever he could, he worked among plants and flowers. But having no garden of his own in which to grow flowers he began to draw and paint them as he saw them in other people's gardens. Once in a town called Minneapolis, Kansas, where he had stopped long enough to finish high school, a lady saw some of his paintings on the walls of her laundress' home. She admired them, and encouraged the young man to keep on painting. For, by now, he was a young man, tall and dark and thin and a little stooped from not having always had enough to eat and from working very hard. Being still curious about the flowers he painted, George wanted to study botany.

One day Carver saw in a newspaper an advertisement of a religious college at Olathe, Kansas, called Highland University. He sent his high school record there and received a letter complimenting him on his good grades and saying that he would be registered. So, in the fall, he journeyed to that town, ready to study. But when he presented himself at the office to enroll, the minister in charge of the college looked at him in astonishment and said, "Why, we don't admit Negroes here!" He would not permit Carver to register. So the disappointed young man continued to wander across the western plains until he became a homesteader on some newly released government land. But he had no tools to develop the claim he had staked out, and no money to pay the taxes, so he lost the land. Although he was now more than twenty-five years old, George Washington Carver was still determined to complete his education. Finally, he gained admittance to Simpson College, near Winterset, Iowa. When he arrived there, so one of his teachers said later, he had only "a satchel full of poverty and a burning zeal to know everything."

Young Carver had but ten cents left after he had paid his entrance fees. With this he bought a nickel's worth of corn meal and a nickel's worth of beef suet which fed him for a week. Somehow he was able to persuade the general store to let him have two tin tubs, a washboard, some blueing, and some soap on credit. And he announced to the other students that he was opening a one-man laundry. That is how he earned his way through his first year of college, using the knowledge Mariah Watkins had taught him about washing and ironing. He had a beautiful high thin tenor voice and a talent for the piano and organ, so he studied music as well as the natural sciences. And, because he liked to paint, he studied art. Curiously enough, it was his painting that led to his further education. When his art teacher discovered his great interest in plants and soil, she wrote to her brother who was a professor of horticulture at Iowa State College at Ames, where there is an excellent agricultural department. Through this teacher Carver was admitted to classes there and became the first Negro to graduate from that institution.

But not all was smooth sailing at Iowa State where colored students were a rarity. Carver was not permitted to have a room in the dormitory. And, when he went into the student dining hall to eat, he was ordered out. But he was determined not to be discouraged, so he got a job as a waiter in the dining room and ate his meals free in the kitchen. Kindhearted teachers or students often wanted to help him with gifts of old clothing or money, but he would never accept charity from anyone. He always insisted on working for everything that he received. His love of plants and painting combined caused him to win several prizes for his still-life canvases at the Iowa Exhibit of State Artists. And four of his pictures were sent to the World's Fair at Chicago. His graduation thesis was "Plants as Modified by Man." He stood at the top of his class in scholarship. And by the time he was graduated in 1894, he had become so popular with his classmates that he was chosen the Class Poet. He ate his graduation dinner with his class in the very dining room that had at first turned him away.

George Washington Carver remained at Ames for two more years to do further study leading to an M.A. degree, and he was made an assistant instructor in Botany and put in charge of the greenhouse. Meanwhile, offers of jobs came to him from a number of Southern Negro colleges. One of his professors at Ames wrote in reply to such a request, "I do not want to lose Mr. Carver from our staff here. . . . In cross-fertilization and the propagation of plants he is by all means the ablest student we have. . . . With regard to plants he has a passion for them, in the conservatory, the garden, the orchard, and the farm. In that direction we have no one who is his equal." But, shortly after he had gained his second degree in 1896, Booker T. Washington came to the campus of Iowa State College and met George Washington Carver. He invited him to come to Tuskegee as head of the Department of Agriculture, director of agricultural research, and a teacher of natural sciences. A pretty heavy program, but, intrigued by the problems of this growing school in the Southland, Carver went, and remained there the rest of his life. It was at Tuskegee that he eventually became as famous as Booker T. Washington.

The two men were very different, and yet they had a great deal in common. Both had come up the hard way. Both believed in and loved working with the hands. Both had a deep feeling for the earth and all growing things. Both wanted to give what they learned to others. But George Washington Carver was a shy man and very quiet. Booker T. Washington was already a great public figure, a speaker able to sway large audiences, and an administrator accustomed to working with many people. Carver preferred to work alone, then present the results of his work to the world. The principal of Tuskegee understood this for he soon gave his new teacher a laboratory of his own, and a sleeping room of his own, and so Carver remained at Tuskegee the rest of his long life, living in one room and working in another. The Bible that Mariah Watkins gave him went with him to Tuskegee, too, resting on his bed table. His college textbooks went, also. But when Carver worked in his laboratory he took no books of any sort into the lab. Every morning before sunrise he sat alone on a stump in the woods just behind his laboratory and talked with God. Then he went to work alone until the hour to meet his students. From Carver's small laboratory at Tuskegee came formulas in agricultural chemistry that enriched the entire Southland, indeed the whole of America and the world.

Tuskegee was situated in the Cotton Belt where everybody had been taught to raise cotton up to the very doorsteps. Cotton had taken all the richness out of the land. Besides, it was no longer as profitable as it had once been. It was a risky crop. One of Tuskegee's problems was to teach the farmers to raise other things, and to save the land by rotating crops. In this Carver's help was inestimable. He showed them particularly the practical value of raising sweet potatoes and peanuts, and the variety of profitable products that could be obtained from these two plants. It was at Tuskegee that he began his famous experiments in finding out how many different kinds of useful things could be derived from the Alabama earth, particularly from the peanuts and sweet potatoes which grew so easily there. Before his death Carver had succeeded in extracting from the peanut such varied by-products as linoleum and metal polish, vegetable-milk and ink, grease, cooking oils, nineteen shades of dyes and stains, food sauces, shampoo, peanut butter, and cheese. Also, he evolved one hundred cooking recipes based on the peanut, from which a housewife could serve a full-course dinner—from soup to nuts!

In his little laboratory near the woods, Carver learned to create from sweet potatoes a valuable rubber compound, starch, imitation ginger, library paste, vinegar, shoe blacking, wood-filler, rope, flour, instant coffee, molasses, and almost a hundred other things. From pecans he produced many varied products. From cornstalks he taught his students how to make insulation wall-boards. Others of his products were synthetic marble from sawdust, plastics from wood-shavings, and writing paper from the wisteria vines that grew in profusion. From the Alabama clay itself, he showed that beautiful dyes of all colors could be made in quantities large enough to dye all the clothes in the world any shades people might desire. "Let down your bucket where you are," became Carver's agricultural maxim. To take what one had and make it yield what one wished became Carver's goal. Using the products of the land in the immediate vicinity of Tuskegee, he eventually benefited not just Alabama but people everywhere. Out of his experiments with the peanut grew a two hundred million dollar industry in the South. When he was called before a Senate Ways and Means Committee in Washington to explain what he had done with peanuts, the busy senators allotted him ten minutes. But once Carver had begun demonstrating peanut possibilities, they became so excited they let him talk for two hours. And, as a result of the information he gave them, they put through a tariff law to protect American peanuts from foreign competition.

Many universities awarded George Washington Carver honorary degrees, including that of Doctor of Science from the University of Rochester, so he became known as Dr. Carver. He was made a Fellow of the British Society of Arts, received the Spingarn Medal for outstanding achievement among Negroes, and many other honors. But he never enjoyed public life and could not often be persuaded to leave his laboratory to make a speech. President Franklin D. Roosevelt stopped at Tuskegee in 1939 to greet Dr. Carver. Henry Ford visited him there and they became great friends. But when Thomas A. Edison sent for Dr. Carver to work in his laboratories, offering him over fifty thousand dollars a year, he would not go. Neither would Carver ever apply for a patent on any of his discoveries. He said, "God gave them to me. Why should I claim to own them?" He cared nothing about money and would never accept a raise in salary at Tuskegee. Often, indeed, he did not even cash his salary checks. Once when asked for a contribution to some fund or other, he said that he had no money. Then he remembered to reach under a corner of his mattress. He pulled out a bundle of uncashed checks and said, "Here, take these. Maybe they are still good."

Although he had no interest in new clothes and never really dressed up, whenever Carver took off his laboratory apron and put on a jacket, he wore a fresh flower in his buttonhole. His speaking voice, like his singing voice, always remained high. Will Rogers once said of him that he was the only man he ever heard who could lecture to a class and sing tenor at the same time. All his life Carver continued to paint, and great museums sometimes tried to buy some of his paintings, but he usually would not sell any. Yet he would give them away, often to farmers or students. As he grew older some people thought he was a very strange old man. Everybody knew he was very famous. So, putting two and two together, they called him a genius. He was. "The wizard of the sweet potato" was a great agricultural chemist who did more in his field than any other single human being to advance the science of chemurgy—which means chemistry at work. When *The Progressive Farmer* once selected him as "the *Man of the Year* in service to southern agriculture" and all the nation's papers carried the news, *The New York Times* asked editorially, "What other man of our time has done so much for agriculture and the South?"

Ten years after his death, the United States government acquired the farm in Missouri on which George Washington Carver was born, and in 1953 it was dedicated by the Secretary of the Interior as a permanent shrine to his memory. On that occasion *The New York Herald Tribune* said:

"It is fitting that there should be a national memorial to Dr. George Washington Carver. He rose from slavery to become a famous scientist. The list of his achievements as a benefactor of mankind is almost endless. . . . Dr. Carver, however, will be remembered in the gallery of great Americans not so much for scientific eminence, but rather for the quality of the man's spirit. He was, as every one knows, a Negro. But he triumphed over all obstacles, including that of racial discrimination. Perhaps there is no one in this century whose example has done more to promote a better understanding between the races. Such greatness partakes of the eternal. Dr. Carver did more than find hidden merits in the peanut and the sweet potato. He helped to enlarge the American spirit."

Robert S. Abbott
A Crusading Journalist

1870–1940

    Robert Sengstacke Abbott was born on St. Simon's Island off the coast of Georgia in 1870, the son of a minister. He grew up in Savannah where he attended Beach Institute, and later Claflin Institute at Orangeburg, South Carolina. Then he went to Hampton where he was graduated as a printer. As a child he loved books and, fortunately, there was a good library in his home. He became acquainted with newspaper work early as an apprentice printer in the shop of the *Savannah News*. But since opportunities for advancement in printing were very limited for Negroes in the South, young Abbott settled in Chicago. There in 1896 he applied for membership in the Printer's Union, but was advised that he would only be wasting his time and money by belonging, since the union did not encourage colored membership. Nevertheless, he insisted on joining since all the big printing shops in Chicago were unionized. But, being a Negro, he found it very difficult to get work. And he learned that the union itself advised shops not to employ Negroes.

    Frustrated in efforts to earn a living at his trade, he turned to the study of law at Kent College, and practiced for a while in Chicago and Gary. But he loved the smell of printer's ink, so he determined to start a newspaper of his own and eventually to buy a printing press. Besides, he felt that with all the problems Negroes had to face, they needed a mouthpiece in Chicago to air their grievances and to work for more democratic conditions in regard to employment, civil rights, and education. On the day that he began his paper he had only twenty-five cents, a desk, and a chair. A woman lent him a basement room on State Street which was at the same time her kitchen. He solicited advertisements, gathered news, wrote editorials, printed, and sold the paper himself. The first issue of *The Chicago Defender,* dated May 5, 1905, consisted of three hundred copies. Its paper and printing cost $13.75. Three friends became subscribers at $1.00 a year. It was to appear weekly at five cents a copy. From the very beginning its issues grew in numbers of copies. Gradually the paper increased in size, too, and its subscribers became more numerous until they eventually numbered a quarter of a million and *The Chicago Defender* became the largest and most influential Negro newspaper in America.

As a boy in the deep South, Abbott had observed that almost the only news which the papers carried about Negro citizens was crime news or lynchings. When Negroes in Savannah died, or got married, or dedicated a new church, there was nothing in the daily press about these happenings. Many Southern papers made it a rule never to publish the picture of a Negro, not even Booker T. Washington's. And in writing about colored people, they usually refused to use the terms Mr. or Mrs. before their names. In the North, general news usually crowded the news of Negro activities out of the papers, unless again these were criminal activities. When colored boys and girls were graduated from high school or college, or won prizes, or gave a party, they liked to see their pictures in the paper, too. So, to supply the Negro community of Chicago with news of its own activities, as well as to provide editorial leadership in its struggle for democracy, Robert S. Abbott started *The Chicago Defender*. Gradually it grew into a national journal on sale on the newsstands of cities and towns almost everywhere. But, because of its strong stand on equal rights for all, various Southern communities refused to permit it to circulate. And, at one time in some counties in Georgia where Negroes could not vote, it was a crime—inciting to riot—for a colored person to possess a copy of this Northern newspaper with its accent on the ballot as the basis of democracy.

When Mr. Abbott began publishing the *Defender,* the Negro population of Chicago was about 40,000. But during World War I there was a great influx of colored people into the North, drawn by the war industries there, so by 1920 Chicago had over 100,000 Negro citizens. Because thousands of men had gone off into the army, thus creating a labor shortage, factories and foundries that formerly had barred colored workers now began to employ them, and the *Defender* urged that more do so. At that time Mr. Abbott wrote:

"There is no line of endeavor that we cannot fit ourselves for. These same factories, mills and workshops that have been closed to us, through necessity are being opened to us. We are to be given a chance, not through choice but because it is expedient. Prejudice vanishes when the almighty dollar is on the wrong side of the balance sheet. . . . Slowly but surely all over this country we are gradually edging in first this and then that place, getting a foothold before making a place for our brother. By this only can the so-called race problem be solved. It is merely a question of a better and a closer understanding between the races. We are Americans and *must* live together, so why not live in peace?"

A firm believer in the power of the ballot, *The Chicago Defender* urged Negroes to register, vote, and elect their own representatives to office. Shortly there were colored aldermen in the City Council of Chicago, Negro representatives in the Illinois State Legislature, and Oscar DePriest was elected the first Negro to serve in Congress at Washington since the turn of the century. In these political gains Editor Abbott's paper played no small part. While urging Negroes to take advantage of their democratic rights, it at the same time continually urged them to shoulder their full civic and national duties, to keep their neighborhoods clean, be thrifty and self-respecting, buy bonds, aid the war effort, and in general be good citizens.

Because, until very recently, the big national advertisers, like the makers of motor cars and breakfast foods, did not advertise in Negro newspapers, these papers had to depend almost entirely on newsstand sales and subscriptions for income. Realizing this, Mr. Abbott instituted colorful and dramatic reporting of news in the *Defender,* the use of big headlines in red ink, and other attention-getting devices. He also kept close to the common people so that he might express in his pages their wants and desires. And, even after he became a wealthy man, he could be found mingling with stockyard workers and steel mill stokers on Chicago's South Side, listening to their problems concerning decent housing, prejudice in promotions, or segregation in unions. Because the *Defender* was for many years the leading newspaper of the Negro masses, it became known all over the country, and has had a very great influence on democratic thinking.

After Mr. Abbott's death *The Chicago Defender* continued under the editorship of his nephew, John H. Sengstacke. During World War II, while pressing for the complete abolition of segregation and discrimination in the armed forces and in industry, at the same time it carried many patriotic editorials in support of the War and conducted vigorous War Bond drives. One of its editorials in 1944 said:

> "Regardless of how deeply we may resent numerous injustices perpetrated against us and how hard we may fight against them, we must admit that this is our war too. Our boys are fighting overseas, facing a dangerous, murderous enemy who will destroy them and us as quickly as he will our white brothers. . . . Participation in this Fourth War Loan drive is not only a patriotic act, but is a matter of self interest."

Chicago's Negro community bought two million dollars worth of bonds. In honor of the newspaper that sponsored this campaign, the United States Maritime Commission named a newly built Liberty ship, launched at San Francisco, the U.S.S. *Robert S. Abbott.*

During his lifetime, Mr. Abbott became the National Executive President of the Hampton Alumni Association, a trustee of the Y.M.C.A, a member of the Board of Directors of the National Urban League, and a Life Member of the Field Museum. Now each year in Chicago a Memorial Award is given in his honor to someone who has made a distinguished contribution toward better race relations in America, and in 1945 *The Chicago Defender* established the Robert S. Abbott Memorial Scholarship at the Lincoln University School of Journalism. Meanwhile *The Chicago Defender* has extended its activities to include a chain of seven other newspapers from New York to Memphis.

Paul Laurence Dunbar
The Robert Burns of Negro Poetry

1872–1906

Paul Laurence Dunbar's father was an escaped slave who took the Underground Railroad to Canada, but returned to fight as an enlisted soldier in the Civil War. He married a woman who had been a slave in Kentucky. Seven years after the War ended, a son was born to them at Dayton, Ohio. His father said, "We will name him Paul after the Apostle Paul in the Bible, because this boy is going to be a great man." His father did not live to see this happen. He died when Paul was only twelve years old. But his prophecy came true. Paul Laurence Dunbar did become a great man.

His mother could not read when Paul was born but, after her marriage, she had begun to learn, and she took pains to send her son to school as soon as he was old enough. As a widow she had to earn her own living, so she took in washing and ironing. Paul called for the soiled clothes and delivered the clean ones to her customers each week. At night together he and his mother studied spelling and young Paul was able to help her learn to write. But with all the work she had to do, she never did learn very well. And once, after her son was grown and away in another city, when a neighbor stopped by her house one morning, she said, "I must hurry up and get my washing done early because I have a hard day's work ahead of me."

The friend inquired, "What have you got to do?"

"I've got to write a letter to my son," said Mrs. Dunbar.

When Paul was graduated from high school, the only Negro in his class, as president of the literary society, he was chosen to write the Class Song to be sung at the graduation exercises. Since the age of seven he had been writing little poems, and he had continued to write in high school where he became editor of the school paper. At thirteen he recited one of his own verses at an Easter Sunday school program. He was sixteen when his first printed poems appeared in *The Dayton Herald*. One of his high school English teachers was so impressed with Paul's talent for rhyming that, after his graduation, when the Western Association of Writers was meeting in Dayton, she arranged for him to compose a poem of welcome and recite it himself. Young Paul was then running an elevator in the Callahan Building on Main Street for a salary of $4.00 a week. He had to beg off from work for a few hours to attend the meeting. The assembled writers were astonished to see a young Negro lad walk to the platform at the opening of their session and greet them in poetry. But they were so impressed with his verses that when the meeting was over many sought to find him. No one in the hall could locate Paul, however, because he had gone back to work. But some of the writers finally found him running the elevator and congratulated him on his poem.

When Paul felt that he had enough poems for a book, he put them together and carried his manuscript to a small publishing house in Dayton where he was informed that poetry was a risky business and that only if he underwrote the cost of publication could they bring out his poems. This would be $125.00. Young Paul did not have a dollar in the world, so he was about to turn away in disappointment when the business manager, who had heard about his talent, called him. Finally this man agreed personally to pay the costs if Paul would reimburse him from the first books sold. Paul gave his word and the little volume, *Oak and Ivy,* appeared in time for Christmas, 1893. Within two weeks, at a dollar each, Paul had sold enough copies to people who went up and down in his elevator to repay the publication costs. And the Reverend R. C. Ransom, who later became a bishop of the African Methodist Church, sold a hundred copies for Paul at his Sunday services.

That year the World's Columbian Exposition opened in Chicago, and Frederick Douglass was in charge of an exhibit from Haiti. Paul went to Chicago seeking better paying work. Douglass gave him a job at $5.00 a week as one of his assistants, and on Colored American Day both Dunbar and Douglass appeared on the same platform. When the Exposition was over Paul returned to Dayton and worked as a page boy at the Court House. The well-known James Whitcomb Riley had somehow heard of Paul's poems, and wrote him a letter of encouragement. As a reader of his own verses, Paul had begun to acquire some reputation in Dayton and surrounding towns, so the head of the State Hospital for the Insane, Dr. H. A. Tobey, arranged for the young man to have a program in Toledo. Its success brought Paul many new friends and through these his second volume, *Majors and Minors,* was privately printed in Toledo in 1895. On Paul's twenty-fourth birthday a famous American writer, William Dean Howells, reviewed this book enthusiastically in *Harper's Weekly,* a widely read national publication, devoting to it an entire page.

It was this review that made Paul Laurence Dunbar nationally known almost overnight. When the article appeared, Paul and his mother were away from home for a few days. On their return he found more than two hundred letters the mailman had stuck through the shutters of the front window. Many of the letters contained money orders for his new book.

Invitations to recite his poems soon came to Dunbar from a number of cities. Many of his verses were in the quaint and charming broken English of the newly freed slaves, such as his mother and father had spoken. Dunbar read these poems very well. And sometimes he even acted them out. When he recited *The Cornstalk Fiddle:*

> "Take your lady and balance down the middle,
> To the merry strains of the cornstalk fiddle. . . ."

he would himself dance the figures of an old-time country dance. Audiences loved him. Soon he had a manager to take charge of his engagements. In New York this manager arranged for him to see the big publishers, Dodd, Mead & Company, who in 1896 brought out the first of his books to be published by a real publishing house. For this volume, *Lyrics of Lowly Life,* William Dean Howells wrote the Introduction. The following year, that of Queen Victoria's Diamond Jubilee, young Dunbar went to London to read his poems. There he was well received, but his manager kept almost all the money so Paul had to cable friends in America for his return fare.

Always an industrious young man, while in London, instead of sightseeing much, he wrote his first novel, *The Uncalled,* which he sold to a magazine as a serial before it appeared in book form. John Hay, the American Ambassador to the Court of St. James, arranged a program for Paul in London and there he met many distinguished people. Just as the English, more than a hundred years before, had welcomed the Negro poet from Boston, Phillis Wheatley, so now they welcomed Paul Laurence Dunbar from Dayton. Luncheons, teas, and banquets were given in his honor, and he was a guest of the secretary of the Royal Geological Society. At that time many upper class Englishmen wore monocles, so Paul wrote home that in London, "the men, poor fellows, did not have enough eye-glasses to go around, so each had *one* stuck in the corner of his eye."

Before he went to London, Dunbar had fallen in love with a beautiful girl from New Orleans who had run away from home to see him off on the boat. So when he returned to America he wanted to get married.

Therefore, he thought he should settle down and take a regular job. With the aid of Colonel Robert G. Ingersoll, he obtained a position as an assistant in the Reading Room of the Library of Congress in Washington at a salary of $750.00 a year. During his first months there he wrote a series of short stories for *Cosmopolitan,* later published in book form under the title *Folks From Dixie,* dedicated to the Toledo doctor who had helped him get started. In Washington he got married, had a fine wedding, and Paul and his bride began to buy a cottage. Perhaps it was then that he wrote:

> "A little dreaming by the way,
> A little toiling day by day;
> A little pain, a little strife,
> A little joy—and that is life.
>
> A little short-lived summer's morn
> When joy seems all so newly born,
> When one day's sky is blue above,
> And one bird sings—and that is love."

For a few months they were very happy—but a few months only—then Paul began to feel badly and to cough a great deal. At first they thought the cough came from the dust on the books at the Library where he worked. But eventually Dunbar learned that he had tuberculosis.

Failing health forced him to resign from the Library of Congress, and for the next eight years he fought against his illness. There were periods when he could do nothing, followed by periods of intense activity. He wrote several more books of poetry and of prose. He read his poems in many cities. At the invitation of Booker T. Washington, he visited Tuskegee more than once and lectured to English classes there. Booker T. asked Paul to write a poem for an annual farmers' conference. He did, and read it to the assembled farmers. He also wrote the *Tuskegee Song* for the 25th anniversary of that famous school:

> " . . . The fields smile to greet us, the forests are glad,
> The ring of the anvil and hoe
> Have a music as thrilling and sweet as a harp
> Which thou taught us to hear and know. . . ."

A student chorus of fifteen hundred voices sang it. The students at Negro schools and colleges all over the South had begun to read Dunbar's poems and to love them. While he was ill in New York in 1899, Atlanta

University awarded him an honorary degree. But the poet could not go South for the ceremonies. He had instead to go West to the Rocky Mountains for his health. Ill though he was, he did not stop writing. In a cottage near Denver he finished another novel, *The Love of Landry,* laid in Colorado.

Although Paul Laurence Dunbar wrote a great deal of prose—four novels, four volumes of short stories, and many articles—and this work appeared in the best magazines and was widely read, it was his poetry that made him famous, that continued to be read after his death, and that is loved today. Many of his poems have been set to music. Especially for the delightful Negro composer, Will Marion Cook, in 1898 Dunbar wrote the lyrics for a musical sketch, *Clorindy—The Origin of the Cakewalk,* which was performed for an entire season at a popular New York music hall. Many of Dunbar's most beautiful poems were written in straight English. But his most popular and charming ones are in the old-time Negro dialect of a sort no longer spoken and rather hard for people to read today. Yet the charm and the humor are still there behind the broken English of that difficult period following the Civil War when a whole race of people was still trying to learn to read and write:

> "Little brown baby wif spa'klin' eyes,
> Come to yo' pappy an' set on his knee.
> What you been doin', suh,—makin' san' pies?
> Look at dat bib—you's ez du'ty ez me.
> Look at dat mouf—dat's merlasses, I bet;
> Come hyeah, Maria, an' wipe off his han's.
> Bees gwine to ketch you an' eat you up yit,
> Bein' so sticky an' sweet—goodness lan's!"

When Paul Laurence Dunbar died in Dayton in 1906 his friend, the Mayor of Toledo, Brand Whitlock, wrote:

> "Nature, who knows so much better than man about everything invariably seizes the opportunity to show her contempt of rank and title and race and land and creed. She took Burns from a plow and Paul from an elevator, and Paul has done for his own people what Burns did for the peasants of Scotland—he has expressed them in their own way and in their own words. . . . There was nothing foreign in Paul's poetry, nothing imported, nothing imitated: it was all original, native, and indigenous. Thus he becomes the poet not of his own race alone—I wish I could make people see this—but the poet of you and of me and of all men everywhere."

Paul Laurence Dunbar was buried on Lincoln's Birthday, and hundreds of people attended his funeral. Beside his grave his mother planted a willow tree, for the site had been selected to correspond to the setting Paul had described in his poem, *A Death Song,* when he wrote:

> "Lay me down beneaf de willers in de grass,
> Whah de branchll go a-singin' as it pass.
> An' w'en I's a-layin' low,
> I kin hyeah it as it go
> Singin', 'Sleep, my honey, tek yo' res' at las'.'"

W. C. Handy
Father of the Blues

1873–1958

Hotel orchestras in Europe frequently strike up *The St. Louis Blues* when they learn that there are American guests in the dining room. Around the world this blues has long been the best known American popular song and the one most often played. Some foreigners are even under the mistaken impression that it is the American National Anthem. During World War II when Hitler's armies invaded France and American jazz music was forbidden on the government radio in Paris, the French continued to play *The St. Louis Blues,* anyway, calling it *La Tristesse de Saint Louis.* When the German censors asked if it was not an American Negro song, the French said, "Oh, my no! Don't you know this song really goes much farther back than that? The man in the song is King Louis the Fourteenth, and the woman with the diamond rings is in truth Marie Antoinette. What a sad ending she had! *Quelle tristesse!*"

The man who wrote *The St. Louis Blues* was born in Florence, Alabama, near the Muscle Shoals Canal, eight years after the Civil War. He was christened William Christopher Handy, in the church which his grandfather had built on a hill called, because his folks had lived there so long, Handy's Hill. All around the house were orchards of peaches, pears, cherries, and plums where birds and butterflies fluttered, lightning bugs glowed in the evenings, and hoot owls sometimes roosted. Not far off were meadows where cattle grazed. And in the bogs and along the canal banks bullfrogs croaked and snakes coiled and hissed. One morning when little William's mother came to wake him up, she found a snake sleeping in the bed with her child. Certainly his early life was spent close to nature. And he was particularly fascinated by the music in the bird calls, the cricket chirps, and lowing of the cattle, and the night cries of owls and frogs.

When William started to school, his favorite class was music. It was his good fortune to have a young man teacher just out of Fisk University who every morning devoted the first half hour of school to singing, without the aid of piano for they had none. This teacher was a lover of great music. He taught the children not only all the gospel hymns, but excerpts from the operas of Wagner, Verdi, and Bizet. He drilled them thoroughly in their scales and in sight reading. Young Handy began to fit what he learned in school to what he heard in the woodlands, searching around in his mind for notes to correspond to those the birds sang or the katydids chirped. Even the mooing of a cow seemed to him to have melody in it, and years later he wrote a piece called the *Hooking Cow Blues.*

But music to his father, a Methodist minister, was something only for church and school. And musical instruments to him were taboo— "instruments of Satan." He did not even permit a piano or an organ in his church. But, nevertheless, little Handy was playing tunes on a fine-tooth comb, or beating out rhythms on his mother's tin pans, or trying to reproduce on a mouth organ the cotton field melodies that he heard rising in the sun-light. And once he tried to make a trumpet from a cow's horn, but it would blow only one note. When he was twelve years old, he got a job as a water boy in a rock quarry near Muscle Shoals at fifty cents a day. There he heard the wonderfully rhythmical songs of the steel-drivers at work:

> "There ain't no hammer. . . . Huh!
> That-a rings like mine, boys. . . . Huh!"

grunting in unison as the hammers fell. It was then that he began to save his money to buy a guitar that he had seen in a window downtown. Finally he had enough cash. But when he came home with the instrument, his father and mother were so shocked they could hardly speak. They called the guitar "one of the devil's playthings," and ordered him to take it out of their house at once. In fact, they made him return it to the department store where he had purchased it and exchange the guitar for something he could use in school—a *Webster's Dictionary.*

In those days in the South actors and musicians as a class were considered trifling people. But it seemed very difficult to teach little Handy that this might be so. One day in school the teacher was asking each member of William's class what careers they intended to follow. Some said lawyers, some said doctors, some nurses, some teachers. When it came his turn he said, "A musician." His teacher was so horrified that he not only scolded him roundly in front of the whole class, but wrote his father a note. That night William's father said that he had rather follow his coffin to the grave than to see him turn out a worthless musician. This had no effect upon the son, especially after a wonderful fiddle player named Jim Turner came to town. Turner was from Memphis where his sweetheart had quit him, leaving him so brokenhearted that he simply went down to the station, pulled out his money, and asked the agent for a ticket to anywhere—just *anywhere* away from there. The agent sold him a ticket to Florence. On his violin Turner could play wonderful waltzes, minuets, mazurkas, and schottisches that fascinated young Handy and made him more determined than ever to be a musician.

A while later a circus was stranded in Florence and its bandmaster, in order to make some quick money, began to give band instructions at night in a colored barber shop. William stood outside the window looking and listening and learning, although he had no instrument on which to play and no money to pay for lessons. One of the members of the band sold him an old cornet for a dollar and seventy-five cents and showed him how to finger the valves. Then William would stand outside the barber shop blowing on this while the men inside practiced with their teacher. Finally they let him come inside and rehearse with the band. Once they needed a player for an out-of-town engagement, so he played hookey from school and went along. He earned eight dollars of which he thought his father would be proud. But no, he was not! And he got a whipping besides from his teacher for missing classes.

When the famous Georgia Minstrels came to town Handy was so impressed by the band, the singers, and comedians like Billy Kersands (who could put a whole cup and saucer in his mouth) that he joined a home-town minstrel show himself and sang tenor in the quartet. When he was in his teens this group went on a tour and got stranded in Jasper, Alabama, where the boys had to sing for their suppers and walk part of the way back home to Florence. His father, frowning on these activities, wanted him to be a minister. Instead young Handy decided to be a teacher. So when he came out of school he took the County Teacher's Examination in Birmingham and got the second highest mark. But when he found out that teachers' salaries were even less than a dollar a day, he decided instead to go to work at a foundry in Bessemer. While there he organized a brass band, a string orchestra, and, on Sundays, played a trumpet in the church choir. But a depression came and he lost his job, the main source of income. Meanwhile, he had organized a quartet and, hearing that there was to be a World's Fair in Chicago that year, the four young men decided to hobo there on a freight train. The brakeman soon put the boys off on a lonely stretch of railroad track in the dark of night. The poor fellows started singing there beside the track. They sang so mournfully that the brakeman took pity on them and let them get back in a box car and ride into Decatur. Handy had twenty cents, so the next morning he bought a loaf of bread and some molasses and sat down beside a spring for breakfast. While they were eating they saw an excursion boat docking and a group of ladies going on board for a picnic outing. Handy ran up and presented them with one of his handwritten cards, *The Lauzetta Quartet,* and the ladies hired them on the spot to sing as they sailed down the Tennessee River. For this the boys got ten dollars and all they could eat from the picnic baskets. Finally, they reached Chicago—only to find that the World's Fair had been postponed for a year.

St. Louis at that time was said to be a very lively town, so they headed there. But it was then in the throes of the depression, too, and nobody had any extra money for music, so the quartet broke up. Jobs were hard to find. Handy slept in the hay of the horses' stalls at the race track and sometimes on the levee of the Mississippi River with thousands of other penniless men. Then he discovered a big pool hall on Targee Street where you could sit and sleep so long as the police did not bother you. He was told that the way the police judged if a man was asleep or not was by whether his feet were moving. Handy learned to sleep with one foot swinging all the time. Sometimes a one-eyed man slept with his hat over his sleeping eye while his glass eye, wide open, was exposed—to fool the cops. The police carried long night-sticks that they loved to use, so nobody wanted to be taken as a vagrant. But neither do homeless men like to be outdoors in the damp of evening. And when it is cold, they dread the coming of nightfall. From his experiences in St. Louis years later Handy derived the opening line of his famous blues:

"I hate to see the evenin' sun go down. . . ."

But he was too proud to go back home to hear his father say, "I told you so! Ruination! Musicians, nothing but bums!"

So Handy did not go home. He hit the road as a freight-train rider again, and found himself one day in Evansville, Indiana, where he got work with a street paving gang. In a little while he was playing with a local band there. One day he went to Henderson, Kentucky, to play for a barbecue. He liked beautiful green Kentucky so well that he stayed, met his wife there, and got a job as a janitor at Liederkranz Hall where a wonderful German singing society rehearsed—just so he could learn from its rehearsals. Meanwhile, he continued to play nights in a little band. One of the musicians from this band had joined Mahara's Colored Minstrels and, when he learned that they needed a new cornet player, he wrote Handy to join the troupe. He did in 1896, and from that time on he was a professional musician.

As a child, his grandmother had always told him that since he had big ears, he must have a talent for music. She was right, for, as a part of a touring minstrel show, his musical abilities developed in many ways, and he became of great value to the troupe, playing solo leads, making arrangements of new tunes, and training quartets. Within a year this talented young man had been made the leader of a thirty-piece parade band, and conducted the forty-two-piece ensemble for the pre-curtain concerts in the evening. For the next four years Handy traveled all over the United States and Canada and into Mexico and Cuba with the minstrels. But, having a little daughter by now, he thought he should settle down, so he took a job as a teacher of music and English at Alabama Agricultural and Mechanical College near Huntsville, Alabama. But the pay was only $40.00 a month, the duties were heavy and worst of all, the president liked only hymns and "classics"—"classics" meaning European compositions. By this time Handy had learned how much audiences all over the land enjoyed American popular music and ragtime. But he was not permitted to teach or play such music at the college. So one day he decided to fool them with his student band. He took a piece called *My Ragtime Baby* and changed the title to *Greetings to Toussaint L'Ouverture, the Liberator of Haiti,* and so it was announced on the printed programs of a college celebration. Not only the students, but the faculty, applauded loudly when the piece was over. They enjoyed it immensely. But, when he told the faculty of the joke he had played on them, it was not appreciated at all. Handy did not remain long at Alabama A. & M. He rejoined the Mahara's Minstrels, and became their star cornet soloist and conductor.

When motion picture theaters began to open up all over the country the minstrels, a form of American entertainment popular for over fifty years, began to decline. The thirty-year-old Handy, with a second child by now, decided to accept the post of bandmaster with the Knights of Pythias Band in Clarksdale, Mississippi. In this city deep in the cotton lands of the Delta, not far from the river, on Saturday nights cotton pickers, roustabouts, and levee camp workers came to town. Handy's band, or the orchestra that he organized from it, made frequent trips into the country to play for picnics or dances. In a region rich with song, he heard the minor melodies of the fields and the river, the Negro work-songs, jailhouse songs, and unwritten blues that were shortly to form the basis for his own compositions. The members of his band and orchestra were all trained musicians, playing by note, and inclined to conventional music. They came mostly from religious homes where playing music was not too highly thought of, anyway, and ragtime and minstrel songs were considered sinful. So by preference they played mostly the standard marches and the more sedate waltzes and two-steps.

But one night, playing for a dance in Cleveland, Mississippi, Handy was asked if he would mind if a trio of local roustabouts contributed a few numbers. Happy to have a rest for his men, he gave the platform up to a group of ragged youngsters who began an endless but very rhythmical tune on their battered string instruments that soon had the whole crowd dancing, swaying, and clapping hands as Handy's own band had not been able to make them do all evening. When the piece was over, the crowd cried for more, and showered the untrained musicians with silver dollars and smaller coins. In the end these boys picked up more money than the Handy band was paid for the whole evening. And the tunes they played were nothing more than those heard every day in the cotton fields and on the levee. That night Handy was more than ever convinced of the pleasure people might find in our own American Negro music, and in the syncopated way in which untrained musicians sang and played.

It was in Memphis, where he had moved to take charge of a band, that Handy had a chance to try out this conviction during a political campaign. There were three candidates for mayor, and each faction hired a band to play at political rallies. Handy's band was employed to back Edward H. Crump, who later became a great power in Memphis politics. Handy wrote a campaign tune for Mr. Crump, based on his memories of the rhythms of the uneducated Negroes. Immediately this composition swept Memphis. White and colored people danced in the streets when it was played. Handy received so many requests for his band to perform in so many places at the same time, that he had to break the band up into several small units. His tune, *Mr. Crump,* with its levee swing and cotton field slurs, was a hit. Mr. Crump himself was elected Mayor of Memphis. And W. C. Handy, as he was known, became famous throughout the Delta. Soon he organized more bands, and all of them were kept busy playing in Memphis or nearby towns. After the campaign was over, the title, *Mr. Crump,* he changed to *The Memphis Blues.* Thus the first famous American blues came into being.

The Memphis Blues was published in 1912. But Handy, not realizing its value, had sold his rights to it for $50.00. So, as its popularity spread across the country, others made thousands of dollars from it while he got nothing. But the tune made him very well known as a song writer, so he determined to follow it up with more compositions. Having by now four children, Handy found it very difficult to compose at home. One night he rented a room over a saloon on Beale Street and stayed up all night writing a new song. The song came out of his deepest memories; the rock quarry melodies of his youth, hoboing on the railroad, tramping from place to place, town to town; the homeless nights in St. Louis when he hated to see the sun go down; a woman he heard once complaining that her lover had a heart as hard as a rock cast in the sea; the women in St. Louis with their diamond rings; the river songs he had heard on the levee. Out of those memories *The St. Louis Blues* was born. The next day he orchestrated it. That night he played it at a dance. The dancers loved it, applauded and applauded, whistled, stamped their feet, and demanded that it be played again and again.

For two days Handy had not been home. When, after the dance, he rushed to the house to tell his wife about his new hit, she met him with a rolling pin! He sang:

> "Saint Louis Blues,
> Just as blue as I can be. . . ."

"Blue, nothing!" his wife said. "I'm the one who ought to be blue. Why didn't you tell me you intended to stay away from home like this? Where have you been?"

Mrs. Handy was not excited about the new song at all, not that night. She was angry. Of course, she and W. C. Handy were both very happy later when thousands of dollars in royalties from sheet music and record sales of *The St. Louis Blues* started to come in. Almost all the leading popular singers and big bands began to record the song. One day the mailman dropped at Handy's house in Memphis a copy of the latest Victor Records catalogue. In running his eye down the list of composers under the letter *H* he saw:

> *Handel*
> *Handy*
> *Haydn*

His name between the names of two of the great masters! When he showed it to his children they said, "Papa, who's them other two men?"

The St. Louis Blues has had over four hundred different recordings. New ones are continually being made not only in English, but in other languages all over the world. From Okinawa during World War II some soldiers sent W. C. Handy a Japanese record they had found in a dugout there of *The St. Louis Blues,* sung in Japanese. Ordinary people and royalty alike have loved the song. King Edward VIII had his Scottish bagpipers play this blues at Balmoral Castle. *Life* magazine reported it as Queen Elizabeth's favorite piece of dance music. Since the 369th Infantry Band introduced it to Europe during the First World War, this blues is said to have influenced the work of such modern composers as Stravinsky, Honegger, and Milhaud. And certainly it influenced George Gershwin, as he himself acknowledged, in his writing of such famous American works as the *Rhapsody in Blue* and *Porgy and Bess.* John Alden Carpenter wrote a symphonic blues, *Katnip Blues.* There have been hundreds of composers who have tried their hand at straight blues or popular songs in the blues style: Hoagy Carmichael's *Washboard Blues,* Clarence Williams' *Basin Street Blues,* Johnny Mercer's *Blues in the Night,* Harold Arlen's *Stormy Weather.* Dorothy Lamour appeared in a motion picture called *The St. Louis Blues,* as did Bessie Smith in an earlier short film of the same title. From tiny night clubs to Madison Square Garden, from river boats to Broadway theaters, juke boxes to films, radio to TV, *The St. Louis Blues* has been sung. Perhaps one of the largest audiences to hear it at one time was at a *Chicago Tribune* Music Festival in Soldier Field when a massed chorus of three thousand voices sang it to an audience of 125,000 people.

W. C. Handy was forty years old when he wrote this song that started him on the road to fame and fortune. Since that time he has become an established music publisher on Broadway, heading the largest Negro publishing firm in the country. He has played his golden horn in all the leading theaters of America, at the International Exposition on Treasure Island in San Francisco, and at the New York World's Fair. He has appeared on every major radio and television network many times. At the age of sixty he toured America with Joe Laurie, Jr.'s *Memory Lane* Company, playing his own blues. Even after he lost his eyesight, Mr. Handy was appearing nightly at Billy Rose's Diamond Horseshoe in New York playing *The St. Louis Blues* as a solo on the cornet. He has composed a great many songs and instrumental compositions, arranged hundreds of others, edited musical anthologies, and compiled a fascinating autobiography, *Father of the Blues.* He was over seventy and entirely blind when he accidentally fell on his head from the platform onto the subway tracks in New York City. For a few days everybody thought he was going to die. But he recovered and returned to his Broadway office and his theater, radio, and TV work.

He was one of the organizers of the Negro Actors Guild. He is also a founder of the W. C. Handy Foundation for the Blind. For a number of years his annual birthday dinners at some large New York hotel have brought in sizable sums for this worthy charity. Now there is a park in Memphis named after him. On the very spot where he slept hungry and penniless as a young man the city of St. Louis is planning a memorial tower with a clock which will chime *The St. Louis Blues.* And in Florence, Alabama, where he was born, there is a beautiful new W. C. Handy School, in honor of the man who has been such a great influence on modern American music—and who first, as a child, began to learn the beauties of our music from the rock quarry and cotton field melodies of his native Alabama.

Charles C. Spaulding
Executive of World's Largest Negro Business

1874–1952

The years immediately following Emancipation were very difficult ones for the newly freed but destitute Negroes. Often they could not afford medical care for the sick, or even to bury the dead. So, to do these things, they had to band together. Therefore, many fraternal groups, mutual benefit organizations, and burial societies came into being, a number of them connected with or growing out of the churches. Even before the War between the States some such groups had been formed among the Negroes of the North. The Free African Society founded in 1787 in Philadelphia was organized "to support one another in sickness, and for the benefit of their widows and fatherless children." Such fraternal lodges as the Masons, the Elks, the Odd Fellows, and the Independent Order of St. Luke, founded by a newly freed woman in 1867 and still in successful operation, had the same objectives. The first Negro-owned insurance, the African Insurance Company, started in 1810 with a capital of $5,000. Today insurance is the largest American Negro business with more than two hundred companies owned and operated entirely by colored people. Their combined insurance in force amounts to more than a billion dollars.

The largest Negro insurance firm in the world is the North Carolina Mutual Life Insurance Company of Durham, North Carolina. Charles Clinton Spaulding was, until his death in 1952, its president. His connection with the company began as its first manager in 1898, and he saw it grow from the ground up. Spaulding had no experience in insurance when he went into the formation of the concern, so he had to learn from scratch. And he had only an eighth grade education as a background. After he became wealthy and famous in the business world, he often said, "The only time I have ever been to college was to deliver a Commencement address."

Spaulding was born on a farm in Columbus County, North Carolina, nine years after Abraham Lincoln was assassinated. He was the third in a family of fourteen children, and being one of the oldest, much of the

85

farm work fell to him. His attendance at school was irregular so, when he became a man, he decided to leave the plow and go to Durham and make a determined effort to at least get through grammar school. In the city Charles got a job at $10.00 a month as a dishwasher in a hotel, and later he became a bellboy in the evenings so he could attend classes by day. He was then twenty-one years old and much too big to be in grammar school with younger boys. But he swallowed his pride and went anyway, finishing the eighth grade—which was as far as Negro boys could go in Durham—at the age of twenty-three. About that time a group of colored men started a grocery store by putting in $25.00 each. They asked Charles Spaulding to be its clerk and manager. None of them had any experience in business, the store soon went broke, and everyone pulled out leaving Spaulding with debts of over $300.00. It took him five years to pay off these debts, but he paid every cent.

Spaulding's integrity and industry attracted the attention of a successful Negro barber, John Merrick, who owned five barber shops in Durham, three for white patrons and two for Negroes, and who was the personal barber to Washington Duke, founder of the American Tobacco Company. Mr. Merrick was interested in starting an insurance company. Dr. A. M. Moore, an uncle of Spaulding's, was interested, too. They both were very busy men so they asked young Spaulding to be the manager. Since he became the only member of the actual working staff, this meant that he also had to be the bookkeeper, typist, field agent, office boy and janitor. His headquarters were a back room in Dr. Moore's office. He once said, "When I came into the office in the morning, I rolled up my sleeves and swept the place as janitor. Then I rolled down my sleeves and was an agent. And later I put on my coat and became the general manager." He was indeed the man of all work.

The first client of the new insurance company was a man who paid 65¢ as the initial premium on a $40.00 policy. Then he promptly died a few days later—before the new company had had a chance to build up any additional funds. When his widow came to claim the insurance, the backers had to dig down into their own pockets to pay the $40.00. But they paid it. Word spread of the promptness and the solvency of the new firm. So young Spaulding did not find it too difficult to sign other policy holders. The first week's income was $29.40. By the end of the year he had taken in $840.00. Not even a thousand, but he was not discouraged because every week, though slowly, the number of policy holders grew. Into the small towns nearby and onto the farms he went, explaining to people the benefits of insurance—who had never heard of insurance before. Twenty years later, when he became secretary-treasurer of the company, his field agents were turning in annually more than a million dollars.

John Merrick, the barber, was the president of the company for twenty-one years. When he died, Dr. Moore succeeded him. Between them they did many good things for the Negro citizens of Durham. Colored people could not get books from the public library, so the two contributed substantially to the creation of a Colored Public Library and Dr. Moore himself gave many of the first books. Since Negro doctors and nurses could not serve on the staff of the City Hospital, they persuaded the wealthy Duke family to aid in the building of Lincoln Hospital for colored patients, where young colored doctors might interne, and nurses be trained. Remembering the bad conditions he had encountered in the rural schools, Dr. Moore personally paid for a year the salary of an inspector of Negro schools so that he might make recommendations to the Legislature for improvements. So successful was the inspector's work that the next year the State made the inspector's position permanent.

When these two good men who founded the North Carolina Mutual Insurance Company died, Charles C. Spaulding carried on their community work in the same spirit of civic responsibility. He not only built the insurance company into one of the most important in America, but he kept up many varied outside interests as well. In 1921 he helped to organize the National Negro Insurance Association and was its first president. In 1926 he became the president of the National Negro Business League. He served as a trustee of the universities of Howard, Shaw, and of the North Carolina State College. He was a member of the National Council of the Young Men's Christian Association, and of the Durham Chamber of Commerce. He was awarded a number of honorary degrees. And in 1926 he received the Harmon Gold Award for Distinguished Achievement.

Out of the North Carolina Mutual Company grew two other major businesses in Durham, the Mechanics and Farmers Bank, and the Mutual Building and Loan Association. In the 1920's Charles C. Spaulding became president of both. One of the purposes Merrick and Moore had in mind when they started their insurance was to provide young Negroes with opportunities to get business training. They wanted also to set up various enterprises where young men and women might get white collar jobs of a sort not generally open to Negroes in the South. They knew, too, that it was very difficult for colored people to get loans on property or secure help in financing the building of homes. To that end they opened their bank, as well as a finance association.

When Charles C. Spaulding died in 1952 *The New York Herald Tribune* reported that the North Carolina Mutual Life Insurance Company with its affiliates was the largest all-Negro business enterprise in the world, having assets of more than thirty-three million dollars, and over 165 million dollars worth of insurance policies in force in eight states. A very modest man, and a firm believer in Booker T. Washington's advice to let down your bucket where you are, Spaulding laid his success entirely to hard work. He had great faith in personal initiative. In giving advice to young people, he often said, "You can't drink from the spring high up on the mountain unless you climb for the water."

A. Philip Randolph
Distinguished Labor Leader

1889–

The first Pullman car in America was named the "Pioneer." And its first porter was a Negro. Since 1867 colored sleeping car porters have been working on all the railroads in the United States. Today they number about 18,000. Most of them belong to the Brotherhood of Sleeping Car Porters, the largest Negro labor union in the world. This union was organized by Asa Philip Randolph.

Randolph was born in Crescent City, Florida, April 15, 1889, the son of a traveling Methodist preacher with several rural churches to pastor. There was a good library of religious literature in the home and, as he grew up, young Randolph used to practice reading aloud from his father's volumes of famous sermons and from Shakespeare's plays. In school he was a good student, but not a brilliant one, and his regular schooling ended with a high school diploma from Cookman Institute in Jacksonville. After he was graduated he decided to seek his fortune in the North, so Philip came to New York where he worked as a bus boy, then an elevator man, meanwhile taking a few night courses at City College. One summer he got a job as a waiter on the Hudson River boats, but was fired for attempting to organize a protest against the hot, crowded quarters allotted to the crew. From his early manhood he was interested in improving conditions for Negroes, especially working conditions, so he soon began to speak from soap boxes on the streets of Harlem. And sometimes he recited bits of Shakespeare to the passing crowds.

In Florida as a child his mother had always forbade her son to ride in the segregated street cars. She said it was better to walk then to be Jim Crowed. So young Randolph was early imbued with an intense dislike of racial discrimination. In 1917 he helped to launch a magazine in New York called *The Messenger* to crusade for the full democratic rights of Negro citizens. Beneath its title was printed, "The Only Radical Negro Magazine in America," and its editorials were bitterly critical of the *status quo*. During World War I it criticized as hypocritical the official slogan, "Making the World Safe for Democracy," while, so *The Messenger* contended, Negro citizens were disfranchised, segregated, and lynched throughout the South. Randolph made very fiery speeches in a number of cities. In 1918 some newspapers termed him "the most dangerous Negro in America," and he was arrested for a talk which he made in Cleveland. But a few days later he was released without being brought to trial. In his talks and editorials Randolph contended he was simply agitating for the fulfillment of our Constitutional guarantees for *all* citizens and the protection of the law for everybody. One of the things he said in his speeches was, "Rights do not mean anything if you cannot exercise them."

After the war Randolph entered politics on the Socialist ticket and ran for a number of public offices without success. Meanwhile, he was in great demand as a speaker before Negro groups and, as such, one night he was invited to the Pullman Porters Athletic Association where he discussed the growing importance in American life of trade unionism. As a result of his address, a group of porters and maids on the trains asked his help in organizing a union. Four times before in various parts of the country the porters had attempted to organize unions but had failed. The best they had achieved was a kind of low-benefit insurance association controlled by the company. But this had not shortened their long hours of work, nor given them sleeping quarters on the trains, nor raised their very low wages. Sleeping car porters were almost entirely dependent on tips for a living, had to pay for meals and lodging away from home, and even had to buy their own polish for shining passengers' shoes.

Randolph himself had never been a Pullman porter, but he had long been interested in labor organizations and in the theories and practices of unionism. He felt that it was high time one of the largest groups of Negro workers in the country be unionized so, when the porters in the New York area invited him to become their general organizer, he went to work at first without a salary. In 1925 at a meeting in the Elks Hall in Harlem, the Brotherhood of Sleeping Car Porters was organized. At first the going was difficult. A number of porters lost their jobs for belonging to the union. A great many others were afraid to join. Some felt that, because many unions would not admit Negroes, no unions were any good. To spread the concepts and values of unionism, labor institutes were organized in the leading cities from Coast to Coast. Randolph traveled a great deal seeking to enlist members, create good will for the new Brotherhood, and explain to colored people the growing importance of labor organizations. He made many talks to religious groups, contending that the church could serve "nobly in championing the cause of labor and yet remain true to its traditions, since Jesus Christ was a carpenter and all his disciples workmen." His magazine, *The Messenger,* became "The Official Organ of the Brotherhood of Sleeping Car Porters." Within two years the new union grew to over two thousand members. But several thousand porters still remained to be organized. With a depression on its way and many people out of work, the fear of being discharged for union activities made many sleeping car workers reluctant to join the Brotherhood. Nevertheless, its membership continued to grow until by 1929 more than half of the porters and maids on the railroads were organized. Then the American Federation of Labor granted the Brotherhood of Sleeping Car Porters a charter—the first such charter to be given to an all-Negro union in America. A. Philip Randolph was its president.

During the depression the young union had such a hard time, with train crews being laid off and many of its members unable to pay dues, that it was not even able to meet its electric light bills. At its New York headquarters, officials had to work in the dark. But they continued to negotiate for better working conditions, and finally, in 1937, the Pullman Company signed an agreement with the Brotherhood which granted porters and maids an annual salary increase of over a million dollars, shorter working hours, less working mileage, and better overtime pay. This, remarkably enough, was achieved *without striking.* Today the Brotherhood of Sleeping Car Porters is considered one of the soundest labor organizations in the country. Of it Leo Wolman, Professor of Economics in Columbia University, has written, "The record of this union affords evidence, if any were needed, of the capacity of Negroes to run a large union democratically and to handle their relations with employers with common sense."

As a labor leader, A. Philip Randolph continued to increase in importance by his enlarged activities within the American Federation of Labor. At its annual conventions he sought to have those member unions that still barred Negro workers drop their color bars. He declared, "Labor can never win fully until it opens its doors freely and equally to all workers." But it was not until World War II, when the federal government took a hand in this, that much headway was made. Because a large number of important defense industries would not employ colored men and women, and because many unions kept Negroes from working in the shops and plants, even before the war Randolph felt that forceful steps needed to be taken. To that end he decided to exercise the old American right of petition for "redress of grievances." He began to organize a protest demonstration of Negro citizens to go to Washington to appeal to the President and Congress to see that Negro workers be employed in defense plants on the same basis as others.

Many organizations, churches, lodges, and newspapers approved of his idea, and large mass meetings were held all across the country in support of what came to be called The March-on-Washington Movement. Hundreds of groups offered to send delegates to Washington, and by June, 1941, some fifty thousand colored citizens were expected to march to the White House with their petitions for "jobs and equal participation in national defense." Government officials began to understand that Negro citizens were very much in earnest and greatly concerned because many airplane factories and munitions plants preparing for the defense of democracy still would not employ them. Just a few days before the March-on-Washington was to have been held, President Roosevelt issued his Executive Order 8802 against discrimination in employment by firms holding defense contracts. This historic order stated in clear language that "it is the duty of employers and labor organizations . . . to provide for the full and equitable participation of all workers in defense industries, without discrimination because of race, creed, color, or national origin." A Committee of Fair Employment Practices was formed in Washington to insure the rights of all citizens to take part in our national defense program. And a clause was written into government defense contracts prohibiting racial bias in employment.

The historian, John Hope Franklin, states in his book, *From Slavery to Freedom,* "Negroes hailed the Order as the most significant document affecting them since the issuance of the Emancipation Proclamation." But he further records that some firms defied the Order. Nevertheless, with governmental recognition and official condemnation of a difficulty that had long plagued Negro workers, the march on Washington was not held. Instead, 20,000 people met in New York's Madison Square Garden to hail Randolph's leadership and to pledge continued support to his efforts for full employment without discrimination. Certainly the doors of industry had been opened to colored workers in greater numbers than ever before. And A. Philip Randolph had moved on from a labor leader to a national leader in the eyes of the Negro people.

Ralph Bunche
Statesman and Political Scientist

1904–

In ancient times Israel, before it was conquered by David, was called the Land of Canaan. Then, according to the Bible, "when David was old and full of days, he made Solomon, his son, king over Israel." Later the country was conquered by Babylon. Still later the Persians and the Macedonians overran it. Then when Jesus was born, Palestine was in the hands of the Romans. In time it came to be called the Holy Land, the name remaining even after the Roman Empire fell and it was taken over by the Mohammedans. During the Crusades the Islamic rulers were driven out, only to come back later to remain until the British took the Holy Land from the Turks during the First World War. The Jewish people in the twentieth century, fleeing from the pogroms and gas ovens of Nazi Europe, wanted to make Palestine their home. The Moslems resented this. So in 1936 serious conflicts began to develop between its mixed population of Jews and Arabs. When the Second World War was over, Great Britain dumped the whole problem of Palestine into the domain of the fledgling United Nations. And eventually it fell into the lap of a young American Negro diplomat at the U.N., Dr. Ralph Bunche. It was Dr. Bunche who brought about first a truce, then an armistice, and in 1949 the end of the Arab-Israeli conflict.

On August 7, 1904, Ralph Johnson Bunche was born in Detroit, Michigan, the son of a barber. He was born in an apartment over the barber shop where his parents, two aunts, and a grandmother lived. All the grown-ups worked, and, at an early age, Ralph began to sell papers to help along the family income. Grandma Johnson not only worked outside the home, but seemed to be the mainstay in keeping everybody—her three daughters, two grandchildren, her son-in-law— and the house neat, clean, and straight. Grandma was the one who always had an extra dollar in her stocking when times got hard. And it was Grandma who took over when both of Ralph's parents became ill and the doctors thought they might get better if they went to the dry climate of the West.

The whole family—father, mother, Ralph and baby sister, two aunts, and Grandma—moved almost all the way across the country to the desert town of Albuquerque, New Mexico, in search of sunshine and dry air. At St. Louis, where the train headed into the South, for the first time little Ralph rode in a Jim Crow car set apart near the engine for Negro passengers. Half the coach was for baggage and the other half for Negroes. It was the first time Ralph had encountered legal segregation, so the boy was glad when the train got out of Texas and into New Mexico where there are no racial segregation laws. The mountains, the deserts, and the Indians of the Southwest thrilled eleven-year-old Ralph. He liked the sunny city and the new school he attended. But it was not long before his mother died of the rheumatic fever they had hoped the sunshine would cure. And only a few months later his father became weaker and weaker from tuberculosis. He died, too. Grandma accepted the job of rearing her two grandchildren. And the first thing she determined was that, no matter what happened, Ralph was to stay in school and get his education. In 1916 Grandma Johnson moved on to the West Coast. And two years later, Ralph was graduated from the elementary school in Los Angeles. Grandma came to the exercises to see him receive two prizes, one in History and one in English.

At Jefferson High School young Ralph went out for the debating team, and for football, basketball, baseball, and track. He was an all-around good athlete and a good student. By her earnings as a seamstress and a houseworker, his grandmother saw to it that Ralph had time for both sports and studies, and she was very proud of his achievements in high school. During the summers, Ralph worked hard and saved for school. One summer he worked in a carpet-dyeing plant; another he was houseboy for a Hollywood star; again he was a messenger in a newspaper office. Once, when the paper gave an outing for its employees, Ralph, of course, attended. But he was not allowed to go into the swimming pool because he was colored. These kinds of discriminations always perturbed him a great deal, and led directly to his early interest in sociology, civics, history, and other studies that might help to explain why democracy put so many stumbling blocks before its Negro citizens. When Ralph came out of high school, he received at graduation a medal for civics and one for debating.

Ralph began to think that perhaps he should now find a full-time job and go to work. But his grandmother said, "Young man, you are going to college." Her tone of voice meant just what she said. So he enrolled at the University of California at Los Angeles, where his athletic abilities in high school had earned him a four-year scholarship. But to make textbook money and spending change, he got a campus job as a gymnasium janitor, getting up at five to wax the floors and keep the mats, bars, rings, and track clean. All went well for a few months, then Ralph developed a mastoid condition from a tiny piece of straw that had worked its way into his ear on a picnic. Two operations, eventual deafness in one ear, and the loss of a whole year in college were the result. Nevertheless, in 1927, he was graduated *summa cum laude,* class valedictorian, and a member of Phi Beta Kappa. This graduation brought five medals for excellence in various studies, plus a scholarship for further work at Harvard University. The Negro community in Los Angeles had grown very proud of this brilliant young student and, before he started off to Harvard, they presented him with a fund of a thousand dollars to help defray his expenses. His grandmother, whose love and faith and toil had meant so much in getting him through school, died just a few days before he started East to attend the great university.

While studying political science in Cambridge, Ralph Bunche got a job as clerk and all-around man in a small book-shop whose owner was quite elderly and could not see very well. However, he liked his young employee's knowledge and courtesy a great deal. But one day some customers must have complained about being served by a colored man. The old proprietor squinted at Ralph's golden skin and finally asked him if he were a Negro. When Ralph said he was, the old man replied that he had never given his racial background a thought one way or another and did not care, anyhow, so just keep on working there. This old New England gentleman remained one of his best friends. In 1928 Ralph Bunche received a Master of Arts degree from Harvard and, from among the several teaching posts he was offered, accepted a position to set up a department of political science at Howard University in Washington, D.C.

Ralph Bunche found Washington more prejudiced in its racial attitudes than any city he had ever known. He said later that he spent most of his free time in the Library of Congress because it was one of the few places a Negro in Washington could go without segregation—since all the downtown theaters, movies, restaurants, and hotels were then closed to colored people. As a political scientist Bunche was interested in getting at the roots of the American race problem, and he found the national capital a good place to gather data. So the twenty-four-year-old teacher was kept busy there—but not too busy to fall in love with a beautiful girl in one of his classes. In 1930 there was a June wedding and the Bunches began to plan a house in Washington. Another year of graduate study at Harvard followed. Then, moving up the academic scale, Bunche became an assistant professor, then Assistant to the President of Howard University. In 1931 a Rosenwald Fellowship enabled him to go to Europe and Africa to gather first-hand material on social problems for his doctorate. And in 1934, at Harvard University, he was made a Ph.D. in political science. Two years later he became a full professor at Howard. Two daughters were born, and Ralph settled down to a life of teaching in Washington. But not for long. By now he was becoming famous as an expert in race relations, and many requests for his services, skill, and information came to him.

In 1936 Dr. Bunche was co-director of the Institute of Race Relations at Swarthmore College. In 1941 the great Swedish sociologist, Gunnar Myrdal, backed by the Carnegie Foundation, was asked to make a comprehensive study of Negro-white relations in the United States. The first person he thought of engaging as one of his chief assistants was Ralph Bunche. Howard University then granted Dr. Bunche a leave of absence and, with Myrdal and others of his staff, he made extended field trips into the South, surveying conditions and asking thousands of questions of Negroes and whites. Myrdal and his staff several times were threatened with violence in more than one backward community that did not wish its ani-Negro practices recorded. But, in the end, the great work, *An American Dilemma,* resulted. For this Bunche prepared more than three thousand pages of detailed reports.

When the Second World War broke out, Bunche was barred from military service by the deafness in one ear. The government, however, requisitioned him for the Office of Strategic Services, and he was put in charge of research on Africa and other colonial areas in which the Allies had military interests. General Bill Donovan called Bunche "a walking colonial institute" since he knew so much that was helpful in planning African bases for an invasion of Hitler's Europe. He could give the general staffs information on African tribal attitudes toward the war, local social customs, native feelings concerning white people, how they would react to airbases in their midst, and much else that was of great value in military strategy. So successfully did Ralph Bunche do this job that in 1944 the State Department selected him for the Associate Chief of the Division of Dependent Territories. Some members of the State Department objected to a Negro having so important a job. But Secretary of State Cordell Hull fought it through and personally phoned Dr. Bunche to inform him of the confirmation of the appointment.

Dr. Bunche then became the first Negro in American history to be in full charge of an office in the State Department.

At the end of the war, Ralph Bunche was assigned by the government as a consultant at the Dumbarton Oaks Conference which was concerned with the economic rebuilding of a war-torn world. When the first meetings to draft a charter for the formation of the United Nations were held at San Francisco, Ralph Bunche was there as advisor to Commander Harold Stassen. Bunche prepared voluminous memoranda for these conferences, particularly concerning the proposed trusteeships of the former colonies of our enemies in the Near East, Africa, and the Pacific. Many of Bunche's recommendations became a part of the Charter of the United Nations, and diplomats of all the governments of the world became aware of this brilliant young Negro in Washington.

In rapid succession various commissions and appointments followed. Bunche was with the United States delegation to the International Labor Conference at Paris in 1945. He was the presidential appointee to the Caribbean Commission in 1946. He was U.S. Commissioner to the West Indian Conference in the Virgin Islands. He went to various United Nations sessions in London and Paris. And in 1947 he was asked by Trygve Lie, then United Nations Secretary-General, to fly to Palestine to aid the United Nations Special Committee in negotiating peace between the Arabs and the Jews. When Count Folke Bernadotte was appointed official Mediator, Ralph Bunche was made chief aide to Bernadotte and the head of his Secretariat. With the Swedish diplomat he toured the battlefields of the Holy Land, their cars bearing the peace flag of the United Nations. They held innumerable meetings with both sides, seeking to end the bloodshed and rancor between the two religious groups who had both occupied the same soil for centuries. Their U.N. cars were often fired upon by snipers. Once the chauffeur who was driving Dr. Bunche was killed at the wheel, and only by quick action did Bunche keep the car from overturning in a ditch. Certainly his Palestine assignment was very dangerous and, so it seemed then, an almost hopeless task. The national, racial, and religious problems involved were extremely complicated ones. Then, to make matters worse, Count Bernadotte was assassinated and several of his staff killed or wounded when their car was ambushed on the road by terrorists. Immediately, the United Nations cabled Ralph Bunche to take over as Acting-Mediator in the murdered Count's place.

It was under such conditions of terror that Dr. Bunche began his personal efforts to bring the Jews and the Arabs to iron out, by conferences rather than bullets, the difficulties between them. Almost nobody believed he could succeed. But he called both Arab and Jew to the Greek Island of Rhodes for a series of talks at the Hotel des Roses. At first the belligerents would not even speak to each other. But by sheer patience, good will, and tact, Ralph Bunche was finally able to bring them together for informal conversations, and, sometimes, a few at a time, for late suppers in his own suite of rooms. At last, he was able to achieve formal meetings to consider a truce. For forty-two days they met, with a crisis coming up almost every day. Sleeping sometimes only three or four hours a night, Ralph Bunche almost exhausted his large staff of advisors and secretaries. But finally he arrived at a partial truce. Then about a month later he secured a cease-fire agreement. But it still took almost another month to get a formally signed armistice. The day before, Bunche, the other United Nations negotiators working with him, the Jews, and the Arabs stayed up in conference all night long—a session of almost twenty-four hours—to finally secure the signing of a peace that was hailed around the world. The leader of the Israeli delegation said that morning that Bunche had earned the gratitude of all humanity. And the Sheik heading the Arab group called him one of the greatest men on earth. Evidently the committee in charge of granting the world's most distinguished award agreed, for they voted him the Nobel Peace Prize in 1950.

Now, as Director of the Trusteeship Division of the United Nations, the ample talents and great scholarship which Ralph Bunche possesses find a wide field of usefulness. His efforts are concerned with the problems of millions of people in various parts of the world whose lands have not yet attained self-government. Dr. Bunche believes that their problems can be solved, and he has written that he has great faith in "the kind of world the United Nations is working incessantly to bring about: a world at peace; a world in which there is full respect for human rights and fundamental freedoms for all without distinction as to race, sex, language, or religion; a world in which all men shall walk together as equals and with dignity."

Marian Anderson
Famous Concert Singer

1902–

When Marian Anderson was born in a little red brick house in Phila-delphia, a famous group of Negro singers, the Fisk Jubilee Singers, had already carried the spirituals all over Europe. And a colored woman billed as "Black Patti" had become famous on variety programs as a singer of both folk songs and the classics. Both Negro and white minstrels had popularized American songs. The all-Negro musical comedies of Bert Williams and George Walker had been successful on Broadway. But no well-trained colored singers performing the great songs of Schubert, Handel, and the other masters, or the arias from famous operas, had become successful on the concert stage. And most people thought of Negro vocalists only in connection with spirituals. Roland Hayes and Marian Anderson were the first to become famous enough to break this stereotype.

Marian Anderson's mother was a staunch church worker who loved to croon the hymns of her faith about the house, as did the aunt who came to live with them when Marian's father died. Both parents were from Virginia. Marian's mother had been a school teacher there, and her father a farm boy. Shortly after they moved to Philadelphia where three daughters were born, the father died, and the mother went to work at Wanamaker's department store. But she saw to it that her children attended school and church regularly. The father had been an usher in the Union Baptist Church, so the congregation took an interest in his three little girls. Marian was the oldest and, before she was eight, singing in the Sunday school choir, she had already learned a great many hymns and spirituals by heart.

One day Marian saw an old violin in a pawnshop window marked $3.45. She set her mind on that violin, and began to save the nickels and dimes neighbors would give her for scrubbing their white front steps—the kind of stone steps so characteristic of Philadelphia and Baltimore houses—until she had $3.00. The pawnshop man let her take the violin at a reduced price. Marian never became very good on the violin. A few years later her mother bought a piano, so the child forgot all about it in favor of their newer instrument. By that time, too, her unusual singing voice had attracted the attention of her choir master, and at the age of fourteen she was promoted to a place in the main church choir. There she learned all four parts of all the hymns and anthems and could easily fill in anywhere from bass to soprano.

Sensing that she had exceptional musical talent, some of the church members began to raise money so that she might have singing lessons. But her first teacher, a colored woman, refused to accept any pay for instructing so talented a child. So the church folks put their money into a trust fund called "Marian Anderson's Future," banking it until the time came for her to have advanced training. Meanwhile, Marian attended South Philadelphia High School for Girls and took part in various group concerts, usually doing the solo parts. When she was fifteen she sang a group of songs alone at a Sunday School Convention in Harrisburg and word of her talent began to spread about the state. When she was graduated from high school, the Philadelphia Choral Society, a Negro group, sponsored her further study and secured for her one of the best local teachers. Then in 1925 she journeyed to New York to take part, with three hundred other young singers, in the New York Philharmonic Competitions, where she won first place, and appeared with the orchestra at Lewisohn Stadium.

This appearance was given wide publicity, but very few lucrative engagements came in, so Marian continued to study. A Town Hall concert was arranged for her in New York, but it was unsuccessful. Meanwhile, she kept on singing with various choral groups, and herself gave concerts in churches and at some of the Negro colleges until, in 1930, a Rosenwald Fellowship made European study possible. During her first year abroad she made her debut in Berlin. A prominent Scandinavian concert manager read of this concert, but was attracted more by the name, *Anderson,* than by what the critics said about her voice. "Ah," he said, "a Negro singer with a Swedish name! She is bound to be a success in Scandinavia." He sent two of his friends to Germany to hear her, one of them being Kosti Vehanen who shortly became her accompanist and remained with her for many years.

Sure enough, Marian Anderson did become a great success in the Scandinavian countries, where she learned to sing in both Finnish and Swedish, and her first concert tour of Europe became a critical triumph. When she came back home to America, she gave several programs and appeared as soloist with the famous Hall Johnson Choir, but without financial success. However, the Scandinavian people, who had fallen in love with her, kept asking her to come back there. So, in 1933, she went again to Europe for 142 concerts in Norway, Sweden, Denmark, and Finland. She was decorated by the King of Denmark and the King of Sweden. Sibelius dedicated a song to her. And the following spring she made her debut in Paris where she was so well received that she had to give three concerts that season at the Salle Gaveau. Great successes followed in all the European capitals. In 1935 the famous conductor, Arturo Toscanini, listened to her sing at Salzburg. He said, "What I heard today one is privileged to hear only once in a hundred years." It was in Europe that Marian Anderson began to be acclaimed by critics as "the greatest singer in the world."

When Marian Anderson again returned to America, she was a seasoned artist. News of her tremendous European successes had preceded her, so a big New York concert was planned. But a few days before she arrived at New York, in a storm on the liner crossing the Atlantic, Marian fell and broke her ankle. She refused to allow this to interfere with her concert, however, nor did she even want people to know about it. She wore a very long evening gown that night so that no one could see the plaster cast on her leg. She propped herself in a curve of the piano before the curtains parted, and gave her New York concert standing on one foot! The next day Howard Taubman wrote enthusiastically in *The New York Times:*

> "Marian Anderson has returned to her native land one of the great singers of our time. . . . There is no doubt of it, she was mistress of all she surveyed. . . . It was music making that probed too deep for words."

A Coast to Coast American tour followed. And, from that season on, Marian Anderson has been one of our country's favorite singers, rated, according to *Variety,* among the top ten of the concert stage who earn over $100,000 a year. Miss Anderson has sung with the great symphony orchestras, and appeared on all the major radio and television networks many times, being a particular favorite with the millions of listeners to the Ford Hour. During the years she has returned often to Europe for concerts, and among the numerous honors accorded her abroad was a request for a command performance before the King and Queen of England, and a decoration from the government of Finland. Her concerts in South America and Asia have been as successful as those elsewhere. Since 1935 she has averaged over one hundred programs a year in cities as far apart as Vienna, Buenos Aires, Moscow, and Tokyo. Her recordings have sold millions of copies around the world. She has been invited more than once to sing at the White House. She has appeared in concert at the Paris Opera and at the Metropolitan Opera House in New York. Several colleges have granted her honorary degrees, and in 1944 Smith College made her a Doctor of Music.

In spite of all this, as a Negro, Marian Anderson has not been immune from those aspects of racial segregation which affect most traveling artists of color in the United States. In his book, *Marian Anderson,* her long-time accompanist, Vehanen, tells of hotel accommodations being denied her, and service in dining rooms often refused. Once after a concert in a Southern city, Vehanen writes that some white friends drove Marian to the railroad station and took her into the main waiting room. But a policeman ran them out, since Negroes were not allowed in that part of the station. Then they went into the smaller waiting room marked COLORED. But again they were ejected, because *white* people were not permitted in the cubby hole allotted to Negroes. So they all had to stand on the platform until the train arrived.

The most dramatic incident of prejudice in all Marian Anderson's career occurred in 1939 when the Daughters of the American Revolution, who own Constitution Hall in Washington, refused to allow her to sing there. The newspapers headlined this and many Americans were outraged. In protest a committee of prominent people, including a number of great artists and distinguished figures in the government, was formed. Through the efforts of this committee, Marian Anderson sang in Washington, anyway—before the statue of Abraham Lincoln—to one of the largest crowds ever to hear a singer at one time in the history of the world. Seventy-five thousand people stood in the open air on a cold clear Easter Sunday afternoon to hear her. And millions more listened to Marian Anderson that day over the radio or heard her in the newsreels that recorded the event. Harold Ickes, then Secretary of the Interior, presented Miss Anderson to that enormous audience standing in the plaza to pay honor, as he said, not only to a great singer, but to the basic ideals of democracy and equality.

In 1943 Marian Anderson married Orpheus H. Fisher, an architect, and settled down—between tours—in a beautiful country house in Connecticut where she rehearses new songs to add to her already vast repertoire. Sometimes her neighbors across the fields can hear the rich warm voice that covers three octaves singing in English, French, Finnish, or German. And sometimes they hear in the New England air that old Negro spiritual, "Honor, honor unto the dying Lamb. . . ."

Friends say that Marian Anderson has invested her money in real estate and in government bonds. Certainly, throughout her career, she has lived very simply, traveled without a maid or secretary, and carried her own sewing machine along by train, ship, or plane to mend her gowns. When in 1941 in Philadelphia she was awarded the coveted Bok Award for outstanding public service, the $10,000 that came with the medallion she used to establish a trust fund for "talented American artists without regard to race or creed." Now, each year from this fund promising young musicians receive scholarships.

Jackie Robinson
First Negro in Big League Baseball

1919–

Cairo is a village in southern Georgia not far from the Florida state line. There, to a poor sharecropping family, on January 31, 1919, John Roosevelt Robinson was born, the youngest of five children. His father died before the boy could learn to remember him, leaving the mother as the only support for her children. So, when little John Roosevelt was about fourteen months old, and the other youngsters ranged from two-and-a-half to ten, Mrs. Mollie Robinson set out with her brood for California where she had heard that times were better and there were good non-segregated schools for children. Mrs. Robinson had a half brother in Pasadena who had promised them a place to stay. The children called him Uncle Burton, and he became like a father to them all, four boys and a girl, sharing with them his two rooms.

They nicknamed the baby Jackie and in the California sunshine he grew strong and healthy. Mrs. Robinson worked sometimes as a domestic servant and sometimes as a laundress, and did her best to keep the children clean and in school. But, with so many, they often did not have quite enough to eat, so little Jackie remembers with particular affection one kind teacher who would sometimes share her lunch with him. And sometimes he bought a nickel bag of peanuts and ate not only the nuts, but the shells, to help fill him up. His wonderful mother washed and ironed their clothes on Saturday night so she might send them neatly dressed to Sunday school and, in every way, she did all that she could to bring them up decently. But she was often away from home working to buy them clothes and food and pay rent on the larger house to which they moved. It was not easy for one woman alone to make enough money to buy shoes for ten active little feet, and keep the pots well filled on the stove, too. It was not her fault if her income did not stretch as far as her love.

The depression of the 1930's made times hard indeed. Still all five of Mollie Robinson's children continued to attend either the Cleveland Elementary School or the Muir Technical High School where Jackie's brother, Mack, became a champion sprinter and broad jumper. Sturdy little Jackie himself was a member of the grammar school soccer team that beat all comers. These two boys of the Robinson family were early known as fine young athletes.

When Jackie was fourteen he entered high school and, following his brother's footsteps there, he became a star athlete, going out for football, basketball, baseball, and track, and playing on all teams. When he was graduated from Muir he was a four-letter man, almost six feet tall, weighing 175 pounds, and still developing. The coaches at Pasadena Junior College welcomed him with open arms, and there he continued to make a distinguished athletic record. In track he set a new junior college broad jump record of 25 feet 6 1/3 inches. In baseball he led the conference with a batting average of .460. And in a single basketball game he broke the individual points record by scoring 28 points in a single game. He was a popular student, good humored, praised for his fair sportsmanship, and not conceited. Since the third grade when he began to play so well on his elementary school soccer team, Jackie had been accustomed to the cheers of his classmates on the sidelines, so he took his junior college triumphs in stride, as nothing unusual at all.

When the two years of junior college were up in 1938, Jackie went to the University of California at Los Angeles to major in Physical Education, riding by bus every morning for more than an hour from Pasadena to the campus. Meanwhile, his brother Mack had taken part in the 1936 Olympic Games at Berlin, finishing second only to Jesse Owens in the 200 meters dash, and setting a new record for that distance at Paris a few weeks later. Jackie adored big brother Mack and continued to try to emulate him. Right away he went out for football at UCLA, and his first season on the team he became a star. As a quarterback in the first big game of the season against the University of Washington, Jackie made the gains that broke a tie score and won the game for UCLA. Before a sprained ankle halted his progress toward the end of the season, Jackie had scored four touchdowns and kicked two points after touchdowns to account for 26 points of his team's total 127. Every time he had gotten the ball he had averaged 12 yards a carry. Out of 14 ball-carryings, he had averaged over 20 yards each time, which set a new record in college football. So Jackie's name became known far and wide as an exceptional gridiron player.

In basketball the same thing happened. Jackie starred in the twelve games that he played, and became the top point scorer that season in the Pacific Coast Conference with 148 points. In track he broke the conference broad jump record, and was a member of the West Coast team that defeated the Big Ten at Northwestern. Then he fell in love with a girl on the campus and began to look forward to marriage. About that time Uncle Burton became ill, and it seemed unfair to Jackie to let his mother carry the whole financial burden of their household alone. So in the spring of 1941 during his second and final year at UCLA, Jackie quit college and went to work at a government Civilian Conservation Corps camp as an athletic director.

When the government camp closed, an offer came to Jackie to play in the *Chicago Tribune* All-Star charity football game at Soldier Field in Chicago. From this came an engagement in professional football with the Los Angeles Bulldogs at a very good salary. But just after a series of games in Honolulu, while Jackie was on the boat coming home, Pearl Harbor was bombed, and America entered the Second World War. Jackie went into the army. He was sent to Fort Riley, Kansas, where Joe Louis, too, was stationed, and the two became friends. Assigned to a cavalry unit, Jackie spent his time vaccinating horses. But when his basic training was over, he applied for officers' school. In 1943 he was commissioned a second lieutenant and was sent to the 761st Tank Battalion at Camp Hood, Texas, where, within a few months his commanding officer commended Robinson for the fine record he made in the training of his men. But his old football injury, the torn ankle, began bothering him and, after thirty-one months service, Jackie was honorably discharged from the army.

The minister of his mother's church in Pasadena had become the President of a small Negro college, Samuel Houston, in Austin, Texas. So when Jackie got home from the army he found a letter offering him the position of athletic director on the faculty there. Since he had enjoyed working with young men in the C.C.C. camp, he welcomed this job with interest. But he did not stay there long for the salary was very low, and at home Uncle Burton was by now bed-ridden, which made it difficult for his mother to continue to go out to work. When the Kansas City Monarchs, a team in the Negro American Baseball League, offered him $400.00 a month as a short stop, Jackie accepted, and began a barnstorming tour from South to North with them. This meant bad hotels, Jim Crow meals, long dusty bus trips, and sometimes six or seven games a week with no rest. But Jackie could send money home and still save something to get married. In 1946 he and Rachel Isum, the girl he had met in college, marched happily to the altar together.

When Clyde Sukeforth, a scout for the Brooklyn Dodgers Baseball Team, asked Jackie on a late afternoon following a game in Chicago to come to New York to see Branch Rickey, President of the Dodgers, Jackie was almost rude. Whether he frowned or laughed in Sukeforth's face is not clear. But at any rate, like most Negro players, he did not like to be "kidded" about the possibilities of playing in the major leagues. To Negroes the "great American sport" was then the "great American *white* sport," since they were barred from teams in the big leagues. Even such really exceptional ball players as Satchel Paige and Josh Gibson had never had a chance to play with the famous major league teams, only with barnstorming Negro outfits. So Jackie thought Clyde Sukeforth was joking the day he asked him to take a train East to talk with the head of the Brooklyn Dodgers. Finally the scout was able to persuade Robinson that he was on the level, and that he had been watching his playing for some time. Having an injured shoulder, Jackie could take a few days off without being fined, so he went to Brooklyn. The rest is history.

World War II had brought about many changes for the better in America's racial climate. The government had ordered war industries opened to skilled Negro workers after A. Philip Randolph's threatened March-on-Washington. The pressure of Negro and white liberals in the National Association for the Advancement of Colored People and other organizations had helped break down the bars of segregation in the Marines, the Air Force, and other branches of the service where Negroes had previously not been permitted to serve. A wave of equality for the darker peoples of the world was sweeping around the earth from India and the Far East to the United Nations. Negro Americans, too, backed by the finest sentiments of many leading Americans in and out of government, were calling for the end of the color bar in voting, housing, education—and baseball. Now, if ever, was the time to begin to admit Negro players to the major leagues. Then, too, the war had robbed the leagues of many of their best players. They were in need of good men. Of the younger Negro athletes, Jackie was certainly a great ball player, a college-trained man, and a gentleman. Branch Rickey completed arrangements for Jackie Robinson to join the Montreal Royals of the International League, a minor league farm team of the Brooklyn Dodgers.

During his first season as second baseman at Montreal Jackie played sensational ball. In his initial game against the Newark Bears he batted out a three-run homer, three singles, stole two bases, slugged in four runs, and scored four times. Montreal won the International League pennant at the end of the season and went on to victory against the Louisville Colonels in the Little World Series. Jackie topped the league with a batting average of .349 and a fielding average of .985. He also led in hits and runs, 155 and 113 respectively, out of 124 games. Despite this record, there was a great deal of opposition inside and outside baseball circles to his being brought into the Dodgers. Some folks said neither the players nor the fans would accept him, and that in cities like St. Louis there would be race riots if Jackie appeared on the diamond. Branch Rickey had to consider all these factors in making up his mind to admit the first Negro player to a big league roster. But on April 10, 1947, Rickey signed Robinson as a member of the Dodgers at a salary of $5,000 a season.

There were no race riots. Box office receipts soared as fans everywhere crowded the stands to see the Dodgers play. And Jackie played brilliantly. He had been asked by Rickey to let his A-1 brand of baseball *alone* answer all slurs, racial jibes, and unfairness that might come up. Most of the fans and most of the players on his own and rival teams treated Jackie fairly. When they didn't, even when someone threw a black cat on the field to taunt him, those first two seasons Robinson kept his head, kept on playing great ball, and steadily built up a reputation as the most valuable player in the National League, whose batting champion he became in 1949. His very first season the Dodgers won the pennant, and Robinson himself was named "The Rookie of the Year." For a time the newspapers devoted more space to Jackie Robinson than to any other sports personality in the United States. And, as Joe Louis had been in the ring, so Jackie Robinson became a symbol to millions in America of the progress which young Negroes in the postwar world might make.

The Dodgers gave Robinson a chance to play before the millions of fans who go to the big league parks. Once the racial ice was broken, other teams followed the Dodgers' example, by employing Negro players. Shortly the Dodgers themselves had signed Don Newcombe, Roy Campanella, and Dan Bankhead. And the "great American sport" had become in truth an *American* sport. Jackie Robinson blazed a trail for democracy when for the first time he went to bat at Ebbets Field.

Famous Negro
Music Makers

(1955)

To Lucille E. Goodloe

Contents

The Fisk Jubilee Singers
The Story of the Spirituals

First tour 1871

> *My Lord, He calls me,*
> *He calls me by the thunder!*
> *The trumpet sounds within-a my soul—*
> *I ain't got long to stay here.*
> *Steal away, steal away,*
> *Steal away to Jesus. . . .*

That was a slave song. Seven of the members of the first group of the Fisk Jubilee Singers were born in slavery. Some were almost grown before they had a chance to go to school. The Fisk School, in Nashville, Tennessee, was established by the American Missionary Association of the Congregational Church in 1866, three years after Abraham Lincoln signed the Emancipation Proclamation. It was a very poor school, and its first classes were held in a wooden barracks abandoned by the Union Armies at the close of the War Between the States. At first, Fisk was a high school, or intended as such. But of the thousand students, old and young, who came to Fisk during its opening year, many could hardly read and write. And some of the old people wanted just to learn to read the Bible before they died. So the teachers had to offer only the rudiments of education to many of their early pupils who were unprepared for higher learning.

There was so little money for books or paper or pencils or fuel to heat the barracks that, at the beginning, it was a great struggle to keep the school open. And many of the citizens of Nashville were hostile to a center of Negro education in their city. It was only the determined pioneering spirit of the white missionary teachers from the North that kept Fisk going. In 1871, however, it established its first college classes, and also set up a normal school to train Negro elementary teachers. By then, Fisk was so short of funds that it was in imminent danger of having to close, and many new applicants had to be turned away. Fortunately, it so happened that the treasurer of the school, George L. White, was also a musician. Through music he thought up an idea that he hoped would raise a little money for the institution. But nobody else among the faculty or trustees had much faith in George White's plans to take a small group of Negro students on a singing tour of the North to campaign for money, so he got little encouragement.

White was the son of a village blacksmith at Cadiz, New York. He had fought at Gettysburg and, after the War, had come to Nashville to teach. Being a singer himself, he was struck by the rich untrained voices of his students at Fisk, so he organized a chorus there and for concerts taught his young singers such songs as *Annie Laurie, Home, Sweet Home,* and *Wine Is a Mocker,* a popular Christian temperance song of the day. In turn, he sometimes heard his students singing the old songs of their parents, such as *Nobody Knows the Trouble I've Seen, A Little Wheel Is Turning in My Heart,* and *Steal Away to Jesus.* But no one thought of these songs as concert material. So at first the school chorus limited its public programs mostly to the songs they had learned out of books or from printed music. But to George White most of the old slave songs seemed very beautiful indeed when, within the schoolrooms, his singers sometimes sang them for him. These young Negro students, however, did not like to sing their songs for other white people outside the school, for fear they would laugh at the dialect—as many of those in Nashville did, being scornful of "slave music." The spirituals and jubilees were not really thought of as serious music then, and the students did not like to be laughed at. But Mr. White did not laugh. Sometimes he cried at the beauty of the singing and the simple poetic words, so they did not mind singing their songs for him. At concerts, however, the students preferred to sing *Moonlight on the Lake* or cantatas like *Queen Esther,* with only once in a while a spiritual on the program.

Whatever they sang, though, was so beautifully done that the group won enthusiastic applause in Nashville and surrounding towns whenever they appeared. This encouraged George White to think in terms of an extended tour, especially since additional funds simply *had* to be raised or Fisk would close. Could they do it? It was a chance. But he prayed that they might. Nine boys and girls, young men and women, volunteered to take the chance with him. But they had no clothes to wear on a trip to the snowy North in wintertime. The white teachers gave or lent them warm dresses and suits. Borrowing what he could from the Fisk treasury and adding to that small amount his own meagre funds, George White bought tickets as far as Cincinnati for the group. On a bleak October day in 1871, they started out. They could not know it then, but this tour was to make musical history for America.

At first things went badly. At the Cincinnati Exposition they sang *Annie Laurie* and people liked this talented group of poorly dressed young men and women, but very little money came in. At Chillicothe, Ohio, they gave a concert which brought in less than fifty dollars, and this they contributed to the victims of the great Chicago fire. The following week, in Springfield, Ohio, only twenty people bought tickets for their program, so the concert had to be cancelled for lack of money to pay the rental of the opera house. Nobody much wanted to hear Negro singers sing *Home, Sweet Home,* even though they sang it beautifully. In vain Mr. White tried to persuade them to include their own spirituals on the programs, along with the other standard songs. But it was not until they reached Oberlin, weary and cold, that the singers realized how moving to a white audience their own songs of the South might be and learned that not all white people would laugh at them.

The Fisk singers had gone to Oberlin, hoping to sing a song or two at a Congregational religious conference—if there were an opening on the program. So they sat in the back of the church all day, waiting for a chance—no opening came, though, and no one called them to the platform. It was the same the next day. But late in the afternoon there was finally a lull in the speeches of the conference when some delay arose over the order of the program. Quickly George White whispered to his singers in the pews at the back of the church to start very softly, *Steal Away to Jesus.* They did, and in a few moments the whole church was quiet as the sweet, soft strains of this old spiritual floated over the assembly. Curious heads were turned, trying to find out where this gentle, almost mysterious music was coming from. It seemed to float out of nowhere, drift up to the rafters like mist, and fall gently around the rostrum. Then one of the girls stood up and threw back her head and sang in a rich, deep contralto voice:

> *My Lord, He calls me!*
> *He calls me by the thunder . . .*

And everybody knew there were Negro singers there at the back of the church.

> *The trumpet sounds within-a my soul!*
> *I ain't got long to stay here . . .*

But the audience wanted the singers to stay as long as they could in Oberlin, so moved were they by these songs new to the North, strange and haunting and beautiful. Nobody laughed, many cried, and the singers themselves were greatly touched by the warmth and friendship that their "slave" songs evoked. After Oberlin they were not ashamed to sing the spirituals for white people again. They realized then that these songs from the dark heart of the South touched other hearts as well. And that was how the spirituals took their first step toward world-wide appreciation.

Up to that time, George White—who acted not only as musical coach of the group but manager, porter, chaperon and caretaker, as well— had been most worried about how to pay their fare from one town to another, about hotels that would give his Negro charges no rooms in which to sleep, although he as a white man could stay there, and particularly about their inability as yet to send even a cent back to Fisk. He prayed all through one night, asking God to help him not to have to cancel the tour entirely. "A more poverty stricken company was never out on a more noble mission," someone said who remembered the group when they first came North. But Oberlin was an artistic turning point, and Brooklyn a few weeks later was the beginning of real financial success.

America's most famous minister of the times, Henry Ward Beecher, the brother of Harriet Beecher Stowe who wrote *Uncle Tom's Cabin,* invited the singers to give a Sunday evening program at his church, Plymouth Congregational, in Brooklyn. When the travelers reached New York they saw announcements of the concert and, for the first time, read in a metropolitan newspaper the new name of their group, The Fisk Jubilee Singers. They had started out without a designation, but one prayerful night, when George White was seeking Divine guidance for his problems, he decided to name them the Jubilee Singers, after the old spiritual about *The Day of Jubilee,* when Moses delivered the Hebrew children from Egypt—just as these singers had recently been delivered from bondage.

Now that they were in Brooklyn, they were afraid that in a big city they would not be successful. But they were. Although on this Sunday night in a church there was no applause, when they had finished singing, hundreds of handkerchiefs were waved aloft, and people began to crowd into the room behind the pulpit to congratulate them. Henry Ward Beecher called them "infants of freedom" and the collection produced baskets full of money. The next day the papers reported that "gray-haired men wept like children" at their "weird and plaintive hymns" such as *Turn Back Pharaoh's Army, Roll, Jordan, Roll,* and *Flee As a Bird to the Mountain.* The New York *Tribune* called their songs, "the only true native school of American music"—those very songs that they had at first been ashamed to sing for any but Negro people were hailed as true American music.

A thrilling New England tour followed for the Jubilee Singers, with large audiences everywhere. Boston cheered. They sang at Yale. At Bridgeport they were housed in the finest hotel. During one week in Connecticut they cleared almost four thousand dollars to send back to their college. This was a great deal of money for that time. Besides, as they traveled, the singers were showered with gifts for the school—furniture, clocks, cooking utensils, and even a great bell which is still used today on the Fisk Campus.

Before the group returned to Nashville for a breathing spell, they sang at the White House, before President Grant, who shook hands with all of them and congratulated them on their stirring rendition of *Go Down, Moses.* By the time that they arrived back in their barracks dormitories in Nashville, they had sent twenty thousand dollars to the Fisk treasury. The money was used to buy a new site for the college, a hill overlooking the city where Fort Gillem had been. And there Fisk University stands today.

Soon the singers, with some new members added, were off on another tour, this time to raise funds for their first building on the new land. This tour, with occasional rest periods, lasted seven years and covered almost all of Europe. The names of the nine who made up the first group of Fisk Jubilee Singers were Ella Sheppard, Minnie Tate, Maggie Porter, Eliza Walker, Jannie Jackson, Green Evans, Isaac Dickerson, Thomas Rutling and Benjamin Holmes. There were some changes in personnel when the group, increased to eleven, went to Europe. Then Ella Sheppard, their pianist, became the musical director. Ella had been born in slavery, but was smuggled away to freedom by her father, who took her as a baby to free soil in Ohio. Showing talent for music as a child, Ella was allowed to study with a white instructor only on the teacher's condition that she come at night and use the back door.

Thomas Rutling's memories of slavery were perhaps the bitterest ones, for he had seen his mother sold away from her family as a punishment after she had tried to escape. Benjamin Holmes, who was forbidden as a slave boy in Charleston to learn to read, did so anyway by always asking people what the street signs said as he ran errands for his master. All the others in the group had experienced similar difficulties and frustrations in their immediate past, so no wonder they could sing with such fervor the old slave songs that contained all the hopes, dreams, and longings of an oppressed people, or make the welkin ring with *Thank God A-Mighty, I'm Free at Last*. Certainly *Nobody Knows the Trouble I've Seen* was much more than just a song to these singers.

In the old days, the slaves had no way of protesting against their fate, without danger of being whipped or even killed, except through their songs. So into the simple lines of the spirituals, short lines repeated over and over, went all the pain and sorrow of their bondage, compressed and intensified into the very essence of sorrow itself. That is why the spirituals are sometimes called *sorrow songs*. In Marsh's book, *The Story of the Jubilee Singers*, published in 1881, concerning the origin of the song:

> *I'm troubled, I'm troubled,*
> *I'm troubled in mind.*
> *If Jesus don't help me,*
> *I surely must die. . . .*

the author writes that the father of the slave woman whom he first heard crooning this song would, after he had been whipped by his master, sit down on a log near his cabin with tears flowing and sing those words. That is where she learned them as a girl, remembered them, and later gave them to the Fisk Jubilee Singers. Truly these songs were *sorrow songs*.

One of the most dramatic of folk songs is:

> *Were you there when they crucified my Lord?*
> *Oh, sometimes it causes me to tremble, tremble!*
> *Were you there when they crucified my Lord?*
> *Were you there when the sun refused to shine?*
> *Were you there when He bowed His head and died?*
> *Were you there when they crucified my Lord?*

Or its companion piece:

> *He never said a mumbling word,*
> *Not a word, not a word.*
> *When they pierced Him in the side,*
> *He never said a mumbling word.*
> *The blood came twinkling down,*
> *And He never said a mumbling word.*

But the slaves of the old South had many joyous songs, too, triumphant jubilees like:

> *Joshua fit de battle of Jericho, Jericho, Jericho*
> *And de walls come tumblin' down. . . .*

and the charming *Little David Play on Your Harp, All God's Chillun Got Shoes, Everybody Talks About Heaven Ain't Goin' There,* and:

> *Why don't you set down?*
> *Set down? Why, I can't set down!*
> *I just got to heaven*
> *And I can't set down.*

because of the wonder of seeing

> *Who's that yonder dressed in white?*
> *It must be de chillun of de Israelite.*
> *Who's that yonder dressed in red?*
> *It must be de band that Moses led.*

With all that excitement on the first day in the heavenly kingdom, who could sit down?

> *Set down? You say, set down?*
> *Go away, don't bother me—*
> *I just got to heaven*
> *And I can't set down!*

Whereas the sad songs made people weep, these happy songs, with their infectious syncopated rhythms, made folks everywhere pat their feet and smile, and feel glad inside themselves. The Northern newspapers began to write a great deal about the young Fisk Jubilee Singers, and people were pleased when they saw them advertised in their communities. By spring, instead of taking up a collection at the *end* of a program, the singers could sell hundreds of tickets *before* a program, even weeks before they got to town. Success was the same in 1873, when they first crossed the Atlantic to Europe, where the spirituals had never been heard before. Lord Shaftsbury sponsored their first tour of England, Scotland, and Wales. They sang for Queen Victoria, the Prince of Wales, and the Duke and Duchess of Argyle. The English portrait painter to the Queen,

Edmund Havell, did an enormous oil painting of them. They gave a program for five thousand school children in London's Crystal Palace, and for seven thousand working people at one of Moody and Sankey's great evangelistic meetings in Glasgow. They sang for criminals in jails and for the sick in hospitals. They dined with Gladstone, the Prime Minister of England. Then, crossing to the Continent, they sang before the Czarina of Russia, the King of Saxony, and in Switzerland and Belgium and Holland and France. When they came to Fisk again, they brought $150,000. They built Jubilee Hall, the large four-story building that still stands on the Fisk campus. And they had made musical history for their country, singing songs of the South into the hearts of half the world—indeed the *whole* world, for since then, as an outgrowth of the impetus they gave them, the spirituals have gone all around the earth, loved and appreciated everywhere.

The Fisk Jubilee Singers were the first internationally acclaimed group of American Negro artists.

James A. Bland
Minstrel Composer

1854–1911

The banjo is an original American instrument, one of the very few musical instruments not brought to this country from Europe. It was first made in crude form by plantation slaves in the deep South. Then, to help syncopate the beat of their music, the slaves also took the small rib bones of a sheep and polished them. With a pair of these bones between their fingers, they beat out very lively rhythms. Bands of slave musicians on the great plantations were often called up to the Big House to entertain the master's guests with banjo and bones, songs, jokes, and jigs. Some slave groups were at times permitted to travel from one large estate to another for a show. Professional white entertainers later began to copy the music and antics of these slave performers, so about a quarter of a century before the War Between the States, the minstrel shows were born. From then on, for more than sixty years, the minstrels were America's most popular form of paid entertainment, with many large companies touring the country to great profit.

At first, minstrel shows were composed entirely of white men who blackened their faces with burnt cork and humorously pretended to be illiterate Negroes. The first such group to invade New York was called *The Virginia Minstrels,* performing on the Bowery in 1843. This troupe consisted of four men, singing and playing a banjo, bones, violin, and tambourine. This burnt cork quartet was headed by Dan Emmett, who wrote *Dixie-land: An Ethiopian Walk-Around* that later became the South's most popular song, known as *Dixie. Swanee River, My Old Kentucky Home,* and most of Stephen Foster's famous songs were also written for minstrel shows. Foster himself labeled them "Ethiopian Songs" and at first did not sign his name, for fear people would think him a Negro. The songs of James A. Bland, a real Negro, whose music has often been confused with Foster's, were also minstrel songs. Both men gave to America some of our most beautiful and best loved compositions. And Bland's *Carry Me Back to Old Virginny* eventually became Virginia's official song.

James A. Bland was born in Flushing, New York, of free Negro parent-age. He was nine years old when slavery was abolished and, by that time, he was going to school in Philadelphia. His father, Allen Bland, had been graduated from Wilberforce University and for a time attended Oberlin College, in Ohio. When young James was about twelve years old, his father was appointed an examiner in the United States Patent Office, in Washington, D.C., the first Negro man to hold such a position there. So the whole family—father, mother, and eight children—moved to the nation's capital, and there James went to high school. By this time he had fallen in love with the banjo and spent more time trying to pick out tunes than he did studying books. Neither his father nor his mother approved of his attraction to this popular minstrel instrument, so they did their best to discourage him. But, in spite of them, James was soon playing very well, and not only playing, but making up tunes of his own. By the time he started college, at Howard University, James had already been earning his own spending change for two or three years by singing and playing on downtown street corners.

One day a white man heard the slender Negro boy strumming his banjo on the street. The man took him to the owner of a large hotel, where he was immediately employed to play for the guests. So, while yet in his teens, James became a professional musician. All the time, he continued to make up songs, but he did not know how to write them down until an elderly Negro music teacher took an interest in him and taught him to put notes on paper. In that day, most college people looked down their noses at the minstrels and thought the banjo an instrument of sin, so Bland received no encouragement at Howard University for his love of popular music. Once when he tried to put on a show there, it was forbidden. And the last thing Bland's father wished his son to be was a minstrel man. Always ambitious, his father entered Howard Law School, and was on his way to becoming a professional man. He wanted young James to follow in his footsteps. Instead, the boy was busy organizing a glee club, plunking a banjo, singing and serenading all over town. And he had written a song called *Christmas Dinner* that he had tried out before the Manhattan Club, to great applause. There was no keeping James from being, as the people said then, a *musicianer.* His heart was set on it. By the time he was twenty-four, he had already composed and published one of his most famous songs, *Carry Me Back To Old Virginny,* and the great George Primrose, a famous white minstrel, had used it in his show. From the beginning, this song was a hit, and it has since become an American favorite.

Even though the minstrel troupes then imitated Negro singers and dancers, and the comedians tried to talk as they imagined the plantation Negro talked, they would not permit a real Negro to be a part of their traveling companies. So Negro men organized minstrel shows of their own. But they could not be as successful financially as the whites because many theaters would not permit Negro companies to perform on their stages. However, there were, in the North, a few successful all-Negro minstrel troupes. One of these, so Bland learned one day, was playing in Baltimore, not far from Washington. Over to Baltimore he went, to strum his banjo and sing his own songs for the white manager. He was engaged at once as a new member of the Haverly Colored Minstrels. Now he was "on the stage." Reluctantly, his parents gave up all hope of making a lawyer or a doctor of their son.

At the height of their popularity the minstrels presented a glittering, gorgeous, slapstick funny singing and dancing show, usually with a very good band that gave a free concert in front of the theater before the performance, preceded by a noonday parade down the main street of the town where they were playing that night. On the stage, the men wore high hats and tail coats and diamond stick-pins in their ties. And all of them, white or Negro, blackened their faces with cork and talked with a broad, uneducated, broken dialect, in humorous imitation of the supposedly "happy-go-lucky" southern Negro man. James Bland, having been to college, did not look like a plantation Negro nor talk naturally in this fashion. Nevertheless, being a good actor, an excellent singer of sweet songs, and a wonderful banjo player, he became a very successful minstrel man. Audiences liked him. And the numbers he composed and performed, *Oh, Dem Golden Slippers, In the Evening by the Moonlight,* and others, soon became popular favorites, used by dozens of singers in many other minstrel shows.

After a summer spent in New York and Brooklyn, the troupe in which Bland was now featured made a cross-country tour all the way to California and back, lasting many months. Then in 1881 the company went to England, to perform at Her Majesty's Theatre, in London. Its comic star was Billy Kersands, who had a mouth so large he could put a cup and saucer in it. There were twenty dancers, a brass band, and a banjo orchestra. One of its comedy bits was a burlesque on the Fisk Jubilee Singers, who had been in England a few years before. And featured on the billboards outside the theater was the name: *JAMES BLAND—The World's Greatest Minstrel Man.* His song, *Oh, Dem Golden Slippers,* became a London favorite.

For the next twenty years Bland was very popular in Great Britain, spending most of his time there. He eventually washed the burnt cork off his face and performed in the music halls as an independent artist, singing his songs to large audiences and earning, for that period, the phenomenal sum of a thousand dollars a month. He became one of the favorite entertainers of the Prince of Wales, later King Edward, and managers vied for contracts covering his services.

In Europe, Bland lived like a star, lavishly. He spent money freely, and was admired as one of the best dressed men in London. His clothes were quiet and well tailored, not at all what people imagined a minstrel man would wear. His tastes were those of a gentleman, and his friends were people of culture and means. But when James Bland finally came back home in the early 1900s, he returned to America with very little money. And, like Stephen Foster, he died broke. Both men were troubadours of the people, making up songs of such simplicity and beauty that the whole world loved them. But these early geniuses of the American popular song cared more for their music than they did for money. Both Foster and Bland often neglected to even copyright their new songs, or to protect them against publication for the profit of others. Of the several hundred melodies Bland is said to have written, less than forty are registered in the Copyright Office in Washington. Even in his own lifetime, other men sometimes put their names on his songs—just as some did with Foster's songs—and published them as their own. And, since Bland's death, many of the melodies have been used by lesser composers without credit to his authorship.

Bland died alone in Philadelphia in 1911 and was buried in the suburb of Merion. There was not even a death notice in any Philadelphia paper, and soon his neglected grave was covered with weeds and poison ivy, in a forgotten corner of the tiny cemetery. But not everyone had forgotten the composer of *Listen to the Silver Trumpets, Pretty Little Caroline Rose* and *In the Evening by the Moonlight,* for *Oh, Dem Golden Slippers* became the marching song of Philadelphia's annual Mummers Day Parade. And years later Dr. Cooke, the editor of the musical magazine *Etude,* began to seek out the facts of Bland's life and instituted a search for his grave, so that a suitable memorial might be erected there. In 1946 the Governor of Virginia, William M. Tuck, headed a delegation to Merion Cemetery for a ceremonial and the placing of a wreath beneath a modest granite slab, newly erected by the Lions Clubs of Virginia and inscribed with the words:

James A. Bland
Oct. 22, 1854–May 6, 1911
NEGRO COMPOSER WHO WROTE
"CARRY ME BACK TO OLD VIRGINNY"

Bert Williams
Artist of Comedy Song

1875–1922

His full name was Egbert Austin Williams, but everybody called him Bert, and that was the name he used in the theater. He was born in Antigua, a tiny Caribbean island in the British West Indies, where his grandfather was the Danish consul, and his grandmother part African and part Spanish. Bert's early childhood was spent on a beautiful plantation overlooking the sea, where white sailboats passed loaded with raw sugar and rum, molasses and tropical spices. But when little Bert was six or seven, his father became ill and the doctor prescribed for his health a more temperate climate than that of the tropics. The family moved all the way to California. Bert grew up in San Francisco when it was still a golden city of the yet Wild West, a center of ships and sailors and fortune hunters, with many gay theaters and clubs and cabarets.

Little Bert had always been musical. In San Francisco he early learned to play several musical instruments, including the banjo. He sang all the popular songs of the day, many of them Irish in sentiment, such as *Little Annie Rooney* and *Slide, Kelly, Slide,* or the ballads of the popular Negro song writer, Gussie L. Davis, who wrote *Wait Till the Tide Comes In* and *In the Baggage Coach Ahead.* When the family fortunes ebbed, little Bert sang and danced in the streets for coins, after school hours. But he had a fairly solid early education and in his childhood learned from his father to love books. As Bert grew older, he acquired a good library of the works of Mark Twain, Voltaire, Goethe, Tom Paine, and even Confucius. Musically, as his voice changed, he developed a rich baritone that pleased the generous patrons of the Barbary Coast clubs where he sometimes sang for tips.

Another brownskin youngster who had wandered away from his home in Kansas teamed up with Bert in San Francisco to sing and dance and crack jokes for the public. His name was George Walker. At first, Walker was the comic half of the team, and Williams the serious singer. But gradually it dawned upon them that, for some reason, people laughed longer and louder at Williams than they did at Walker, so they switched roles, and Bert became the comic, still singing, but with George playing the straight part. When they were scarcely in their twenties, this pair of young Negro performers became so popular on the Coast that they traveled East to New York, to augment their fortunes. Singing a song called *Dora Dean,* about a beautiful Negro cakewalker of the time, and doing the cakewalk themselves, with a couple of charming brownskin girls, the two boys performed at Koster and Bial's Theater for a record run of more than six months without a break. The minstrels had already made the old plantation dance, the cakewalk, very popular, and Williams and Walker made it more so. The cakewalk became a New York fad, taken up by high society, and was featured at every fashionable ball. As a publicity stunt, the prancing young Bert Williams and his partner, Walker, challenged the wealthy young William K. Vanderbilt of Fifth Avenue to a cakewalk contest. Their challenge went unanswered, but their names were in all the papers as a result and more people than ever crowded the theater, to see them dance and to listen to their songs.

As a part of their act, Bert Williams gradually began to develop a slow, sad, mournful way of singing absurd songs that made people laugh—and sometimes almost want to cry, too—songs like *I Don't Care If You Never Come Back* and *You're in the Right Church but the Wrong Pew,* or *I May Be Crazy but I Ain't No Fool,* for which he wrote the music himself. Williams and Walker took their songs and the cakewalk to London. When they came back they were starred in their first full-length New York show, *The Sons of Ham,* a musical farce that ran for almost two years. This was followed in 1902 by another musical called *In Dahomey,* which they took to England. There the King heard of it during the summer and they gave a command performance of the show in the garden of Buckingham Palace.

In putting up the scenery out of doors on the palace lawn that day, everything went wrong. Late in the afternoon, a stout man in a red vest came out of the palace and asked the Negro stage manager in charge how things were going. The man answered, "Very badly," and he said that his English helpers did not seem to know how to do anything right. In fact, he raved and ranted. The stout man smiled and went away. That night, when the stage manager peeped through the curtains just before the show started, to see what the King looked like, he was amazed to see that the King was the man to whom he had so soundly berated the English that afternoon! But all the royal family were so entertained by the show that nobody mentioned that awkward incident afterwards. And the

King was frequently entertained by Williams and Walker in the months that followed.

At first, Bert Williams did not perform on the stage in burnt cork as the minstrel entertainers did. In appearance he was just his natural self. But, because the public then expected all Negro comedians to look like coal black minstrels, Bert began to blacken his olive skin and paint his lips white. And it was as a blackface comic that he later achieved his greatest fame. But the half century vogue of the minstrel was passing and, at the turn of the century, the era of the big and lavishly costumed musical shows was coming into being. In 1906 and 1907, Williams and Walker starred in such big, beautifully staged musicals in New York, with gorgeous costumes and choruses of lovely Negro girls. These shows also featured excellent music by Will Marion Cook and other highly talented Negro composers. And the women stars were always very good singers like Abbie Mitchell, or wonderful dancers like Ada Overton Walker, whom George Walker had married. Only the comedians in such shows now wore burnt cork and rags. Bert Williams was a comedian.

For a man who read good books and had never heard the broken speech of plantation dialect in the West Indies or California, the part Bert played on the stage was not, as many people thought, a "natural" part. It was only because he was such a good actor that he made it seem natural when he told a story in dialect or sang a minstrel-type song. But for years, those of the public who did not know the man thought he was playing himself. And the long years of the minstrel shows had so fixed in the public mind the stereotype of the drawling, lazy, uneducated, always funny Negro, that many people never dreamed a man of that race read Mark Twain or Confucius. This sometimes worried Bert Williams. Late in life, he thought of doing serious dramatic plays as a straight actor without hiding his face behind a mask of burnt cork. But, right up to his death, his popularity as a black-face comedian was so great that he never got around to portraying anything else on the stage. This, his friends knew, sometimes made him very sad. Another great comedian, the white star, W. C. Fields, once said, "Bert Williams was the funniest man I ever saw—and the saddest man I ever knew."

But Williams was not without honor in his own country. He became a very famous Broadway star, using his beautiful baritone voice to almost talk rather than sing the quaint comedy songs that made him the highest salaried Negro performer in America. It was as a singer of these humorous songs that he eventually saw his name go up in great big lights on Broadway—as a star and the only Negro performer in otherwise all-white shows. When his partner, George Walker, was forced through illness to retire, Bert Williams, in 1910, signed a three-year contract with the *Ziegfeld Follies.* He remained with various editions of this famous Broadway revue for ten years, and traveled with its companies all across America.

In black face, and in dark clothes, but always wearing white gloves, his comic figure, before and during the First World War, became as well known on the stage as is that of Danny Kaye on the screen today. And such Bert Williams songs as *Nobody,* whose music he wrote, *Woodman, Spare That Tree* by Irving Berlin, *Oh, Death Where Is Thy Sting,* and *You're on the Right Road but You're Going the Wrong Way* tickled the nation. His famous musical pantomimes of the card game and the dinner party were talked about and written about from coast to coast. And his entrance on the stage became a kind of trademark. As a star, Williams did not appear until late in the show. The lights would go down, a spotlight would make a great white circle against the black velvet curtains at the left of the stage, the orchestra would strike a few chords. Then out from the wings would protrude a lone hand in a white glove, then another white-gloved hand with slowly moving fingers. And just the droll motion of those two hands, *before* Bert Williams himself came into view, would make an audience howl with laughter. Then Williams would emerge, sing a little and talk a little and disappear. As a star, he often did not have to perform more than fifteen or twenty minutes a night. His records sold by the thousands. And at one time his salary equaled that of the President of the United States. For any actor, and particularly a Negro actor at that period, he had come a long way up the ladder of success.

Yet, at the peak of his fame, only a few days before he was stricken suddenly with a fatal illness on tour in the Middle West, Bert Williams wrote to a friend, "I was thinking about all the honors that are showered on me in the theater, how everyone wishes to shake my hand or get an autograph, a real hero you'd naturally think. However, when I reach my hotel, I am refused permission to ride on the passenger elevator, I cannot enter the dining room for my meals, and am Jim Crowed generally. But I am not complaining, particularly since I know this to be an *unbelievable* custom, I am just wondering. I would like to know when (my prediction) the ultimate changes come . . . if the new human beings will believe such persons as I am writing about actually lived?"

It was very hard for Bert to believe that he could be so famous on the stage, yet so ill treated on account of his color in many public places, particularly in hotels where, if he were accepted at all, he would often have to use the alley entrance and the freight elevators, rather than go through the lobby, as the rest of the members of the famous *Ziegfeld Follies* did.

"It is no disgrace to be a Negro," Bert Williams once said, "but it is very inconvenient."

In the show in which he was appearing when he became ill, Bert Williams was singing a little comic song called *Puppy Dog,* whose refrain contained the lines, "When you die no one will care—they'll just say puppy's gone." But when Bert died in a New York hospital at the age of forty-six, a great many people cared. Papers across the nation headlined his death, and the great of the theatrical and professional world paid him tribute. Of this singing comedian the *Literary Digest* wrote, "No man in the theater of our day could tell a story as well." And another publication remembered that a few years before, the great Negro educator at Tuskegee, Booker T. Washington, had said, "Bert Williams smiled his way into people's hearts. I have been obliged to *fight* my way." That smile which Bert Williams passed on to others over the footlights still lives in theatrical history.

Bill Robinson
Music with His Feet

1878–1949

Bojangles was his nickname. His dancing feet were clicking on the cement pavement of a street corner one day, tapping a fast and lively beat, when somebody cried, "Bojangles! That's who you are! Do it, Bojangles!" He had never been called that odd name before, but from that day on it stuck. Bill Robinson was his real name. Neither he nor anyone else ever knew why an onlooker on a street corner, watching him dance, suddenly christened him Bojangles. Maybe it was because the light, quick, jingle-jangle of his tapping feet suggested such a combination of syllabic sounds. And Bo, from *hobo,* has always been a name for wanderers. Perhaps because he looked like a wandering dancer, the name Bojangles descended upon him out of the blue as he danced. Anyhow, in the years that followed, patrons of the theater knew that nickname as well as they did his real name. Sometimes the playbills announced: BOJANGLES, WORLD'S GREATEST TAP DANCER.

Born in Richmond, Virginia, on a bright day in May, 1878, Bill Robinson was soon an orphan. Both of his parents died while he was very young. An aged grandmother, who had been a slave, tried to raise him. But Bill was an unruly little boy whose teachers from the first grade on found him a trial and tribulation. At the age of eight, he wanted to ride race horses, so he left school and started carrying water for the grooms in a racing stable. From the stable boys he learned to buck-and-wing and cut a few other cute dance steps that were rewarded with showers of pennies when he did them on street corners. When a show called *The South Before the War* came through town, little Bill joined it and traveled all over the country. Being a bright-eyed small brown boy, his flying feet added humor and color to the old plantation scenes as he jigged. For ten years he knocked about the land with various traveling shows. Then when the Spanish-American War broke out in 1898, Bill went to war— although not officially. The Army did not seem to want him, but he went along anyhow. He was not wounded in battle, but somewhere along the line he got shot in the knee in a dance hall. By this time Bill was a very good dancer. However, the bullet, which remained in his knee, never seemed to affect his tapping. After the War he continued to work in traveling shows.

Bill was a rough and ready youth, anxious to battle at the drop of a hat, but ready to smile and crack a joke just as quickly. His fights from coast to coast were many, and he was shot, shot at, cut, and upper-cut more than once. In later life, he had so many scars on his body that he could not remember where they all came from. He was a valiant battler, but he did not hold grudges long. And he loved the police. Oddly enough, as Bojangles became better and better known as a dancer, he knew more and more policemen in more and more towns—not as enemies, but as friends. When he became a famous vaudeville star, many police departments across the country presented him with honorary badges and New York County made him a Special Deputy Sheriff. In spite of a quick temper and a boxer's pugnaciousness, his spontaneous wit, ever-ready smile, and dancing feet kept him out of any serious trouble. Once, at the opening of a new police station in Harlem, Bill Robinson danced up the steps and into a cell, where he was photographed through the bars as the first honorary prisoner!

Bill Robinson was a great singing and dancing clown. But he was first and foremost a dancer, a tap dancer—and his dancing was music. Robinson could dance, and often did, without accompaniment. His feet made their own music. He so developed the expert timing of his taps, mostly with his toes, but sometimes bringing the heels into play as well, that he produced the most charming of syncopated rhythms, audible from the stage of the biggest theater high up into the top balconies. Almost any sound or rhythm that could be produced by a snare drummer, Bill Robinson could produce with his feet tapping on a bare floor, a table top, a chair, a pair of stairs, or a cement pavement. His was *human percussion.* No dancer ever developed the art of tap dancing to a more delicate perfection, creating little running trills of rippling softness or terrific syncopated rolls of mounting sound, rollicking little nuances of tip-tap-toe, or staccato runs like a series of gunshots. Bojangles, dancing alone on a stage with the orchestra quiet, could make tantalizing, teasing off-beats, sometimes merging into a series of restful continuous bars of sound that would build up in tempo and volume to a climax like a burst of firecrackers. Some writers on American Negro jazz have classified the percussion rhythms of Bill Robinson's feet as among the finest of sounds in jazz music.

Certainly, his feet produced happy sounds, and he was aptly termed by theater critics as a "bundle of joy." One said that Bojangles looked always as if "he were treading on coiled springs." As light and quick and delicately balanced as a young boxer, Robinson had a joyousness in his dancing that was gaily infectious and that filled a theater with audible rhythms and visual grace. For fifty years he danced his way across the stages of America. His was one of the longest continuous careers in the history of show business. From a jigging lad in *The South Before the War* to a headliner at the Palace on Broadway, from tent shows in Dixie to the World's Fair in New York City, from carnival midways to Hollywood, Bill Robinson danced, tap-tap-tapping along until his nickname, Bojangles, became a household word. His musical shows included *Brown Buddies, Blackbirds, The Hot Mikado,* and *Memphis Bound.* Some of his Hollywood films were *The Little Colonel* with Shirley Temple, and *Stormy Weather* with Lena Horne. He made records and tapped on the radio and television.

By the time he was sixty (and looking half his age) Bojangles Bill Robinson had earned—and spent—almost a million dollars. He lived with his wife in a small apartment in Harlem, but he had a long foreign-made Duesenberg car and a charming California bungalow. He wore a pearl-handled, gold-inlaid pistol in a fine leather holster, since he had been twice threatened with kidnapping. He had given his hometown of Richmond a set of traffic towers out of love for the city of his birth. He had donated money and time to good causes all around the world. He had invented a word, *copacetic,* meaning all right, O.K., fine, wonderful, that found its way into some dictionaries. He had created a delightful staircase dance, tapping up and down a tall flight of stairs at center stage, which was copied by many other dancers. He had taught such popular stars as Eleanor Powell, Ruby Keeler, Sammy Davis, Jr., and Dorothy Stone how to tap. And he had eaten thousands of gallons of ice cream, his favorite food. Bill slept about four hours a night, never smoked or drank, and held the world's record for running backwards against any and all challengers. He loved to play pool, at which he was an expert, and liked to bowl. He once donated a lot of prizes to a bowling tournament, then went to the tournament and himself won most of them back! In Pittsburgh, he took six shots at a robber he saw holding up a woman in the street, but in turn was shot by a policeman, who did not know why Bojangles was shooting. Bill never learned to read and write very well, but at the height of his fame he earned sometimes as much as four or five thousand dollars a week. He enjoyed spending it, and often said, "You can't take it with you when you go."

Certainly the audiences that made Bojangles rich enjoyed him. Mary Austin once wrote that his feet could "produce and coordinate more distinct simultaneous rhythms than any other American dancer. And by the postures of his lithe dark body and the motions of his slender cane so punctuate this rhythmic patter as to restore, for his audience, the primal freshness of their own lost rhythmic power. It is only by the sincere unconsciousness of his genius that he is able to attain that perfection of stage performance, in which his audience is made happily to participate."

When Bojangles died at the age of seventy-one, *Life* magazine published a page of pictures of some among the thousands of New Yorkers who passed his bier, or lined the route of his funeral procession. His funeral was one of the largest ever held in New York City. As the hearse passed the Palace Theater, near Times Square, where his name had often been up in lights, a band there played *Give My Regards to Broadway* and a group of chorus girls threw roses into the path of his cortege. There was music as Bill Robinson went to rest, although the music of his dancing feet could be heard no longer, except on some of the recordings he had made. There, on records, his feet still make music.

Leadbelly
The Essence of Folk Song

In the 1880's–1949

Charged with murder and assault with intent to murder, Leadbelly went to prison three times before he became famous as a folk singer. In his youth he was a fighting man, who did not mind using knife, gun, or fists, sometimes winning, sometimes losing his battles, and sometimes being carted off to jail. He was born in tough days in tough country— in the 80's in the backwoods of Louisiana. As a boy, he wandered all over Texas and the Delta lands, back and forth, working on plantations, in lumber camps, and on the levees of the Mississippi. He was never sure how old he was. Some printed stories of his life give his birth date as 1882, others as 1885, and still others as 1888. When he died famous in New York in 1949, the papers said he was about sixty. His real name was Huddie Ledbetter. But early in his life his last name got changed to Leadbelly, perhaps because Ledbetter sounds like Leadbelly, and also probably because he was hard as nails, tough as steel, and durable as lead, having suffered many vicissitudes in his life, from long prison sentences to serious accidents, and near fatal knife and gunshot wounds. On his phonograph records you will see in large letters the name: LEADBELLY.

He was almost six feet tall and solid muscle. He once claimed that he could pick a thousand pounds of cotton a day. On a chain gang he was the lead man, swinging his pick deeper than anybody else's, and singing along with it. He could work from sunup to sundown, then play and dance and joke the night away. He was a big man with a big voice, full of energy and song. Perhaps if he had not been a singer, he would have been dead twice as soon. Songs were his salvation. He knew a thousand songs and, with those songs, he often sang his way out of difficulties— and eventually out of jail to fame.

When Leadbelly died he had a long list of phonograph records in the catalogues. He had been heard in folk concerts, on the radio and TV, and had put on tape almost two hundred American folk songs for the Library of Congress Archives. He was called "The King of the twelve-string guitar." He was a natural musician, who never had a lesson in his life. And his songs were the true folk songs of the deep South, learned from thousands of anonymous singers in thousands of different places—in levee camps, chain gangs, sawmill shanties, roadside taverns, country churches, little jails, big penitentiaries, and from blind beggars. For forty years Leadbelly was a roustabout, a roamer and a "rounder."

During the later years of his life, in New York and Hollywood, Huddie Ledbetter was a tall, solid, handsome, mahogany-colored man with short cropped white hair, with eyes that seemed to be looking a long way off in a stern but at the same time gentle face. And almost always strung across his shoulders by a long cord was his big long-necked beautiful guitar. Without the aid of an amplifier, he could make the vibrant strings of his guitar sound across great distances, and his rough booming voice could fill the largest hall. He had been accustomed to singing in the fields and on the roads under the open skies, so he had no need of electronics to carry his songs to listening ears. He could make the very walls vibrate. In recording studios, the microphones were never placed close to Leadbelly. He loved to sing, and, at parties or on platforms, once he got started, it was hard to stop him. Some of his songs had dozens and dozens of verses, so he did not fit easily into the limits of professional programs or recording sessions. And he seldom sang the same song the same way twice, so no one ever quite knew what he was going to sing or do. For example, his versions of *John Henry* vary a great deal on different records which he made.

Out of his long life, Leadbelly remembered many ballads, field hollers and blues that most other people had forgotten, and that no one had ever bothered to put down on paper. Thanks to records and the tape recorder—and to the devoted interest particularly of John and Alan Lomax, distinguished folk song collectors—dozens of old American songs have been preserved through Leadbelly that otherwise might have been lost. And even well-known songs like *John Henry* were given a new and unique charm through the additional verses that Leadbelly remembered or made up as he sang. True folk singers often change or add to songs if they feel in the mood, or if they forget the words they heard before. That is why there are so many different verses to the anonymous song-stories of the people, and why folk music has about it a kind of continuous freshness and spontaneity. It is not easy to make a professional singer of a folk singer because on days when such a singer does not feel like singing much, he won't. On the other hand, on days when he *does* feel like singing he may not want to stop for hours. Leadbelly generally felt like singing, and he sang a great deal—for nothing, for pay, for just one friend, or for big audiences, for children or for old folks, in hospitals for the sick on Welfare Island or at private parties for the rich in Hollywood. He just naturally liked to sing, twang his guitar, pat his foot, and let the music rise.

Frank Warner of the New York Folklore Society wrote of Leadbelly, "At his best, with his guitar organically fused into himself and his wild uninhibited voice in full cry, Leadbelly brought a spine-tingling, hair-raising impact to people who had never listened to unadulterated back-street, rock-breaking, swamp-grown Negro singing. He translated a way of life into music. He spoke true."

Among the many American folk songs which Leadbelly sang, usually in versions peculiar to himself, are *Green Corn, Take This Hammer, Old Riley, The Cotton Song, The Gray Goose, Rock Island Line, Good Night, Irene,* and *You Can't Lose Me, Cholly.* He sang many old children's songs, church songs, spirituals, and blues, too. *Good Mornin', Blues* was one of his favorites:

Good mornin', blues,
Blues, how do you do?
I'm doin' all right—
Good mornin', how are you?

I laid down last night,
Turnin' from side to side,
Just turnin' from side to side.
I was not sick—
I was just dissatisfied.

When I got up this mornin',
Blues walkin' round my bed,
Old blues round my bed,
I went to eat my breakfast
The blues was in my bread.

I got a new way of spellin'
Memphis, Tennessee,
Aw, Memphis, Tennessee—
Double E, double T,
Double N-X-Y-Z.
Ow-ooo-o, blues!

Just as Leadbelly could sing hundreds of songs, he could tell thousands of stories out of his past, adventurous and dramatic stories of wanderings, fights, flights, parties, work, sugar cane, cotton, levees, steamboats, fun, love, and revenge. Perhaps not all of his tales were exactly and entirely true, but they were fascinating.

Students of his life, however, have definitely ascertained that his early childhood was spent on a farm in Louisiana, where the cotton grew right up to the very door of his father's shack, and where he learned to play both a guitar and an accordion, which he called a "squeeze-box." While still a boy, he played well enough to be in demand for Saturday night dances all up and down the countryside. These Saturday nights were often pretty rough—mule drivers, cotton pickers, river roustabouts, and drunken gamblers raising sand. Brawls and free-for-alls were not uncommon—a *free-for-all* being a fight in which almost everybody took part. It was such a fight which first sent Leadbelly to jail. Nobody knows who started it or why, but when it was over a man was dead. Nobody knows who killed the man either, but Leadbelly was the boy they sent to jail. Leadbelly says he escaped from one of the prisons he was in, with the guards firing their rifles at him as he ran, yet he got away. He was always handy at getting out of jails.

The girls liked young Leadbelly's music. By the time he was sixteen he was married. But by the time he was twenty, he had wandered away. From Blind Lemon Jefferson, a street singer in Texas who needed a boy to lead him about, Leadbelly learned many songs like *Jack O'Diamonds Blues* and the *Mosquito Moan*. Leadbelly says he heard jazz music played by a whole band for the first time in Dallas. And it was in Dallas, too, that the police carted Leadbelly off to a state prison farm. More than once, Leadbelly was in prison. From other prisoners, he learned many of his songs. In 1925, Governor Pat Neff of Texas, who said he would *never* pardon a man, pardoned Leadbelly, whom he had heard sing, setting him free of Shaw State Prison. But he soon got in trouble again, and was confined in a penitentiary in Louisiana. This time the elder Lomax, on the trail of folk songs, heard him sing. Because Leadbelly knew so many songs and sang so wonderfully, John Lomax arranged for him to sing for another governor. This time Governor Allen of Louisiana set him free. He came out with more songs. For the first time then, Leadbelly went North, to New York, in 1935, and started cutting records instead of people. He put his knife away, didn't carry a weapon of any kind any more, and eventually settled down to a peaceful married life with a good and helpful woman, Martha Promise, who described her husband as "built like King Kong."

During the years that followed, Leadbelly sang and played his guitar for folk song collectors, lecture audiences, night club patrons, and college students interested in native American music. Between songs, he would tell of the sources and background of his music. Sociologists and musicologists became interested in him, as did the radio and record executives. Well in his forties at that time, his professional musical career began. Before his death at Bellevue Hospital, in New York City, Leadbelly had recorded several hundred numbers. Folkways Records issued a memorial album of ninety-four of his songs.

Cold, hunger, knives, pistols, fights, chain-gangs, long years in prison, hard work all day and playing all night did not kill Leadbelly. He was hardly ever sick a moment until a strange illness with a strange name struck him down. There is a disease that doctors say very hard and healthy and active men are more likely to get than others. It has a long name, *amyotrophic lateral sclerosis*. Huddie Ledbetter, like the famous baseball player, Lou Gehrig, was stricken with this disease, and he died.

Jelly Roll Morton
From Ragtime to Jazz

1885–1941

New Orleans was a good-time city when Jelly Roll Morton was a boy. It was full of music and dancing and bands, river boats coming and going, money flowing, ocean steamers sailing up the Mississippi to the Queen City of the Delta, and people from all the world walking the streets. French and Spanish, Creole and English were the languages. Ferdinand Joseph Morton, later called Jelly Roll, was a mixture of the various bloods under the various flags that had floated over his home town—for New Orleans had at first been French, then Spanish, then American, so no wonder races and languages were mixed. The city had also harbored thousands of African slaves. The Mortons were only part African, and Jelly Roll was quite light in complexion. He looked as Spanish as he did anything else.

Slavery under French and Spanish masters was not as harsh and brutal in some ways as was bondage under the Anglo-Saxons. The children of Latin race masters and African women were often set free, and sometimes sent abroad for education. In New Orleans, before Emancipation, there was a large class of cultured free mulattoes with Creole ancestry. There were poets and playwrights among them and even a large symphony orchestra. New Orleans was a musical city, loving opera and symphony, so from the time of his birth there in 1885, young Morton heard all around him music, classical and popular, Spanish and French, African and Afro-American.

In slavery days, Negroes gathered in a large open park called Congo Square, on Sundays, to play drums and dance. When freedom came, their African drum rhythms affected the music of the free Negro bands that played for dances, parades, and funerals. As a child, Jelly Roll often heard these bands, and liked their rhythms. As a piano student of ten, learning to play French quadrilles, for fun he often gave his pieces an African rhythm. As a young composer, he wrote a piece called *The Tiger Rag,* which combined French and Afro-American influences into a jolly kind of composition that people then called ragtime. Jelly Roll Morton became one of the first of the great ragtime pianists.

His parents spoke Creole French and, when he was born, the family name was La Menthe. This, Jelly Roll said, he changed to Morton because he did not like to be called *Frenchy.* He was a sensitive boy, in love with music. With a Spanish teacher, he first studied the guitar because in those days the piano was thought "sissy" and he didn't want the other boys to make fun of him. He had heard a man playing a piano at the old French Opera House, in the *Vieux Carre,* who had long hair like a woman, and it was not until he heard another man playing a piano at a party who had short hair and played ragtime that he decided he would take up the piano. His father was a budding contractor and expected his son to take up his trade. But, in the family, there were always musical instruments around the house, harps and mandolins and accordions, and at his uncle's barber shop, too. As an apprentice at the shop for a time, Jelly Roll strummed his guitar between haircuts. He soon played well enough to join a child trio and serenade grown-up friends. And he studied the piano with a teacher from St. Joseph's Catholic University.

His first job was as a dishwasher in a restaurant, after school, for three dollars a month. But he ate so much that the owner refused to pay him. Besides, he liked music better than he did work or school. By the time he was sixteen, he was playing the piano for tips in cafes and cabarets and staying out so late at night that his parents did not like it. So he left home.

New Orleans was a very gay city then and a great many ragtime pianists were playing all up and down the busy midnight streets. Jelly Roll listened to their music, and learned to play like them. There was a Negro band then too, called Buddy Bolden's, which took piano-ragtime and turned it into the kind of music that was later to be called jazz. Jelly Roll often heard that band play and adopted its style to his piano. As a boy, he went from the classics to ragtime to jazz. And so, before he was a man, he could play all kinds of music on his piano. But the only places where Negro musicians could play were night-life spots—bars, cafes, cabarets, and such, catering to the pleasure seekers. So in such places on Basin Street young Jelly Roll began to earn his living. Sometimes he supplemented his income by day as a pool shark, challenging other players for bets. At other times he sold to the gullible what he called a "consumption cure," made of Coca-Cola and salt in little medicine bottles. And on special occasions he took part in piano battles, each pianist trying to outplay the other, for applause and money.

During his teens young Jelly Roll wandered all up and down the Gulf Coast, from Biloxi, Mississippi, and Gulfport, to Pensacola, Florida, listening to and playing with other wandering piano players like Skinny Head Pete, Florida Sam and Baby Gryce. In Mobile, Alabama, he met, admired and worked with Porter King, a wonderful ragtime player after whom, in later years, Jelly Roll named one of his compositions, turning the name around into *The King Porter Stomp*. The great Tony Jackson, a ragtime genius, was one of his idols. All of these men, some of whom became famous, were creating and popularizing a then new kind of syncopated American music eventually to be called jazz. The whole Mississippi Valley was alive with ragtime with its marching bass and rippling trebles and syncopated counter melodies. Up the river as far as St. Louis, this music was enlivening the nights. And in a few years, on the perforated paper rolls of the recently invented player pianos, it was to enliven the days, as well, in family parlors across America.

In Sedalia, Missouri, a Negro composer-pianist had written a piece called *The Maple Leaf Rag*, published in 1899, which was sweeping the country. This very popular tinkling piano music, in combination with other instruments, gradually acquired the characteristics of blues and boogie woogie, and became jazz. Jelly Roll made this transition in styles, too, and some of our earliest recorded jazz band music is of Morton's composition, with himself at the piano. On one of his records, Jelly Roll demonstrates the steps from ragtime to jazz by playing *The Maple Leaf Rag* in both styles.

Of ragtime, Hiram K. Moderwell wrote, "To me ragtime brings a type of musical experience which I can find in no other music . . . I love the delicacy of its inner rhythms and the largeness of its rhythmic sweeps. I like to think that it is the perfect expression of the American city, with its restless bustle and motion, its multitude of unrelated details, and its underlying rhythmic progress toward a vague Somewhere. Its technical resourcefulness continually surprises me, and its melodies, at their best, delight me."

The three Negroes who were ragtime's most famous exponents, both as composers and pianists, were Tony Jackson, Jelly Roll Morton, and Scott Joplin. Scott Joplin's *Maple Leaf Rag*, named after a pleasure club in Sedalia, became the basis for the expansion of a small white music firm in that city. From the *Maple Leaf Rag*, John Stark & Son became wealthy. They moved to St. Louis, where they bought a printing plant, and by 1900 were among the leading music publishers in America. Their success derived from the ragtime compositions of Scott Joplin and other Negro and white writers. Scott Joplin's fame as a composer preceded that of Jelly Roll Morton. But soon, both in the ragtime and jazz fields, Morton was to catch up with, and surpass, Joplin.

Jelly Roll could compose spontaneously at the piano, and most of his published compositions were no doubt "played out" first, before they were written out. Like many early popular musicians, he did not always publish all his work under his own name, or take the trouble to copyright it. He claimed late in life that many of his pieces were plagiarized by others. He was a bad business man. But there are 120 copyrighted compositions to his credit in Washington. However, whenever he made any considerable sums from his playing or his compositions, he would put the money into some sort of business, attempting to double it—and would invariably lose it. He was not good at finance. But he did acquire three or four fine automobiles, a large wardrobe, and a diamond inserted in one of his front teeth—which truly gave him a brilliant smile!

During his lifetime, Jelly Roll Morton made hundreds of phonograph records, so many he could not remember them all. The early recordings of his small band, the Red Hot Peppers, made in the 1920's are among the best and most authentic renderings of unadulterated Dixieland jazz. And in 1938, he made a monumental contribution to the preservation and documentation of early jazz when, for four weeks, under the direction of Alan Lomax, the Curator of the Archives of American Folk Song at the Library of Congress, Morton recorded 116 sides for posterity, with a running commentary of his own, at once personal and historical. The story of early ragtime, blues, and jazz, demonstrated at the piano by this great old master, has been termed "a priceless musical, historical, and social document." A commercial recording company later selected a number of these records and issued them in album form. And from it all Alan Lomax, using mostly the composer's own words, wrote the story of Morton's life, times, and music, under the title of *Mr. Jelly Roll,* with printed examples of some of the music maker's most famous compositions and arrangements at the back.

It was a good thing for American music that these Library of Congress recordings were made in 1938, for, three years later, poor and ill and neglected in a new era of sweet swing music, Jelly Roll Morton went to Los Angeles, driving across the country alone in winter, and died.

Considered by a younger generation of jazz fans and musicians as old-hat and "corny," the man who had been one of the greatest individual influences on the whole field of jazz passed away with but scant attention from the newspapers. But since his death, there has been a revival of interest in his music. Sigmund Spaeth, in his *History of Popular Music in America,* says of Morton, "He was unquestionably the best all-around musician produced by the classic period of New Orleans jazz." And the excellent discography, *A Guide to Longplay Jazz Records,* by Frederic Ramsey, Jr., lists a large number of new releases of Morton's best performances. Certainly, as Mr. Ramsey writes in his record notes, "Ferdinand Jelly Roll Morton's place as composer, arranger, and player of New Orleans jazz has been firmly established." Along with the recordings of King Oliver, Bunk Johnson, Kid Ory, and Louis Armstrong, those by Morton constitute a rich library of basic jazz. As a commentator wrote in the English magazine, *Jazz Music,* a few years after his death, "Band styles changed with the times, but Jelly Roll's piano and compositions did not. They were the firm, reliable base upon which could be made a variety of designs in a variety of colors."

Roland Hayes
Famous Concert Artist

1887–

Roland Hayes was born in Georgia. After he became an internationally famous singer, he wanted to live near his birthplace again, so he bought a farm there. But one day, when he went into a shop in a near-by village to buy some shoes for his little daughter, not thinking, the famous singer sat down on a bench intended only for white people. A young clerk struck him in the face and he was thrown out of the store. The police did nothing, and the townfolk criticized him as being a Negro "who did not know his place." Roland Hayes, a small, kind, cultured and very gentle man, was emotionally deeply hurt by this, and frightened for the sake of his wife and daughter. So in 1942 he sold his farm in the state of his birth and took his family to live in a suburb of Boston, where Negro people are not treated so rudely in public places. He never went back to his home state.

There is an old saying to the effect that, "It is an ill wind that blows nobody good." The repressive color line in the Deep South was partially responsible for Roland Hayes becoming a great concert singer. When he was a young man at Fisk University, the concert halls of America were not open to Negro singers generally and the booking agents would not handle Negro talent. The excellent Fisk Jubilee Singers had by then so popularized the spirituals that audiences wanted, anyhow, only to hear Negroes sing the traditional slave songs in concert. In the theater, Negro performers were expected to do minstrel numbers. But Roland Hayes had fallen in love with the great classical music of the famous composers of Europe, Schubert and Brahms, Beethoven, Verdi and Monteverdi and Glinka and the arias of the great operas. Yet there was in America almost nowhere for a Negro to sing these songs or operatic arias professionally, or to appear in a concert presenting music of such calibre. Early in life Roland Hayes determined to break the color bar in the concert field. So his career is not only a musical career of distinction, but one of historical and sociological importance as well. He blazed the trail for many fine young Negro artists to follow later, from Marian Anderson, Dorothy

Maynor, and Camilla Williams to William Warfield and Robert McFerrin. From the cotton fields of Georgia to Carnegie Hall is a pretty big step.

Shortly after the War Between the States, in a roadside camp for freed slaves, just north of Atlanta, William Hayes met and wooed a little brown woman named Fannie. They had several children. One of them was Roland, born in a two-room cabin on a ten-acre farm, three miles from Little Row, Georgia, in the shadow of Horn Mountain. Roland's father was a great hunter and a pretty good farmer, though not a very energetic one. There was a big bell on the neck of their plow-ox which Roland suspected his mother had put there so she could tell from the cabin when the bell was still that neither the ox nor her husband was working. His father figured out a way, however, of sitting down in the shade and ringing the bell at the same time—until his wife caught him! A great lover of nature, Roland's father taught him how to imitate all the bird calls of the region, the orioles and tanagers and meadow larks. Little Roland's first music was the music of the birds. And his mother, who was a pillar of Mount Zion Baptist Church, taught him the songs of the church and the old spirituals of her slave days. There were, too, autumn barbecues and country dances where little Roland heard the "sinful" music of the fiddle and the banjo. And once a man came to board with his family who taught Roland how to read the printed notes in a hymn book.

While Roland was still a boy, his father died, and his mother worked the farm herself for two years, to pay off the debts of his illness. But when the ox died, their only plow animal, Roland and a brother, Robert, barefoot boys in their early teens, had to hire themselves out for wages. When Roland was almost fourteen the whole family and a cow moved to Chattanooga, to live with an Aunt Harriet. There he saw the bright lights of a city for the first time, acquired a pair of yellow shoes that squeaked, and met a beautiful little girl whom he married, years later. Roland's mother took in washing and he got a job in a foundry, distributing hot liquid metal into moulds with a hand ladle. Scars from the red hot iron spilling on his feet have remained with Roland Hayes all his life. Sometimes he went to school and by the time he was sixteen he had moved as far as the third grade. Then he got caught in a conveyor belt, was badly mangled, and was out of work and out of school for months. He got religion early and was baptized in the Tennessee River and gave up dancing. But he was singing in a quartet and, fortunately, his religion did not require that he give up music.

One Sunday, Roland sang the solo part in an anthem at church and, for the first time, someone noticed the peculiar richness of his young tenor voice—a teacher named Arthur Calhoun, who offered to coach him for fifty cents a lesson. This young Negro teacher arranged for Roland to hear, on an old-fashioned phonograph with a big horn, the records of the great opera singers of the day—Scotti, Melba, and Caruso. It was the first time young Roland Hayes had ever heard any classical music. He was so thrilled by the arias of Puccini and Verdi that he made up his mind then and there to be a singer himself. This uneducated foundry boy in Tennessee dared to dream that he, too, could some day sing the songs of a Caruso.

At eighteen, with only a fifth grade education, but with fifty dollars he had managed to save, Roland Hayes set out for Nashville and the University for Negroes there, and saw for the first time Jubilee Hall, which the Fisk Singers had built from the spirituals. He could not enter college, being unprepared, but he was admitted to special music classes and elementary academic instructions. He studied hard and worked hard, tending the furnace and waiting on table for his room and board, in the home of some white aristocrats a long way across town.

Roland remained at Fisk for four years and learned to sing Mendelssohn, Haydn, and Beethoven. When he moved on to Louisville, Kentucky, in 1911, he was singing so well that he attracted the attention of a white theater owner there. But since he was a Negro and therefore could not openly sing on the stage of a white theater in Louisville, he was offered work at forty dollars a week, singing operatic arias *behind* the motion picture screen. This seems hard to believe, singing behind a screen, but it is told in his life story, *Angel Mo' and Her Son, Roland Hayes,* by MacKinley Helm.

Some months later, when he was offered the chance to tour with a new group of the Fisk Jubilee Singers, at a salary of fifty dollars a month and expenses, Roland Hayes stopped by Chattanooga, feeling that at last he was on his way to becoming a professional singer. His mother did not give him her blessing. She told him that white people would never listen to serious music from a Negro and that he was, she thought, wasting his time.

A few months later, in Boston, some of the best music teachers there were willing to accept him as a student, but he was told quite frankly that, in their opinion, it was next to impossible for him to be accepted by the white public as a concert artist. Nevertheless, for eight years, Roland studied singing with one of the finest teachers there. Meanwhile, he booked himself on concert tours in the Negro churches and schools of the South, usually on an uncertain percentage basis. But his beautiful tenor voice and his repertoire of both foreign language songs and native Negro spirituals delighted his audiences, made up almost entirely of his own race. When Hayes attempted to persuade the white concert managers of Boston to book him, they shook their heads. One told him that Negro audiences were the best he could hope for in the United States. Then it was that he decided to try his luck abroad.

In 1920, Roland Hayes went to London. Unknown, his first concerts were not sensational. But gradually more and more people began to hear of his soft, clear, lovely tenor voice and the gentle yet intense spiritual quality in his singing. Whether in English or German, French or Italian, or the broken dialect of the Negro spirituals, each of his songs seemed to move even the most callous listener. Here was a singer with a wistful brown face, a wonderful lyric voice, and a varied program of both classics and folk music. The newspaper critics came to hear him and commented favorably. And within a year the royal family learned of his presence in Great Britain. King George V commanded him to sing at Buckingham Palace, and American newspapers reported this concert. It took an English king to break the color bar for Roland Hayes in America—for, when he came back home to the United States, professional managers who formerly would not book a concert for a Negro singer were now ready to arrange his tours. And concert halls whose stages had heretofore been denied to Negro solo artists were now open to Roland Hayes, who had sung for a king. With a series of highly successful appearances in Europe behind him, and a press book filled with laudatory clippings from London, Glasgow, Dublin and Paris, Roland Hayes came back to his own land in 1923. For a quarter of a century thereafter, he was a top-ranking concert attraction—even in the city of Louisville, where he once had to sing behind a screen.

Unique in content for a Negro concert artist at that time, a typical Roland Hayes program might begin with the *Ah, Spietato* aria from Handel's opera, *Amadigi*, or with Mozart's *Si Mostra La Sorte*. Then perhaps would follow songs by Franz Schubert or Claude Debussy, or the famous *Dichterliebe* of Robert Schumann set to poems by Heine. A middle section might be the Russian songs of Tchaikovsky, the charming English lyrics of Quilter, or a group of Creole folk songs arranged by Camille Nickerson. And always, for the conclusion of his solo appearance, would come the beautiful old Negro spirituals of his childhood, sung as he had heard them in Georgia. But it was primarily as a singer of art songs that Roland Hayes sought—and achieved—recognition. His diction in foreign languages was unsurpassed, critics said. His feeling for the songs of Italy or Germany or France was deeply moving to the citizens themselves of those countries. The great tenor arias of opera found in Hayes a sensitive interpreter. Someone once declared, "Roland Hayes sings, not with his voice, but with his soul." And the *Boston Transcript* said, "No one can fail to wonder anew at the miracle of his art."

William Grant Still
Distinguished Composer

1895–

The most prolific of American Negro composers, William Grant Still, was born on May 11, 1895, in Woodville, Mississippi. His father, who had been an instructor of music at Alabama Agricultural and Mechanical College, died when William was only three months old. Then his mother moved to Little Rock, Arkansas, where she found work as a public school teacher. A grandmother and an aunt helped to bring little Bill Still up in a home full of good books. When he was nine years old, his mother married a postal clerk who had a great love for operatic music and acquired a large collection of classical records, played on a phonograph cranked by hand. This stepfather bought opera librettos and explained the stories to Billy, and often the whole family went to concerts together. The little boy liked the violin and, with his stepfather's tools, tried to make himself one. He played his homemade instrument along with the phonograph records, until the noise drove his parents to buy him a real violin. By the time he was sixteen, graduating from high school as the valedictorian of his class, he had made up his mind to be a musician.

William's parents, as most parents did in those days, looked upon music as an insecure profession. They discouraged him. His mother wanted him to be a doctor or a teacher. To please her, when he registered at Wilberforce University, in Ohio, he took up science—in the classroom. But outside he organized a string quartet and he was the violinist. He also played in the college band—all the reed instruments at one time or another—and he amused himself with the piano as well. He learned to arrange and orchestrate, and eventually became the leader of the band. He composed pieces for the band, too, and once an entire program of his student works was given at Wilberforce. He wanted to transfer to Oberlin College, where there was an excellent music department, but his mother insisted that he continue at Wilberforce, with physics, chemistry, and mathematics, so that he might have a sound way of making a living. But music, and music alone, soon had such an appeal for young Still that he quit college, married, and went to work in the music publishing firm of W. C. Handy, "the father of the blues," in Memphis. He made arrangements for Handy and traveled on the road, playing with his band. After six years of this, he finally went to Oberlin and studied composition. During the First World War, Still served in the United States Navy as a messman.

W. C. Handy had moved his music business to New York, so after the war, Still went there and again worked with the famous blues composer. In the orchestra of *Shuffle Along*, a Negro musical hit of the early 1920's, he played the oboe and the same instrument in the band at the Plantation Club, on Broadway. With the money thus earned, he entered the New England Conservatory of Music, in Boston. Subsequently he studied with the modernist composer, Edgar Varèse. Having worked a long time with W. C. Handy in the field of popular music, studied for several years in the serious idioms, and played in all types of bands and orchestras, Still developed such talent as an arranger that many singers and conductors sought his services, from the vaudeville star, Sophie Tucker, and the Broadway and Hollywood producer, Earl Carroll, to the band leaders, Paul Whiteman, Artie Shaw, and Don Voorhees. The large radio networks employed him frequently. And he became the first Negro man regularly to conduct a radio station orchestra in New York City.

Shortly before World War II, William Grant Still moved to California, where he composed and arranged for Hollywood pictures, married a second time, set up housekeeping in a Los Angeles bungalow, and began to pursue the career of a serious composer. There he conducted the Los Angeles Philharmonic Orchestra in a program of his own compositions. He also led the orchestra at Hollywood Bowl's "Symphony Under the Stars." Of his former staff member, W. C. Handy said that Still was "a composer who can qualify as one of the most graceful conductors ever seen on a podium."

Today, William Grant Still is known chiefly as a composer, following the path of such other serious composers of Negro ancestry as London's Afro-English Samuel Coleridge-Taylor, South Carolina's Edmund Jenkins, Tennessee's Clarence Cameron White, Chicago's Margaret Bonds, John Work of Fisk, and William Dawson of Tuskegee. In 1944, Still received the first prize in the Cincinnati Symphony Orchestra's Composition Contest. He was the recipient of Rosenwald and Guggenheim Fellowships. He became a member of the American Society of Composers, Authors and Publishers. His work has been commissioned by the Cleveland Symphony Orchestra, The New York World's Fair, the League of Composers, and the Columbia Broadcasting Company. Leopold Stokowski, and also the Eastman-Rochester Symphony under the baton of Howard Hanson, have recorded his compositions.

Still has written many songs and short pieces. His longer scores include the ballets, *La Guiablesse* and *Sahdji;* the operas, *Blue Steel, A Bayou Legend,* and *Troubled Island,* with libretto by Langston Hughes, which was performed by the New York City Center Opera Company in 1949; and four symphonies. Some of Still's librettos have been written by his wife, the pianist, Verna Arvey. Still's *Afro-American Symphony* was performed by the New York Philharmonic and the Philadelphia Symphony, as well as other large orchestras in America and abroad, where the European critics have received his work with acclaim. In Berlin, an enthusiastic audience broke a long-standing tradition by demanding with bravos an encore of the scherzo from this symphony. Still's *Symphony in G-Minor* was given its world premiere by Leopold Stokowski and the Philadelphia Symphony. In Belgium as a tribute to the composer's 59th birthday, the Brussels radio broadcast an extensive program of the works of William Grant Still. Wilberforce, Howard, Oberlin, and Bates College have awarded him honorary degrees. Howard Hanson has described Still as one of the four leading composers in America today.

His complete list of compositions is a very long one, and ever growing. A recent bibliography of Still's works, the majority of which are issued by various leading American publishers, indicates thirty compositions for large orchestras, three for small orchestras, one for a brass band, five works for small combinations, seven individual pieces or suites for piano, eighteen songs for the solo voice, ten chorus works, four operas, four ballets, and twenty-four arrangements of Negro spirituals. This does not include the bits of incidental music or background material, or the hundreds of unsigned arrangements which Still has done for orchestras, dance bands, and motion pictures or radio. He is a hard worker, a skilled professional musician, and a very serious composer.

A quiet, golden-skinned, rather distraught looking man, Still lives with his wife, two children, and a dog, in a house behind a high wire fence with a locked gate, in Los Angeles. He avoids visitors who have no appointments. He composes for several hours in the morning, and arranges or copies in the afternoon, working on a musical typewriter. For recreation, he tends his vegetable garden, makes much of his own furniture, and carves out little wooden toys—animals, trains, and whole villages—for his youngsters. Occasionally, he writes an article for some musical magazine. Still is a religious man and at the end of every new composition, when the last note is down on the manuscript, he writes, "With humble thanks to God, the source of inspiration."

Bessie Smith
"The Empress of the Blues"

About 1896–1937

She had one of the most powerful singing voices in the whole world. When Bessie Smith sang in a theater, you could sometimes hear her out in the street, and all up and down the street. People did not always have to pay to go inside the auditorium to listen. She was a large woman, almost six feet tall, very dark, with a round pleasant face, and big arms that she carried slightly akimbo, yet hanging down at her sides. She sang blues. She is remembered in the annals of folk music and jazz as the greatest of all blues singers. During her lifetime, she was called, "The Empress of the Blues." After her death, Columbia Records issued a long playing album of her blues, *The Bessie Smith Story,* containing forty-eight of her songs. And new releases of her old records continue to come out, now almost twenty years after Bessie Smith is gone. She died tragically.

Never so famous in her lifetime as she became after death, Bessie Smith sang mostly for Negro audiences. While she was living, Broadway hardly paid the least attention to her. She did sing once in a downtown New York night club. But most of the time she sang in tents and little theaters and open air shows all over the South. She was a great favorite with the simple people of color. She sang their songs, the blues. The blues are mostly very sad songs about being without love, without money, or without a home. And yet, almost always in the blues, there is some humorous twist of thought, in words that make people laugh. They have a very definite lyric pattern, the blues, one long line which is repeated, then a third line to rhyme with the first two. Sometimes, but not often, instead of being repeated, the second line is omitted. The music is slow, often mournful, yet syncopated, with the kind of marching bass behind it that seems to say, "In spite of fate, bad luck, these blues themselves, I'm going on, *on!* I'm *going* to get there." One very beautiful old blues, *Trouble in Mind,* has the refrain, "The sun's gonna shine in my back door some day." That's the way the blues are, about trouble, yet looking for the sun.

Genuine blues are folk songs, anonymously created. Commercial writers have greatly distorted and vulgarized the blues, and the term is often used loosely to mean almost any type of loud, jazzy, popular Broadway song. But the true folk blues are very simple, direct, and beautiful. Nobody knows who made up the first blues, sixty or seventy or eighty, maybe a hundred years ago. The form seems to have become standardized in the late 1800's. But it was not until about 1910 that W. C. Handy, in Memphis, wrote down on music paper the words and notes of a blues. The blues were then considered backwoods music, river music, bad people's music. Just as no one paid much attention to hillbilly music until recently, so no one except the singers and creators of blues themselves paid that music any attention. It sometimes takes a citizenry a long while to appreciate its folk heritage. But the blues have been in the hearts of the unsophisticated Negroes of the South for a long time. Gradually they began to creep into the hearts of all America. The blue note drifted up the Mississippi into the heart of American music, became a standard note in jazz, and went on into the serious compositions of George Gershwin and others. The warm, deep, harsh, slurring singing voice of the blues has been copied by thousands of popular singers on the radio and in the theater. In 1955, a vogue called "rhythm and blues" took possession of Tin Pan Alley, as Broadway calls that section frequented by popular song writers. And Helen Traubel of the Metropolitan Opera House has sung the *St. Louis Blues* in a night club. If Bessie Smith were still alive and singing, she would be a very rich woman. She never became really rich while she was alive.

Bessie Smith was born into the world toward the end of the nineteenth century, in Chattanooga, Tennessee. The exact date of her birth is unknown. Where she lived as a child and how she grew up is almost equally obscure. But somewhere along the line, the great old-time blues singer, Ma Rainey, took the girl under her wing, encouraged her to sing the blues, and Bessie traveled throughout the South with Ma Rainey's Rabbit Foot Minstrels. As she grew into her late teens, she traveled with the Florida Cotton Blossoms and other tent shows, and gradually she worked up to being a star attraction on the leading Negro vaudeville circuit, which booked performers into theaters, not tents. This circuit was a combination of white managers and owners of Negro playhouses, known as the Theater Owners Booking Association, T.O.B.A.—which Negro performers said meant, "Tough On Black Actors," since that circuit often meant working many shows a day, in hot, over-crowded theaters, with only a cubby hole for a dressing room. But the top stars were well paid, and Bessie was a top star. She "packed 'em in" and audiences wept, shouted, screamed, and cried at her songs, the deep, earthy Southern blues out of their own hearts. With her enormous frame planted in the center of tiny stages from Newark to New Orleans, Chicago to Dallas, hardly moving at all as she sang, her arms curved at her sides, Bessie would throw back her head and let the blues roll out.

All the sorrows of the poor, the friendless, the deserted and betrayed, the lonely and the homesick were in her songs: *I'm so downhearted, heartbroken, too. . . . I hate to see that evenin' sun go down. . . . You got a handful of gimme and a mouthful of much oblige. . . . I love you, baby, but I can't stand mistreatment any more. . . . The mail man passed but he didn't leave no news. . . . Nobody knows you when you're down and out. . . . I hate a man that don't play fair and square.* Or her great song of the Mississippi floods:

> *When it rained five days and the sky turned black at night. . . .*
> *When it thundered and lightened and the wind begin to blow. . . .*
> *Back water blues done caused me to pack my things and go*
> *'Cause my house fell down and I can't live there no more.*

Bessie Smith eventually became the highest paid entertainer in Negro vaudeville and, due to her vast public, her very first record, *Down Hearted Blues,* made in 1923, sold over two million copies, mostly to Negroes. During the years that followed, Bessie made an amazing number of records, and her greatest buyers were still members of her own race. The plain, ordinary Negroes loved her discs and recognized, long before white America did, the wonderful playing of the men who often accompanied her recording sessions—Louis Armstrong, Charlie Green, Buster Bailey, Fletcher Henderson, Clarence Williams, Chu Berry, Joe Smith, James P. Johnson, Frankie Newton, the white trombonist, Jack Teagarden, and on one record, Benny Goodman—a kind of honor roll of selected masters of jazz. These great records, distributed and sold almost exclusively to a Negro market, were best sellers. For ten years Bessie, in her way, "lived high." She was a kind and generous woman who gave much of her money away, helping or treating friends. But a great deal she "sported" away, too, having a good time. She lived "not wisely, but too well." Her voice grew rougher and harsher, but never weak or tired. Her last recording session was in 1933, just ten years after her first record was made.

By this time, Carl Van Vechten and other famous music critics had written about Bessie Smith—of "her magnificent voice, big enough to fill a dance hall, warm enough to enfold the whole suffering world," as the *New York Times* later described it—for her name and her fame had begun to spread from Negro circles to white. She made a short film of the *St. Louis Blues*. She sang for the United Hot Clubs of America, one of the first groups to consider jazz a serious art. She had one unsuccessful engagement at a Broadway club, where the hard simplicity of her primitive blues was not appreciated. Back she went to the road again, to sing for her dark public in the deep South, doing one-night stands, traveling fast and hard, losing sleep and driving long distances to make engagements. In an automobile crash in Mississippi, in the middle of the night, Bessie had an arm almost torn from her body. For a long time she lay bleeding in the road. When they finally got her to a hospital, it was a white hospital which would not treat Negroes. An attempt was made to get her to Memphis, where there is a Negro hospital. On the way she died.

An authority on jazz, John Hammond, wrote, "To my way of thinking, Bessie Smith was the greatest artist American jazz ever produced. In fact, I am not sure that her art did not reach beyond the limits of the term 'jazz.'" And Mezz Mezzrow commented that "She didn't have any mannerisms . . . to send those golden notes of hers on their sunshiny way. She just stood there and sang, letting the love and laughter run out of her, and the heaving sadness, too . . . and swayed just a little with the glory of being alive and feeling." And the jazz man, Zutty Singleton, said, "Yes, I remember Miss Bessie Smith. . . . I remember she had a beautiful dress she wore for the show. It was white. But when the electrician turned a certain kind of spotlight on it, Bessie's dress would shine with beautiful colors which the special light brought out. With the dress she wore a big headdress—like the Queen of Sheba—and she was a queen, a magnificent woman. . . . She brought out those blues right from the heart. . . . No wonder everybody loved to listen to her sing. Yes, I remember Bessie Smith. . . . Man, I'm sure sorry for the folks who missed seeing her."

Duke Ellington
Composer and Band Leader

1899–

"The best records of Duke Ellington . . . may be taken definitively like a full score, and they are the only jazz records worth studying for their form as well as their texture. . . . I know nothing in Ravel so dextrous in treatment as the varied solos in the middle of the ebullient *Hot and Bothered,* and nothing in Stravinsky more dynamic than the final section. . . . He has crystalized the popular music of our time and set up a standard by which we may judge not only other jazz composers, but also those high-brow composers, whether American or European, who indulge in what is roughly known as 'Symphonic jazz,' " so wrote the English composer, Constant Lambert. "In the exploitation of new tone and coloring, he has proceeded further than any other composer, popular or serious, of today," said R. D. Darrell. And the European jazz critic, Robert Goffin, wrote that Ellington rationalized the technique of jazz production and "gradually placed intuitive music under control."

Duke Ellington was a young soda fountain clerk in the Poodle Dog Cafe in Washington when he formed his first orchestra. Born in the nation's capital, he was christened Edward Kennedy Ellington. His father was a well-salaried employee of the Navy Department of the Government, and the boy was always nicely dressed—so well dressed, in fact, that his schoolmates nicknamed him Duke. At the age of six or seven, his mother arranged for him to start taking piano lessons after school. Little Duke, however, wanted to be a commercial artist, so, for a while during his teens, he studied painting and sketching in high school. But baseball took up as much of his time as did painting. He was a good center fielder, and sometimes played second base, as well. But he continued to study the piano. His scholastic record in high school was not notable, and sometimes in classes Duke and the boys around him would set up such a racket, beating out ragtime rhythms on their desks, that the teacher would have to call for order. When Duke told one of his teachers that he was organizing a little band, the teacher helped him to get engagements playing for parties. Before he was twenty, Duke was a part-time band leader.

He was a good looking, well-dressed youth, popular with his friends, and often invited to parties, where he would play for dancing and entertainment, just for fun. But many Negro parents of middle-class standards in Washington looked askance at ragtime, and sometimes young Duke would be invited *out* of the house for filling it with too much syncopated melody. James P. Johnson, a great Harlem piano player, had made hundreds of player piano rolls. One of them, *Carolina Shout,* was a favorite with Duke, who played it over and over, then tried to reproduce its lively rhythms with his own fingers. He also tried to compose pieces in the same sparkling idiom. Since he worked at a soda fountain after school, one of Duke's first compositions was called *The Soda Fountain Rag.* By the time he was eighteen, young Ellington's little band had been developed into a six-piece combination, Duke's Washingtonians. By the time he was twenty, he was making enough money to get married. His son, Mercer, was born the following year. In 1922, Duke, his family, and the Washingtonians invaded New York.

Nobody in Manhattan paid much attention to the Washingtonians. The great New Orleans trumpeter, King Oliver, was playing at the Savoy Ballroom in Harlem. Fletcher Henderson, pianist and extraordinary arranger, had his band downtown at the Roseland. And Paul Whiteman's Palais Royal Orchestra was the toast of Broadway. The competition was keen for the young men from Washington, and the first year proved rough going. Sometimes a hot dog and a toothpick was a whole meal. Then Barron Wilkins, who owned one of Harlem's most popular night clubs, gave the band a job. In that smoky basement, many musicians and theatrical people heard them play, and a Negro cabaret producer brought them from Barron's to the Hollywood Cafe on Broadway, where there was a Negro show. There young performers like Jimmy Durante, Al Jolson, the Dolly Sisters, and even popular Paul Whiteman heard Duke's music. The word got around Broadway that a wonderful little Negro band was playing at the Kentucky Club—for the cafe changed its name to Kentucky to give it a more "southern" atmosphere, in keeping with its new Negro show and music. This club soon became known as a place where people could enjoy some of the most enticing jazz in New York.

One night, while the band was playing Handy's *St. Louis Blues,* a Broadwayite named Irving Mills came into the club. Mills was so struck by the sweet syncopated moaning of Duke's musicians that he asked them about making records, and said that he could arrange it. He did. Irving Mills became the band's manager, and was for many years the publisher of Ellington's music. In 1927, Duke Ellington and His Kentucky Club Orchestra began to record for Columbia Records, Vocalion, and later for Victor. Among the excellent Ellington records of that period, with himself at the piano, are *The Black and Tan Fantasy, The Blues I Love to Sing,* and *The East St. Louis Toodle-Oo.* Since then the Duke has made hundreds of discs, some of the most famous being *The Mooche, Echoes of Harlem, Mood Indigo, Do Nothing Till You Hear from Me, Take the A Train,* and *Black, Brown, and Beige.*

There was in Negro Harlem, in the period of the "roaring twenties," an expensive night club called the Cotton Club. There excellent shows were given and the best Negro bands played. But Negro patrons were not welcome at this club, unless they were celebrities like the dancer Bill Robinson. Its clientele was drawn almost entirely from monied whites, wealthy bootleggers, gangsters, and famous Broadway performers. But it was an excellent showcase for a new band on the way up in those mad-spending days, just before America's great depression began. Duke Ellington's Cotton Club Orchestra, as his group was renamed, became a great success. Nation-wide radio broadcasts were arranged, directly from the club. Records of the band began to sell better than ever. Duke Ellington's name became known far and wide. When the depression deepened and not so many people had money to spend on shows, dancing, or music, the Ellington band was one of the few that kept right on going. The Duke and his music were firmly established in public favor. And for more than a quarter of a century, he remained a popular favorite, his music always keeping its distinctive flavor, yet changing just enough never to be behind the times. For Duke this was not difficult because some of the most effective qualities of his musical arrangements were far ahead of the times when he first played them, in the twenties.

In 1933, the Duke Ellington band toured Europe and left a deep impress upon music there. Some European writers called Ellington the greatest living American composer, and declared that the new and unique harmonies and tone color which he brought to orchestral jazz were like a fresh wind blowing away the old conventions of musical composition. Almost immediately the influence of American jazz, and of Ellington's work in particular, began to be observed in the output of many serious young composers abroad. Jazz began to creep into modern music. And Ellington himself in time began to work in larger and more serious forms extending his range beyond the limits of the dance composition or the popular song. Some of his longer works are *Black, Brown, and Beige, New World A-Comin'* and a *Tone Poem to Harlem.* At Carnegie Hall, in 1955, the Symphony of the Air, augmented by the

Ellington band, introduced Duke Ellington's *Night Creature*, a tone parallel for piano, jazz band, and symphony orchestra.

As well known as are Ellington's orchestral compositions, his songs are perhaps better known. Thousands of professional singers have sung them and millions of ordinary people have hummed them around the world. As a popular song writer, Ellington ranks with the top ten in America—such men as Irving Berlin, Cole Porter, Richard Rodgers, Hoagy Carmichael, W. C. Handy, and Harold Arlen. Ellington's *Solitude* received the ASCAP Award as the best popular song of 1934. His *Sophisticated Lady, Mood Indigo, Don't Get Around Much Anymore, I'm Beginning to See the Light, Rocks in My Bed, I Ain't Got Nothing but the Blues, I Let a Song Go Out of My Heart, I Got It Bad and That Ain't Good, Little Brown Book,* and *In a Sentimental Mood* are widely known. Ellington also did the music for a revue, *Jump for Joy,* in which he appeared with his band in Los Angeles, and also the score for *Beggar's Holiday,* on Broadway.

Jazz purists contend that Duke Ellington's sweet swing and sophisticated blues are not really jazz. But other musicologists say that Ellington has lifted jazz to new heights and indicated its future form and direction. Certainly Ellington's way of composing has in it one of the old elements of jazz, improvisation—but more *before* a performance than during performance—in that he often works with the various excellent instrumentalists in his band, accepting their ideas and interpretations, before putting a piece together. The work is then written down on paper, already arranged in large part during rehearsals, with leeway left for individual improvisation.

Ellington has had excellent and inspiring musicians with whom to work. The core of Duke's band was for many years, with variations at times in personnel, composed of such sterling jazzmen, long accustomed to playing with each other, as Ray Nance, Harry Edison, Cootie Williams, Bubber Miley, and Rex Stewart on trumpet; Lawrence Brown, Sam Nanton, and Juan Tizol on trombone; Johnny Hodges, Harry Carney, Al Sears on sax; Otto Hardwick on sax; Barney Bigard on clarinet; Wellman Braud on bass; and the famous Sonny Greer on drums. Musicians and the public alike have long regarded the Ellington ensembles as among the best in the field.

Most of Ellington's composing is done on the move, in hotels, in theater dressing rooms, on trains between engagements, or in his dressing gown before going to bed in the wee hours of the morning. Up early the next day, perhaps to make a train and invariably running late, Duke has often been known to clutch his manuscripts of the night before in one hand and a piece of toast in the other and finish his breakfast in a taxi on the way to the station. The composition he is working on might be finished on the train. Ellington estimates that he has composed about fifteen hundred pieces. He has made so many records that he himself cannot enumerate them and he does not own half of them. In fact, he learned once, when he was in England, that the late King George had a larger collection of Ellington records at Buckingham Palace than he himself owned!

Suave, neat, habitually well dressed, with more than a thousand ties in his wardrobe, Duke Ellington, in spite of a full and hectic life, always looks impeccable, cool, and calm. Even-tempered and likeable, he has long been one of the most popular men in the entertainment world. Once when the French idol, Maurice Chevalier, was about to open on Broadway in a solo show of his own with the Ellington band, the Gallic singer shook with fright at the prospect of facing an American audience that might, he feared, not like him or his songs. Reassured by Duke's calmness and encouraged by his encouraging smile, the Frenchman went out on the stage, singing to Ellington's music, and was a great hit. Once when jitterbugs shook the floor down in a southern dance hall, and it caved in, Duke and his men kept right on playing. He seldom gets excited. When Ellington was thirty-five, critics said he was at the peak of his career. When he was fifty, younger commentators of musical subjects said the same thing. Certainly, since his rise to fame in the twenties, Duke has never gone downhill in critical or public estimation. On his fiftieth birthday, the leading magazine of jazz, *Downbeat,* devoted an entire issue to Ellington's Silver Jubilee. His picture was on the cover.

The Duke seldom writes anything other than music, not even a letter. But he did once write an article on jazz for the magazine *Etude*. In it he said, "Jazz means simply freedom of musical speech. In opening the way for many kinds of musical expression, jazz is peculiarly American—even the Negroid element in jazz turns out to be less African than American. The pure African beat of rhythm and line of melody have become absorbed in its American environment. It is this that I have tried to emphasize in my writing."

Peculiarly American, says Duke—that is jazz.

Ethel Waters
Singer of Popular Songs

1900–

For a long time, one likely way to make a new song into a hit was to get Ethel Waters to sing it. Then, when she became a dramatic actress, the same might have been said about a play were a producer to contract her as its star. But Miss Waters first came to fame as a singer of popular songs, rather than as an actress. She introduced *Stormy Weather* and, almost immediately, it became a nation-wide success. She sang Irving Berlin's *Heat Wave* in the Broadway revue of 1933, *As Thousands Cheer.* It became a hit. The same was true of *Taking a Chance on Love,* which Miss Waters premiered in *Cabin in the Sky.* Her records of these and other songs were best sellers. Her melodious voice, with its varied inflections, sweet high notes and warm deep tones, has entertained many thousands of people during her long career in show business.

Miss Waters made her debut at the age of seventeen, on the stage of the Lincoln Theater, in Baltimore. For the occasion, she had bought a dress at a rummage sale. Being tall and lanky, she was billed as SWEET MAMA STRINGBEAN, and she sang *The St. Louis Blues.* She received eight dollars a week, whereas her managers got twenty-five. Miss Waters came up the hard way in show business, often cheated, underpaid, stranded, singing in smoky night clubs and cheap theaters, living from hand to mouth. She was born in a rundown tenement, in the slums of Chester, Pennsylvania, and knew neither love nor care as a child. Her surroundings were evil, ugly, and sordid. She was often beaten and half-starved. In her early teens, she worked as a maid in a Philadelphia hotel, earning less than $5.00 a week. When she told of these hardships in her autobiography *His Eye Is on the Sparrow,* the book critic of the *New York Times,* Charles Poore, wrote, "Miss Waters has survived a dozen catastrophes that would have killed off whole armies." Because of her brave story of great triumphs over desperate odds, from the slums to stardom on Broadway and in Hollywood, Mr. Poore suggested her book as a candidate for the Pulitzer Prize. *Stormy Weather,* Miss Waters said, might have been the theme song of her life. Yet, in thousands of theaters, her sweet and gentle smile, the friendliness of her personality, and the rich warmth of her voice have made audiences all across America feel happy and relieved of their own cares.

Ethel Waters sang many happy songs in clubs and theaters, songs like *Dinah, Joy to My Soul,* and *You Can't Stop Me from Lovin' You.* But there were always the sad songs, too, like *Stormy Weather,* about a broken love, or *Travelin' All Alone,* or Irving Berlin's memorable *Supper Time,* a song of a southern Negro woman who learns as she is setting the supper table that her husband has been lynched—and so "won't be comin' home no more." Into the short thirty-two bar choruses of these brief songs, Ethel Waters could pour all her own memories of grief, sorrow and loneliness, and make of them unforgettable vignettes of great dramatic intensity. The American popular song, often of Tin Pan Alley origin, is seldom more than sixteen lines in length, with perhaps a short verse preceding the chorus. With only these sixteen or twenty lines of doubtful poetry to work with, Miss Waters has made of many of these songs such intensely human pictures of love and tragedy that audiences who have heard her will never forget them. Before she turned most of her attention to the dramatic theater, Ethel Waters was a great singer of popular songs.

As a singer, Miss Waters was a vaudeville headliner, a star in *Africana, Blackbirds of 1930, Rhapsody in Black,* and at the Cotton Club and Plantation Club, in New York. As a singing comedienne she appeared with Clifton Webb and Marilyn Miller in *As Thousands Cheer,* and in 1935 she was co-starred with Beatrice Lillie in *At Home Abroad.* In the John La Touche musical, *Cabin in the Sky,* she toured from coast to coast. And in 1954 she did a similar tour in her own one-woman show, *At Home with Ethel Waters,* alone holding audiences enthralled for an entire evening, with the accomplished musician, Reginald Beane, her accompanist at the piano.

As a serious actress, beginning with the role of the mother in *Mamba's Daughters,* in 1939, and continuing through that of the servant in *The Member of the Wedding,* in 1950, in the full-length play Miss Waters found ample scope for her great histrionic powers. Critics immediately hailed her as a dramatic star. Even without the use of songs, she filled theaters to capacity. But when she did sing the simple little spiritual, *His Eye Is on the Sparrow,* in *The Member of the Wedding,* it became one of the high points of her performance. And in this drama at the Empire Theater, in New York, Ethel Waters was the star of an otherwise almost entirely white company. Of her acting ability, the critic, Brooks Atkinson has said, "Miss Waters, powerful in both body and spirit . . . is larger than life." In Hollywood, Miss Waters made several films, *Tales of Manhattan, Stormy Weather, Cabin in the Sky, Pinky* and *The Member of the Wedding.* She has been a guest star on numerous radio shows, and was for a while a regular feature of the *Tex and Jinx Show* on television, singing and telling stories.

At one time or another, Ethel Waters has adopted twelve children, all needy youngsters whom she hoped to give a happier start in life than she herself had as a child. In theatrical circles, her generosity is legendary. She is a devout Catholic and her heart and her purse strings are always open to the appeals of priests and nuns working among the poor. After several long Broadway runs in hit shows, Miss Waters purchased, besides her New York home, a beautiful house in California. In contrast to her poverty-stricken youth, she now lives well, but she has not forgotten hunger.

A newspaper man who interviewed Ethel Waters recently reported that when he asked her what the big sparkling diamond ring meant on her finger, she replied, "Success!" Unlike the poor heroine of one of her musicals, Miss Waters did not have to wait for a cabin in the sky to be happy. Certainly, in the eyes of an admiring public, her success and her happiness are well deserved.

Louis Armstrong
King of the Trumpet Players

1900–

Louis Armstrong's life spans the whole history of orchestral jazz. It roughly followed its geographical course as well, up the Mississippi from New Orleans to St. Louis and Chicago, thence eastward to New York, westward to the Coast, and over to Europe and Asia. On the Fourth of July, 1900, at about the time that jazz was crystallizing into orchestral form, Louis was born in the very city that did the most to give birth to jazz, New Orleans. That is why Louis Armstrong and jazz are in a sense one and the same. Louis heard jazz all his life, played it most of his life, and became the greatest jazzman of the twentieth century. He played in St. Louis and Chicago when jazz was young, in New York and California later, and finally in Europe and Asia. Louis Armstrong has been America's leading ambassador of our most popular music in its original form. He has lifted his trumpet and blown to the four corners of the earth.

The first time Louis possessed a horn was in the Colored Waif's Home, in New Orleans. He was not an orphan, but he was sent there for firing a pistol in the streets for fun on New Year's Eve—for the Waif's Home was also a kind of reformatory. Louis was not a bad boy, but the police thought he must be, shooting off a big gun in public at the age of twelve. They hauled him off to jail and thence to the Home. This was bad for Louis, but good for jazz—in that it was there that he learned to play the cornet, and to be part of a band.

James Alley, where Louis was born, was a slum. His people were very poor, and his father was sometimes home, sometimes not. Finally he wandered away from Louis's mother for good. His mother had to work hard all day, cleaning or cooking for white families across town, so Louis was left to his own devices as he grew up. That he got into no more serious mischief than that of firing a pistol for fun is amazing. Perhaps his love of music prevented delinquency. As a small boy, he had formed a little band with four other boys and their homemade instruments, serenading on New Orleans corners for pennies. Louis's mouth was very big. His pockets were very raggedy—pennies might fall through. But his mouth could hold quite a few pennies. Early in life, Louis acquired the name Satchelmouth, shortened eventually to Satchmo. Sometimes his friends called him Dippermouth, too. He had a bright, good-natured smile, all the wider because his mouth was so large. And even as a little boy, selling the *Times-Picayune* at a newsstand on a busy Canal Street corner, Louis had a deep gravelly voice that could be heard yelling, "Paper, paper! Latest paper!" above all the traffic. When he sang, he could be heard up and down the street.

The same Buddy Bolden who enthralled with his trumpet an older boy, Jelly Roll Morton, in musical New Orleans, also enthralled Louis. Summer nights, old Mr. Bolden would lift his horn to his lips and blow far away in Lincoln Park, and that horn could be heard way across town, where Louis lived. Louis fell in love with horns and used to follow the Negro marching bands to the cemeteries as they played slow dirge-like music for funeral processions. On the way back—"going to town," for that's how this saying originated—the bands would strike up happy syncopated tunes, marching quickly into the city. Louis and dozens of other raggedy little boys and girls would prance along in the dusty streets beside the band. These children were called "the second liners," the band itself being, of course, the first line. With the bass drum booming, clarinets shrilling, slide trombones *ummping*, and golden trumpets blaring, the bands made a mighty noise, syncopated, ragged, jazzed—although the word jazz had not as yet come into being. It was wonderful music to march to, to dance to, or just to listen to—except that almost nobody could keep still just listening.

Louis wanted more than anything in the world to blow a horn. The story is told that when he was finally handed a cornet in the reform school, he kissed it. But he had been there for several months before this happened. At first Louis was permitted to play a small drum in the Waif's Band, beating out terrific rolls throughout the school's favorite piece, *At the Animals' Ball*. Then Louis became the official bugler, waking everybody up in the morning. But a bugle is a very inflexible instrument, not like a cornet or a trumpet. When at last Louis was allowed to have a real band horn—on loan, since it belonged to the school—he filed notches in its mouthpiece the better to fit it to his large lips. The Waif's Band sometimes marched in parades in the city. Soon all of Louis's friends, and many older people, too, were talking about the sweet, loud, wonderful playing of one of the boys in the band—Louis Armstrong. Louis was in his seventh heaven, in the white jacket and dark trousers of the band uniform, prancing proudly through the streets at Mardi Gras and other holidays. When Louis had served his time at the home and was released, he cried because he hated to leave his horn and the band behind.

To aid his mother and younger sister, he went to work as a helper on a coal wagon, yelling, "Coal! Coal! Basket of coal!" But times were hard and he did not earn enough money to buy himself a trumpet. So when the horn player in a little band in a corner cafe near Louis's home became ill, and somebody suggested him as a substitute, he had no horn to blow. The Italian owner of the place bought one for him second-hand, from a pawnshop, and Louis's career as a professional musician began, at fifty cents a night. But, not having played in many months, his upper lip soon got so sore that he could hardly make a note. Instead, he filled in the trumpet part with his gravelly voice, singing from the bandstand. This amused the patrons, but not the boss. However, when the proprietor discovered that there was something appealing to his customers in Armstrong's rough, funny-sounding, sandpaper growl, he let him keep the job until his lip healed and he could play again. In the months that followed, Louis's playing began to attract Negro musicians from all over New Orleans, and even the great King Joe Oliver came to hear him. Other jobs soon came his way. Playing with Kid Ory's Brownskin Band, and later with Fate Marable, on the Mississippi River boats as far upstream as St. Louis, young Armstrong, who couldn't read a note as yet without a struggle, absorbed by ear all the happy music of the period and could reproduce it on his horn. As a boy, standing outside the swinging doors of Basin Street bars, he had heard young Jelly Roll Morton and other fascinating ragtime pianists. Through the windows of dance halls on Rampart Street and Perdido, he had listened to Bunk Johnson and other great New Orleans jazz makers. All this music had gone in both ears and out none. By the time he was twenty, Louis could play by ear hundreds of tunes, blues, ragtime, spirituals, funeral marches, and he began to invent his own embellishments on these traditional melodies. He is credited with having created, early in life, some of the most exciting and original passages in jazz.

When the popularity of this syncopated Dixieland music spread to the North, King Oliver, in 1921, sent for Louis Armstrong to join his band playing at the Lincoln Gardens, in Chicago. By 1924, Louis was with Fletcher Henderson's Orchestra at the Roseland Ballroom, in New York. On Broadway, for the first time he played with a band that used written arrangements, leaving little room for free spontaneous improvisation. Yet Louis fitted in well, and later played with many such tightly orchestrated bands. A musician who once worked with him in such a band says that one day when a new piece was being rehearsed, while the arranger was still writing out the parts for the various instruments, Louis listened to the melody on the piano. When the whole band ran through it, some with scored parts, others without, Louis could be heard swinging out beautifully on his horn at just the right places. A bit later that day, however, when he was handed the written trumpet part, Louis saw so many notes on the paper that he said, "Man, you know I can't play this with all those notes!"

The arranger looked at him and said, "Why, you've already played it—and more, too." Louis's musical sense was so true that he had created that day a more exciting trumpet part than even the composer or arranger had written. Throughout his long career, no matter what groups he has played with, foreign or domestic, big or small, Louis Armstrong has stood out as a thrilling performer. His rough and rumbling singing style, too, has delighted audiences everywhere, and his famous "scat singing" of pure nonsense syllables has been widely copied. His shining trumpet, big smile, and white handkerchiefs have become his trade marks. Because Louis blows very hard when he plays, giving unstintingly to his music, he perspires a great deal on the bandstand. So he always has a dozen or so gigantic white handkerchiefs at hand to wipe the moisture away.

In theaters and night clubs, on television and the radio, Louis Armstrong is a long-time headliner. In motion pictures, he is a featured performer. His repertoire of songs ranges all the way from genuine blues and spirituals like *Nobody Knows* to popular numbers such as *Them There Eyes, Pennies from Heaven,* and *La Vie en Rose.*

Louis's discography, dating from 1923, is a very long one, and his records are sold around the world. George Avakian has re-recorded and annotated some fifty outstanding examples of the best of his famous old recordings. On eight long-playing sides, this historic album has been issued under the title of *The Louis Armstrong Story.* Here, playing with Louis, are some of jazzland's finest musicians—Johnny Dodds, Baby Dodds, Kid Ory, Johnny St. Cyr, Lil Hardin, Honore Dutrey, and Earl Hines, among others. And such old standbys of jazz as *The Twelfth Street Rag, Heebies Jeebies, Muskrat Ramble,* and *The Sugar Foot Strut* are performed, as well as *The Basin Street Blues* and the classic *West End Blues.* On other records, Louis's trumpet has spun golden notes behind the voices of many famous singers, from Ma Rainey and Bessie Smith to Frances Langford and Bing Crosby.

London, Paris, Copenhagen, Tokyo, and Rome have heard Louis's horn. He has twice written his autobiography, and other books have been written about him. *Trumpeter's Tale,* by Jeanette Eaton, is his story, written especially for young people. In 1950, when Louis Armstrong was fifty years old, and jazz about the same age, *The Record Changer* devoted a whole issue to articles and tributes about him, in honor of his Golden Jubilee. Its editorial page termed Armstrong "the man who represents the greatest in jazz." Earlier commentators had even gone so far as to say that Louis was the artist who "brought respectability to jazz." Concerning his playing, Wilder Hobson has said, "I have always felt that the most ecstatic passage in jazz—the adjective is not used lightly—is Armstrong's last trumpet chorus in *Struttin' with Some Barbecue.*" Both at home and abroad, many have pronounced Louis "the greatest trumpet player in the world." Others have declared that only Gabriel can outblow him! Concerning all this, Louis Armstrong says, quite simply, "Me and my horn, we come a long ways together."

Marian Anderson
Metropolitan Opera Star

Early 1900's–

When the great brocaded curtains of the Metropolitan Opera House in New York parted on the second scene of the first act of Verdi's *Un Ballo in Maschera,* on the evening of Friday, January 7, 1955, a precedent-shattering moment in American musical history occurred. A Negro singer for the first time appeared on its stage as a featured member of the Metropolitan Opera Company. That singer was Marian Anderson.

Abroad, and with lesser opera companies in the United States, Negro singers had sung leading roles. And the Metropolitan had signed a prima ballerina, Janet Collins, of color. In Europe, Madam Lillian Evanti, an American Negro woman, had starred at leading opera houses before World War II. And after the War, in 1953, Mattiwilda Dobbs, a young Negro coloratura from Atlanta, Georgia, sang a leading role in Rossini's *Italiana in Algeri* at La Scala, in Milan. The same year another young Negro singer and graduate of Fisk University, the soprano, Leonora Lafayette, sang Aida at London's Covent Garden. Katerina Yarboro had sung the same role with the New York Hippodrome Opera Company, under the direction of Alfredo Salmaggi, in an enormous theater—and an enormous production which advertised performances of this opera as having elephants, camels, horses—and the former heavyweight champion of the world, Jack Johnson! Muriel Rahn also sang Aida with otherwise white companies. And the New York City Opera had taken the lead in integrating Negro singers into its municipally controlled City Center company from the beginning. At the City Center from 1948 on, the soprano, Camilla Williams, sang not only the dusky Egyptian role of Aida, but leading roles in *La Bohème* and *Madame Butterfly,* also. Todd Duncan appeared in *Pagliacci.* And the baritone, Lawrence Winters, in *Carmen, The Tales of Hoffmann, Turandot, Aida, Die Meistersinger* and as one of the Three Wise Men in Menotti's *Amahl and the Night Visitors.* But not until 1955 did the chief of American opera houses, the Metropolitan, drop its color bar. That year, not only was Marian Anderson engaged, but the Negro baritone, Robert McFerrin, made his appearance there as Amonasro in *Aida*. The Marian Anderson debut was of such significance in the history of American race relations that it was given a front-page story the next morning in *The New York Times*, with a picture of Marian Anderson and her mother photographed after the performance.

Miss Anderson's mother had been a schoolteacher in Virginia before Marian was born, but her three daughters came into the world in Philadelphia. Marian's father died when she was a child, and her mother went to work in a large department store, making sure that her children were well cared for and that they attended school and church regularly. At church, Marian sang in the Sunday School Choir and by the time she was ten knew a great many hymns and spirituals by heart. Even as a girl, she had a very beautiful singing voice. Her first music teacher felt that she was so talented that she would not accept any pay for instructing her. Marian's church, however, had raised a fund for her musical education, and this they put in trust for her future study. The Philadelphia Choral Society, a Negro group, further sponsored her training, after she graduated from high school. By 1925, Marian felt herself ready to enter the New York Philharmonic Competitions in New York. She won first place. More years of study, and of small concerts in Negro churches, followed until, in 1930, on a Rosenwald Fellowship, she embarked for Europe. In Berlin, Miss Anderson made her concert debut, followed by a tour of Scandinavia that was so successful that she returned there in 1933, on a second trip to Europe. That year she was decorated by the King of Sweden and the King of Denmark, and gave almost a hundred and fifty concerts. Later, she sang in Paris and in all the other European capitals. And Toscanini called the rich velvet of her contralto a voice of the sort that might be heard but once in a hundred years.

On her return to America for a New York concert, armed with a brace of wonderful press notices, and already a seasoned concert artist, Marian Anderson fell during a storm at sea and broke her ankle. Nevertheless, she went ahead with the concert, propped up in a long gown against the piano, so that the audiences did not see the plaster cast, nor know that she was suffering. She sang so well that the *Times* review of her program said her music making "probed too deep for words," and the other papers the next day were equally enthusiastic. A very successful coast to coast tour followed.

Since that year, 1935, Marian Anderson has been one of America's favorite concert artists. Just as Roland Hayes, in 1923, became the first Negro man to sing in our major concert halls, so Marian Anderson became the first Negro woman. Since that time, however, many excellent Negro singers have emerged in the concert field in America, foremost among them being Dorothy Maynor, Carol Brice, Adele Addison, Leontyne Price, Mattiwilda Dobbs and William Warfield.

Only a very few singers have had so consistent a box office appeal as Marian Anderson, filling enormous auditoriums over so long a period of years. *Newsweek* recorded in 1949 that her annual gross was more than $265,000 from concerts alone, and much more if her radio and record fees were added. Her famous recording of Schubert's *Ave Maria* had then sold more than a quarter of a million copies. At one time Miss Anderson gave as many as a hundred concerts a year, but later limited herself to not more than fifty or sixty a season. Sometimes within a single season these concerts were as far apart as Boston and Tokyo, Vienna and Buenos Aires. Marian Anderson has sung in almost all the large cities of the world, and many of the small ones. Her largest audience was, however, at a free concert in Washington, D.C., given outdoors in the plaza before the statue of Lincoln, arranged in protest against the barring of Negro singers from Constitution Hall. There, on an Easter Sunday, in 1939, Marian Anderson sang to seventy-five thousand people. Since her marriage in 1947, she has acquired a lovely country home in Connecticut, but much of her time is still spent on tour. She travels without a maid and always carries along her own portable sewing machine. She lives simply and quietly. Her friends say that she is a very kind and generous woman, but her only publicized patronage is that granted through the Marian Anderson Scholarship Fund, which she established some years ago for "talented American artists without regard to race or creed."

As have all Negroes, Marian Anderson has known many of the harsher aspects of the color bar, and some of her unhappy experiences in this regard are recounted in a book which her long-time accompanist, Kosti Vehanen, wrote about her. So, when the gorgeous curtains of the Metropolitan Opera House parted on that historic evening and for the first time from that stage a Negro diva faced its Diamond Horseshoe filled with distinguished people, with a brilliant audience above and below the boxes, it was truly an epoch-making moment for America, and a great moment in Marian Anderson's life. She received a tremendous ovation. Her role was that of Ulrica, the Sorceress, and she looked very beautiful, like a bronzed gypsy.

Once Marian Anderson had said, "Years and years ago, I had hoped to some day sing in opera. Later . . . it did not become a necessity." Perhaps she had never believed it would become a reality for her in her own country. But it did become a reality. "For Marian Anderson it was the culmination of a brilliant international career as a concert performer," reported the *New York Times,* and "for other Negro singers, it was the opening of a big new door to opportunity." Marian Anderson, Metropolitan Opera Star.

Bennie Benjamin
Broadway Song Writer

1907–

A few blocks from Times Square, in New York, there is a stretch of Broadway where many of the publishers of popular tunes have their offices. This section is known as Tin Pan Alley. Its heart is the Brill Building. Here song writers are a dime a dozen, and on sunny days they may be seen standing all along the sidewalks, manuscripts in pocket or briefcases in hand. To achieve success as a writer of hit songs is a long, hard road and there is a great deal of competition.

Bennie Benjamin says that when, just from the West Indies, he first tried to sell a song, the doors of the publishing houses in New York seemed to be made of cement. He had worked at being a song writer for ten years without success, and the manuscript of his first hit he carried from publisher to publisher for three years before it was accepted. Meanwhile, in collaboration with others, it was reworked and revised. Finally, *I Don't Want to Set the World on Fire* came out—and it went like wildfire. From then on Bennie Benjamin didn't have to worry much about getting into publishers' offices. Today he is a top Broadway song writer, and certainly one of the most successful of the younger men in that field.

Since the days of James A. Bland of the minstrel shows, who wrote *Carry Me Back to Old Virginny* and *Oh, Dem Golden Slippers,* there have been many famous Negro writers of popular songs in the United States. Gussie L. Davis wrote two of the biggest hits of the gay 90's, *Fatal Wedding* and *In the Baggage Coach Ahead,* also *Lighthouse by the Sea,* and *Wait Till the Tide Comes In.* Bert Williams and Alex Rogers wrote *Nobody.* Tom Lemonier wrote *Just One Word of Consolation.* Will Marion Cook composed *Rain Song* and *Bon Bon Buddy.* W. C. Handy wrote innumerable blues, including the great *St. Louis Blues.* Rosamond Johnson wrote *Lil' Gal* and *Under the Bamboo Tree.* Shelton Brooks wrote *Some of These Days* for Sophie Tucker. Cole and Johnson composed *The Maiden with the Dreamy Eyes* and *My Castle on the Nile.* Alberta Hunter and Lovie Austin put down *Nobody Knows You When You're Down and*

Out. Lucky Roberts wrote *Moonlight Cocktail.* Una Mae Carlisle wrote *Walking by The River,* and Maceo Pinkard wrote *Mammy,* the famous Al Jolson number. Joe Trent wrote *Muddy Water;* Fats Waller and Andy Razaf, *Honeysuckle Rose* and *Ain't Misbehavin'.* Sissle and Blake wrote *I'm Just Wild about Harry* and numerous others. James P. Johnson wrote *Old Fashioned Love* and *The Charleston.* Jimmy Davis and Ram Ramirez wrote *Lover Man.*

Whereas many of the Negro song writers of a past generation had in their compositions much of the flavor of the spirituals, blues, and early jazz, Bennie Benjamin has in his songs almost none. Although he is Negro, in his music the "Negro" flavor is lacking. Coming from the West Indies rather than the South, and landing as a young man in New York, he is more influenced by Broadway than he is by Dixie, and by the commercial ballads of Tin Pan Alley more than by the jive and jam of Harlem. But within the narrow limits of the Broadway commercial song, Benjamin is a master and, together with George Weiss, has turned out some of the catchiest tunes of our times.

Benjamin came to New York from the Virgin Islands when he was about twenty. He was born at Christiansted, St. Croix. His father was the captain of a small ship that was wrecked off the coast of his homeland when Bennie was a baby, and his father was drowned. The very year that young Benjamin came to the United States, the depression was beginning and soon many people were out of work. Bennie had hard going during his early years on the mainland. At home, in the West Indies, as a child, Bennie had learned to play a banjo, but he never had any music lessons, and banjoes had gone out of favor, in America, anyway, with the passing of the minstrel days. In New York, Bennie managed to purchase a guitar, and he used this instrument to pick out the tunes of his songs. His second song hit was written during the wartime dimout, and was called *When the Lights Go on Again All over the World.* It caught on immediately, and had a number of recordings, but before Bennie could collect any money from it, he was taken into the armed services. When he reached Europe, he heard his fellow G.I.'s singing his song. And he enlivened the barracks there with his guitar. Bennie could play well.

When the War was over Bennie Benjamin returned to New York. One day, while walking down Broadway, he ran into a young white man whom he had met shortly before the war in a record shop owned by the young man's father. They had interests in common and had become friends. George Weiss was a student at the Juilliard School of Music, had studied composition and arranging, and worked for such well-known band leaders as Vincent Lopez and Stan Kenton. Bennie Benjamin had never had a lesson in musical theory in his life, but he possessed a natural talent for making up tunes. Together Benjamin and Weiss formed a song writing team that has since become one of the most successful in the business. Young George Weiss wanted to write songs. Combining their talents, that of Bennie for melody making and those of George for arranging music and rhyming words, the two men, one white and one Negro, have produced a dozen or more really big hits, many other published songs, and some filed away and as yet never published at all. But their names are familiar the length and breadth of Tin Pan Alley, and the best of their many songs are known everywhere.

Among their top tunes are *Rumors Are Flying, Oh, What It Seemed to Be,* and *Surrender,* all three hits in the same year of 1946. These were followed by, among others, *Speaking of Angels, These Things I Offer You,* and *Wheel of Fortune.* The credit line on their title pages reads: *Words and music by Bennie Benjamin and George Weiss.* Dozens of well known singing stars recorded their *Wheel of Fortune,* even before it had appeared on the market, and it was sung in night clubs from coast to coast. Walt Disney asked the collaborators to write the title songs for his films, *Fun and Fancy Free* and *Melody Time.* They now have an office on Broadway for, in less than ten years, the team of Benjamin and Weiss has sold millions of records and stacks of sheet music. Their work has been called "a slot in the arm to juke boxes." Probably, around the clock, twenty-four hours a day, some juke box or another somewhere is playing their records. For the year 1946, *Billboard* rated them the top song writing team in America. Both men are members of ASCAP, the society which collects performance rights for music from night clubs, theaters, TV and radio. From this source, and record and music sales, Mr. Weiss and Mr. Benjamin collect a pretty penny. Their greatest ambition now is to write the songs for a big Broadway show. No doubt, they will in time. Meanwhile, they continue to turn out hits.

Mahalia Jackson
Singer of Gospel Songs

1911–

Among Negro musicians in the popular fields of music there seems to be a tendency to employ terms of royalty as a part of their names: King Cole, Duke Ellington, Count Basie, Lord Invader, Sir Charles Thompson, Princess Stewart, also Lady Day. Mahalia Jackson is *not* known as Queen Mahalia, but she is called the "Queen of Gospel Singers," just as Bessie Smith was called the "Empress of the Blues." As a child in New Orleans, Mahalia Jackson heard many of the early Bessie Smith records, liked them, and, in a religious rather than a worldly way, developed as she grew older a singing style not unlike that of the great Bessie. Bessie Smith had a strong, rich, deep contralto voice. So has Mahalia Jackson. Bessie Smith had an innate feeling for rhythm. Miss Jackson has, too. Bessie Smith's voice slurred and slid and curved from one note to another in a way that made it impossible to put down in musical notation exactly what she was singing in a blues. So curves and slides Mahalia Jackson's voice when she is singing a church song. But of the blues Mahalia Jackson says, "Anybody that sings the blues is in a deep pit, yelling for help." Of her own gospel singing she has stated, "I try to give it the way I *feel,* and most of the time I feel good." She explains her way of projecting a song as simply "accelerating the beat of the music, and putting joy into the voice. Sort of 'making a joyful noise unto the Lord,' as David said." Or as the old Fisk Jubilee Singers did when they sang their jubilees.

But gospel songs are not spirituals. They should not be confused with folk songs at all. The spirituals were created by a great body of unknown singers, as is all true folk music. Gospel songs are modern *composed* songs, most of them written by living men and women since 1925. They originated with Negro writers and Negro singers in Negro churches. Thomas A. Dorsey of the Pilgrim Baptist Church in Chicago is a leading gospel song writer, the composer and former publisher of such well known tunes of that genre as the widely sung *Precious Lord, Take My Hand, We Will Meet Him in the Sweet By and By,* and *Someday, Somewhere.* Other gospel writers are Roberta Martin, Theodore Frye, Jobe Huntley and Clara Ward.

Before he went into the church, Thomas A. Dorsey was a piano player for one of the first of the famous blues singers, Ma Rainey. He composed one of her most popular songs, *The Stormy Sea Blues*. At that time his nickname was Georgia Tom, and he was known far and wide to tent show and theater audiences as a player of joyous, rocking, foot-patting piano music. This happy quality Dorsey has carried over into the music of many of his church songs, and they are sung in thousands of congregations whose members believe that "religion is a joy." The more sedate Negro churches do not have gospel choirs, nor employ such music. They stick to the traditional hymns. Gospel songs are unknown in the Episcopal, Presbyterian, or Congregational churches. But among the masses of the Baptist, Methodist, and Sanctified sects they are widely used. Concerning these songs, the distinguished author, Arna Bontemps, has written an analysis called *Rock, Church, Rock,* in which he traces their development. Gospel songs are of such a nature that often, literally, churches do rock. But the composers and singers of gospel tunes, at least most of them, resent their music being confused with secular or sinful music, and have considered ways of preventing this at their annual Convention of Gospel Choirs. One excellent Negro gospel singer, Sister Rosetta Tharpe, has had for years very successful engagements in theaters and night clubs—just as the white Los Angeles evangelist, Sister Aimee Semple McPherson, carried her songs and sermons into the show at the Capitol Theater on Broadway during the 1920's. But most gospel singers do not approve of this merging of the church and the entertainment fields. Mahalia Jackson has stated as her conviction, "The church will be here when the night clubs are gone." And she has turned down very lucrative offers to sing in places of amusement.

Once, on a cold winter night in Chicago, before she became nationally known, I went to hear Miss Jackson give a program of her religious songs in a small South Side church. It was a chilled audience and, due to the weather, a small one. But Mahalia warmed the church with the intensity of her singing. When the program was over, a poor little woman came up to her and said that her mother was very ill and might never hear Mahalia Jackson sing again. She asked timidly if she would come home with her and sing just one song for her mother. Through the biting cold of the Chicago streets, at midnight, Mahalia Jackson trudged, then up a dimly lit flight of stairs to a poor apartment where the sick woman lay. There she sang not one song, but several, and prayed with the woman before she went home.

It is said that when Mahalia Jackson was contracted in 1954 to appear on a series of transcontinental radio programs for the Columbia Broadcasting System, her newly acquired managers suggested that perhaps she might arrange during the series, for the sake of variety, a few light non-religious programs. Her answer was, "I can't let CBS dominate the Lord." And, although Miss Jackson did sing some songs that were not formerly a part of her church programs, such as the folk air, *Danny Boy,* and a thrilling rendition of *The Battle Hymn of the Republic,* she refused to do any number of a crassly worldly nature or purely for the sake of entertainment.

In the New Orleans of Mahalia Jackson's childhood, it would have been impossible not to hear the jazz or blues for which that city is famous. And on a sensitive child with a musical ear, such music was bound to make an impression. But Mahalia grew up singing in a church choir. And her father, who was a dockworker by day and a barber by night, on Sundays became a preacher in a small church. In her early teens, Mahalia was already singing "the Lord's songs," as she terms them, so beautifully that the little church was crowded with people who loved to hear her. At sixteen, she migrated to Chicago, intending to study beauty culture, or else become a nurse, she was not quite sure which. Meanwhile, she took jobs in domestic service to earn a living. The first week in the North, she joined the church and went to choir rehearsal. In the familiar old Baptist hymns, her deep strong voice soared above all the others. She became a soloist with the choir. And soon the director had formed a quintet of gospel singers around her, which was quickly in demand for appearance at revivals and programs in other churches.

For many years Mahalia Jackson was widely known in the large and small Negro churches of Chicago as a stirring singer of their songs. When the popularity of gospel music began to spread in Negro church circles all over the country, requests for her services began to come to Miss Jackson from congregations in other cities. She traveled a great deal, singing. Then in 1945 she made a record called *Move on Up a Little Higher,* which overnight became a phenomenal best seller—almost entirely to Negro buyers. Eventually this record sold over a million copies. Its slow, syncopated rhythms caught the fancy of jazz fans too, who bought it, not for religious reasons, but as a fine example of a new kind of rhythmical Negro singing. The gospel song began to reach a public for whom it was not intended at all, and its vogue has been mounting ever since.

When her records were released in Europe, publications there devoted to popular music immediately hailed Mahalia Jackson as a great new

American artist. These comments drifted back to America, and booking agents and radio executives began to inquire into just who Mahalia Jackson was and where she might be contacted. The spotlight of publicity began to center upon her. From the churches to larger auditoriums she moved with her modern religious songs. In New York she gave a gospel concert at Carnegie Hall. It was sold out. A second religious concert a year later was packed to the doors and hundreds of people were turned away. Then she went to Europe. One publication reports that a half hour after the advance ticket sale began for her five concerts in Copenhagen, all the tickets were sold for all the programs. She gave crowded concerts in England and France, too. Then she treated herself to a trip to the Holy Land and on Christmas Eve she sang *Silent Night, Holy Night* in Bethlehem.

Mahalia Jackson can, if she chooses, buy a great many things with the money that came from her singing. But she remains in the same apartment where she has lived for many years in Chicago. And she could not buy the kind of goodness, about which she never boasts herself, which led her one cold winter night to walk through the snow to sing for just one poor woman alone, whom she had never seen before. From this quality within herself comes the powerful intensity and deep conviction which Mahalia Jackson puts into so simple a lyric as:

> *I'm so glad salvation is free!*
> *So glad salvation is free!*
> *Yes, Salvation is free*
> *For you and me!*
> *I'm so glad salvation is free!*

Dean Dixon
Symphony Conductor

1915–

Dean Dixon was born in New York City. His father died while he was a child. His parents were of modest means, but his mother had a love of music which made her a frequent patron of the symphony concerts at Carnegie Hall. Some of Dean's earliest memories are of holding her hand as his little legs toddled up the long steps to the balcony. Sometimes he would go to sleep as music filled the vast hall. But early in his childhood he, too, learned to love this music, and gradually acquired an appreciation for the great classics. He could read music as soon as he could read his ABCs, and before he was six years old his mother had started him on the violin. When, a few years later, his teacher told her that Dean was not suited to the violin, she simply changed teachers. At home, he was surrounded by an active lot of neighborhood boys and girls, since his mother was a great church worker, and community groups and youth clubs often met at her apartment. Little Dean grew up in an atmosphere of art and activity, surrounded by the cultural opportunities of Manhattan.

Dean played in his high school orchestra, and began to be interested in all the aspects of orchestration and instrumentation. Before his graduation, he had organized a little chamber orchestra at the Harlem Y.M.C.A., with himself as conductor, using a pencil for a baton. It was composed of amateur musicians in various stages of development, grownups and children, Negro and white, male and female. He enjoyed working with them and often used his own money to buy music. At seventeen, he was graduated from high school and took the auditions for admittance to the Juilliard School of Music. Among others, the famous conductor, Walter Damrosch, examined him that day and passed upon him approvingly. As a student at Juilliard, Dean continued with the violin, but took courses in musical pedagogy and all the fields relating to the materials of music that he could cover. He became especially interested in conducting, and at Juilliard was afforded the chance to extend his already considerable skills in this direction. Upon his graduation in

1936, he was offered a scholarship in conducting, for further study. At the same time, he took graduate work at Columbia University. Meanwhile, he continued to lead his own orchestra of old and young, Negro and white, in Harlem, which by this time was called the Dean Dixon Symphony Society, and was sponsored by a committee of sympathetic women. Free tickets were given to school children, for one of the things young Dean Dixon was trying to do was to bring symphonic music to a jazz conscious community.

When Dean Dixon was twenty-three, he was invited to conduct a Town Hall Concert of the Chamber Orchestra of the League of Music Lovers. In the spring of 1941, in an auditorium on the edge of Harlem, he had his own inter-racial orchestra of seventy men, women, and children, the youngest being twelve and the oldest seventy-two years of age, in a full evening's program of the works of Beethoven, Haydn, and Tchaikovsky. The wife of the President of the United States, Mrs. Eleanor Roosevelt, was in the audience. The head of the National Broadcasting Company was there, too. He was so impressed with the concert that Dixon was invited to be a guest conductor of the NBC Summer Symphony. And the following winter he conducted the NBC Symphony Orchestra over a nation-wide hookup. He conducted the orchestra of the briefly-lived musical *John Henry*. In 1943, he was a conductor of the Shoestring Opera Company. His greatest ovation up to that time had come, however, when, in the open air at Lewisohn Stadium one summer Sunday night, he became the first Negro in the one hundred years of its history to conduct the famed New York Philharmonic Symphony—the orchestra that had played under the direction of such great conductors as Toscanini, Koussevitzky, and Stokowski. When the slender brown young man lifted his baton and the beautiful music of that distinguished group of musicians rose into the night air, another page had been turned in American musical history.

One of the most interesting adventures of the young conductor's life was his leading of the National Youth Administration Orchestra. With a large and heterogeneous company of boisterous youngsters of all races, and limited rehearsal time, Dean Dixon was nevertheless able, through patience, humor, and above all competent and respected musicianship, to weld them into an interesting symphonic group. In 1944, he organized the American Youth Orchestra, which played Mozart and the Beethoven Seventh Symphony at its debut in Carnegie Hall. Olin Downes of *The New York Times* called their performance musicianly, sensitive, and effective, and he found in Dean Dixon "the stuff of a real conductor."

But young Dixon was interested in more than music for its own sake. In the first place, unlike many orchestras, his orchestra was open to all young people, regardless of race, creed, color, or sex, and its objectives were to provide good music free—or at very low cost—and to assist and encourage American composers and performers, using as much good American music as possible. It gave "Concerts for Three Year Olds," especially for very young children, even allowing them to sit on the stage beside the musicians. And it inaugurated a series of "Symphonies at Midnight" for people whose working hours did not permit them to hear good music at any other time. It became the conductor's pleasure to introduce new works by a number of previously unplayed young composers. These unusual aspects of the American Youth Orchestra, under the direction of its youthful Negro conductor, attracted much comment in the metropolitan press. Seldom before had the community uses and social possibilities of good music been so vigorously presented. Dean Dixon received the ASCAP Award of Merit for outstanding work in the musical education of young people. But as its program grew and costs mounted faster than public support, its funds dwindled. Dean Dixon had to earn a living. In 1949, at the invitation of *Radiodiffusion Française,* he went to Europe.

After conducting a very successful series of radio concerts in Paris, the thirty-four-year-old conductor was invited to lead some of the most famous orchestras in Italy, Austria, Israel, and the Scandinavian countries. Later he was invited to become one of the three permanent conductors of the Göteborg Symphony Orchestra, a post which Dean Dixon accepted. He now lives in Sweden and has married a Scandinavian woman. He is established there and throughout Europe is a great drawing card. His interest in modern American music continues unabated, and he is credited with introducing to European music lovers within the last few years more of the works of our composers than any other conductor. In the courtyard of one of the ancient palaces of the Doges in Venice, he conducted George Gershwin's *An American in Paris,* and the world premiere of Gordon Parks' *Symphonic Set for Piano and Orchestra*. In Scandinavian cities, he has presented an all-Negro program, which included William Grant Still's *Old California,* Amadeo Roldan's Afro-Cuban *La Rebambaramba,* the *Suite for Orchestra* by Ulysses Kay, and Howard Swanson's *Short Symphony.*

Most symphony programs limit themselves largely to the old masters, for the concert stage at home and abroad has long been dominated by the three B's—Bach, Brahms, and Beethoven. Dean Dixon has performed pioneer service in the presentation of serious new American music. But his interests and abilities are by no means confined solely to the work of his countrymen. The Norwegian newspaper *Dagbladet* calls his conducting of a Brahms symphony "gracious, poetical and bold, magnificently and finely chiselled in its dynamic figuration, and with a mellow sound that delighted every lover of Brahms." And a Swedish paper says that Dixon has an "outstanding capacity to interpret the nuances in Mozart." A Finnish paper says, "He is an artist radiating such power of spirit that it goes through every man in the orchestra like an electric shock and spreads throughout the hall." After his conducting of the *Brandenburg Concerto,* Rome's *Il Momento* called him "a conductor with an enormous talent."

"He can give a new and particularly melodious aspect to universally well-known works," a Paris critic wrote. Whether the compositions which Dean Dixon selects to conduct in Europe are old or new, established or ultra-modern, European or American, his public reception and critical acclaim is great. In a survey of his musical triumphs in far away lands, many miles from Harlem, Gladys Graham of the Associated Negro Press terms Dean Dixon "America's musical Ambassador." Certainly he is carrying goodwill and good music with him wherever he goes. And, having been the first distinguished Negro symphonic conductor in America, he has opened the doors for others of his race to enter that field. A young Negro man, Everett Lee, has recently been appointed one of the conductors of the orchestra of the New York City Opera Company. Dean Dixon, Everett Lee, and the English Negro conductor, Rudolph Dunbar, are examples that Negro musical talent embraces not only the spontaneity of jazz, but the discipline of the symphony, as well.

Lena Horne
Singing Star of Hollywood

1917–

When the beautiful face of Lena Horne flashed on the motion picture screens of the world in *Panama Hattie,* in 1942, it was the first time that a Negro woman singer had been permitted by Hollywood to appear with white actors as a featured star, without the benefit of apron or bandanna. Up to that time, Negroes had been limited almost entirely to the roles of servants or clowns on the American screen. In spite of the fact that there were by then in the United States thousands of Negro teachers, doctors, lawyers, nurses, firemen, mailmen, mechanics, business men and women, students and writers, no one would ever know this from looking at a Hollywood picture. Only menials appeared on the screen. There was a very definite color line in characterizations and casting in the cinema capital. Negro writers and technicians were never employed, and Negro actors and actresses rarely, and then only in stereotyped roles. Lena Horne is credited with breaking the color bar in Hollywood and establishing a precedent for the presentation of Negro beauty and talent without resort to kitchen scenes.

Lena Horne was born in Brooklyn, New York, during the First World War. Her father and mother separated when she was barely able to walk, and little Lena was brought up by various relatives. Her mother had been an actress, and Lena herself started her career in show business when she was only sixteen, as a chorus girl in an Ethel Waters revue at Harlem's famous Cotton Club. Lena was a strikingly beautiful golden girl, with a snub nose and a sprinkling of freckles. She could dance, and she had much more of a singing voice than the average young lady in a night club chorus. Attracted by her voice, the Negro band leader, Noble Sissle, secured her services as a vocalist. And in 1940 the famous white band, Charlie Barnet's, contracted her, one of the very few times up to that date that a Negro soloist had sung with a white jazz orchestra. Radio and recording dates soon followed and the name of Lena Horne began to be widely known.

Before her dance band days were over, Lena Horne was asked by several managers of night clubs if she would consider appearances in their establishments. The Trocadero in Hollywood, and the Mocambo were among the first to star her. The California columnists and newspaper critics extolled her beauty and said that this charmingly dressed golden girl had a voice like dripping honey. Soon the Metro-Goldwyn-Mayer studios signed her to a long-term motion picture contract. With Ethel Waters and the dancer, Katherine Dunham, Miss Horne starred in *Cabin in the Sky,* and in *Stormy Weather,* with Bill Robinson. She was a featured performer in *Broadway Rhythm, Ziegfeld Follies, Till the Clouds Roll By,* and other lovely Technicolor pictures. Meanwhile, her name went up in lights as a stage performer in feature presentations in leading motion picture houses across the country using live shows as well as films.

In 1943, Miss Horne received the Page One Medal of the New York Newspaper Guild as the brightest singing star of the season. And she was engaged at the most fashionable of the night clubs from Cafe Society and the Copacabana in Manhattan to those of the Champs Élysées in Paris. Busy years of flying from continent to continent followed. At the ANTA Album show in New York, in 1955, seen both in a Broadway theater and on a closed circuit television across America, Helen Hayes and Lena Horne were the two stars who received the greatest ovation. Faultlessly gowned and "pretty as a picture," the lovely Miss Horne was the only singer forced to take more than one encore. The artist John Vogel selected Lena Horne as "the most beautiful woman in America." And she has been photographed and painted innumerable times.

Lena Horne's singing of *Stormy Weather* has been surpassed by no one save Ethel Waters, who introduced the song and whom Lena Horne admires greatly. *The Man I Love, Honeysuckle Rose, One for My Baby, Good for Nothin' Joe,* and *Old Fashioned Love* are other songs of hers in which her audiences revel. And her interpretations of Duke Ellington's and Cole Porter's numbers delight their composers. Broadway song writers vie with each other to get Miss Horne to present their songs. She is a favorite entertainer on charity shows and benefits and, like most theatrical people, gives generously of her time and talent to help good causes. Lena Horne has been very active in combating race prejudice and bigotry in and out of show business. In recent years, she has refused to appear before segregated audiences or in places where her own people could not be admitted. She has turned down numberless lucrative engagements for this reason and refused a well-paying Miami Beach contract because no hotel there would admit a Negro guest and she would have had to find sleeping quarters miles away.

Negro theatrical people often have great difficulties in finding housing and eating accommodations when traveling. But the twists and turns of the color line are not without humorous aspects. Once during the Second World War, on a USO tour of the South, volunteering her services to entertain our soldiers, Lena Horne found herself grounded for hours at a small airport that had no restaurant. When she asked where she might get something to eat, she was sent across the road to a little cafe. But she was refused service. Negro people could not eat there. Yet as she left, one of the white customers on a stool at the counter recognized her as a movie star. He came running to the door with a pencil calling, "Please, could I have your autograph?"

In California, Lena Horne lived in a pretty stucco house in Hollywood's Nichols Canyon, with Humphrey Bogart and Peter Lorre as near-by neighbors. She has two charming children, a boy and a girl, by an early marriage. Miss Horne is now married to her musical director, Lennie Hayton. The films in which Lena Horne appears are especially popular with the Negro audiences of the West Indies, Africa, and Asia, and the theaters are crowded when her name is shown on the posters. She was Hollywood's No. 1 Negro star and, as such, made history. But throughout her brilliant career, Lena Horne has been worried, really worried, about one thing—that people might like her looks better than her singing!

Famous Jazz Musicians
Congo Square to Carnegie Hall

1800–1955

They must have been pretty good, those African drummers who, as slaves in old New Orleans long before the War Between the States, drew crowds of people to Congo Square on Sundays to listen to their syncopated rhythms, played for their own amusement. The rhythms must have been unusually tantalizing and powerful because they are still echoing in the widely popular music of America today—jazz—a music that has gone around the world. The old slave songs, shouts and field hollers, the blues and spirituals, musicologists now acknowledge as having possessed great intensity and beauty. And there are living people who still remember—and still play—the lively New Orleans music of the turn of the century that became Dixieland jazz. The trumpeter, Louis Armstrong, is one of these people, as are the trombonist, Kid Ory, the drummer, Baby Dodds, and the clarinetist, Sidney Bechet. These are famous contemporary musicians whose lives began back in those old days when ragtime was new and jazz was just being born.

The word *jazz* itself is only about forty years old, as applied to music, and at first it was spelled *jass*. Its origins are obscure, but some say it came from the fact that there was a Spasm Band player once in old New Orleans named Jasper—Jas for short. Others say his name was Charles, which he wrote Chas., and the illiterate, who couldn't read very well, called this Chass, which got changed to *jass*. Another theory is that a little band around 1900 called Razz's Band somehow got twisted into Jazz Band. Still others say the word has an African origin. However that may be, by the time Dixieland music reached Chicago in the early 1920's, people were calling it jazz. Now it is a word that is the same in every language in the world.

From the drums in Congo Square to the Negro marching bands of New Orleans, from the plantation music and levee chants, the spirituals and the blues, came the rhythmic and melodic elements that eventually blended into jazz. The joyousness of early ragtime piano playing went into it, too. Who the Congo Square drummers were, or the plantation singers and banjo players, or the original makers of spirituals and blues, nobody knows, other than that they were slaves. They were "the black and unknown bards" that James Weldon Johnson wrote about in his beautiful poem on this music. But the original makers of ragtime in the late 1800's are, many of them, well known—Tony Jackson, Scott Joplin, and Jelly Roll Morton are the best remembered, not only for their brilliant pianistics recorded on player piano rolls, now reproduced on records, but for their printed compositions and their long performing careers, as well.

New Orleans marching bands still exist, and some of the old musicians of the turn of the century still play in them. The influence of the syncopated music of these bands is felt in the playing of the older of today's jazz artists. The great cornetists, Buddy Bolden and King Oliver, are gone, but their styles still live in Armstrong and others, from whom younger players continue to learn. When jazz moved up the Mississippi to St. Louis and Kansas City and Chicago, then eastward and westward to both coasts, dozens of big name bands and hundreds of little bands came into being. Most of the more exciting bands were Negro, but some good white bands developed, too, in the first quarter of the twentieth century. Eventually, out of the West, between the two World Wars, came such Negro musicians and band leaders as Count Basie, Andy Kirk, Mary Lou Williams, Buck Clayton, and the boogie-woogie players, Meade Lux Lewis, Albert Ammons, Pete Johnson, and Jimmy Yancey. The blues singers from the deep South who had a great influence upon jazz included Blind Lemon Jefferson, Ma Rainey, and the three great Smiths— unrelated—Bessie, Mamie and Clara. When these people began to make records in the 1920's and 30's, the influence of their musical styles spread all over America and was absorbed by thousands of young jazzers, Negro and white, and soon infiltrated Broadway and Hollywood.

Unfortunately, in the old days there was in jazz music, as in most of American life, a color line. White musicians and Negro musicians did not play together. Nevertheless, each learned from the other. And the large number of exciting Negro jazz musicians greatly colored all of American popular music. For example, the famous Louis Armstrong breaks, or interludes between musical phrases, which he and other old Dixieland musicians improvised, have become standards in contemporary jazz, and are widely used now by anybody who can play them. It was in the 1930's that the clarinetist and band leader, Benny Goodman, formed his famous inter-racial quartette as a part of his band. From then on the color bar in the performance of popular music began to disappear. In this group, the Negro pianist, Teddy Wilson, the drummer, Lionel Hampton, and the guitarist, Charlie Christian, beat it out in happy rhythm with the white Benny Goodman, backed by other white members of his band. Lena Horne appeared as a singer with the white Charlie Barnet Orchestra. Cozy Cole, the drummer, and other Negro players of jazz, were engaged by various formerly all white groups. John Hammond and other prominent jazz authorities, by their influence and writing, aided greatly in bringing about this musical integration. When be-bop came in around 1942, none of the younger jazz players thought of the color line any more. The great bop musicians, white and Negro, played together. And many of the modern jazz or progressive combinations are today racially mixed. Some believe that jazz has done more in twenty-five years to bring people of all racial backgrounds together in musical friendship than classical music ever did in all its long history. In reading the pages of *Downbeat, Metronome,* or *The Record Changer*—magazines devoted almost entirely to jazz—it is no longer possible to tell which musicians are Negro and which white, so integrated now are the rosters of many jazz bands and small combinations.

In the ragtime tradition, but not of it, there have been many fine Negro pianists in the last quarter of a century. Among them are the musical clown—but at the same time able musician—Fats Waller, his mentor of Harlem, James P. Johnson, and Willie "the Lion" Smith. Among women are Kansas City's Mary Lou Williams, Lil Armstrong, and Hazel Scott. Teddy Weatherford, Fletcher Henderson, Earl Hines, Teddy Wilson, Erroll Garner, Nat King Cole and Oscar Peterson have been top-flight piano folks, too. Drummers to remember, other than those already mentioned, include Chick Webb, Sidney Catlett, Jimmy Crawford, Joe Jones, and the Cuban, Chano Pozo. A great old-time banjo player was Johnny St. Cyr, and more recent ones are Elmer Snowden and Dave Wilborn. The late Charlie Christian is remembered as one of the finest guitarists ever in the jazz field. And other excellent Negro guitarists are Oscar Moore, Teddy Bunn, Lonnie Johnson, Brownie McGhee, and Carl Lynch. Distinguished bass players include Wellman Braud of New Orleans, perhaps the originator of the "plucking bass," and that great old-timer, Pops Foster, also John Kirby out of the past, and in the present Ray Brown, Jimmy Blanton, Oscar Pettiford, and Slam Stewart. Tyree Glenn, Lionel Hampton, and Milt Jackson are terrific pounders of the vibraharp. Sonny Terry blows a great blues harmonica. Ray Nance, Stuff Smith, and Eddie South play syncopated violins. The great trumpet names include Bunk Johnson, Freddie Keppard, Papa Celestin, Sidney

De Paris, Bubber Miley, Rex Stewart, Charlie Shavers, Harry Edison, Roy Eldridge, Frankie Newton—and the one and only Dizzy Gillespie, who was among the originators of bop. A list of trombonists could hardly leave out J. C. Higginbotham, Dickie Wells, Lawrence Brown, Amos Gilyard, Bessie Smith's Charlie Green, Wilbur de Paris, or Benny Morton. Besides Bechet, the clarinetists must include Omer Simeon, Barney Bigard, George Lewis, Edmond Hall, and Jimmy Noone. And of saxophonists, tenor, baritone, or bass, there have been hundreds of exciting performers. To name a few, Chu Berry, Benny Carter, Coleman Hawkins, Don Redman, Wardell Gray, Johnny Hodges, Ben Webster, Lester Young, Don Byas, Charlie Parker, Joe Thomas, James Moody, and Willie Smith. Jazz singers, too, have not been without influence on the development of this music. Louis Armstrong, Cab Calloway and his hi-de-hi-de-o, Ray Nance and Joe Carroll, Dizzy Gillespie's oo-papa-da, and Florence Mills, Adelaide Hall, Alberta Hunter, Baby Cox, Billie Holiday, Babs Gonzalez, and Ella Fitzgerald have all been outstanding jazz vocalists.

In spite of the fact that many distinguished musicians and writers have expressed admiration and high regard for jazz, some people still claim that it has little importance as music. Of course, as a matter of taste, one has a right to like or dislike whatever one chooses. But simply because one does not like something does not make it insignificant. The late Serge Koussevitzky, former conductor of the Boston Symphony, termed jazz "an important contribution to modern musical literature. It has an epochal significance," he said, "it is not superficial, it is fundamental. Jazz comes from the soil, where all music has its beginning." Dimitri Mitropoulos has shown his interest in jazz by conducting the New York Philharmonic and the Sauter-Finegan Band in a Carnegie Hall presentation of Lieberman's *Jazzband Concerto*. And the famed conductor Leopold Stokowski has said, "Jazz has come to stay because it is an expression of the times, of the breathless, energetic, super-active times in which we are living. . . . The Negro musicians of America . . . are not hampered by conventions or traditions, and with their new ideas, their constant experiment, they are causing new blood to flow in the veins of music. The jazz players make their instruments do entirely new things, things finished musicians are taught to avoid. They are pathfinders into new realms."

What might have been called the first concert of symphonic jazz, had the word *jazz* been in general usage at that time, was given in Carnegie Hall in 1912, when the Clef Club's Syncopated Orchestra of 125 Negro musicians gave a *Concert of Negro Music* there, with Will Marion Cook and James Reese Europe in charge. During World War I, James Europe directed the famous Fifteenth Regiment Band of the 367th U.S. Infantry, which introduced syncopated band music abroad. In France, many people did not believe that the Negro musicians were playing on ordinary band instruments, but thought they had had them especially constructed, so unusual were the musical effects that these Negro soldiers produced. So they borrowed instruments from the French bands and played the same way on them, to show that it was not the instruments, but the music and the musicians that made the difference. The happy rhythms of jazz had invaded Europe by way of the American army. And in the decades that followed a number of serious European composers began to be influenced by jazz, including Darius Milhaud, Dana Suesse, and Kurt Weill, who later came to America to write Broadway shows. In our own country, John Alden Carpenter combined the classical and jazz styles, as have at times Louis Gruenberg, Aaron Copland, and Leonard Bernstein. George Gershwin wrote his famous *Rhapsody in Blue*, introduced at Aeolian Hall in New York, in 1924, by Paul Whiteman and his Orchestra, of which the critic Henry O. Osgood wrote, "It is jazz—but it is serious jazz . . . and the thing is unbelievably American." Jazz had gone, early in its career, from the dance hall to the concert hall.

In the years that followed, that jazz has not only given dancing pleasure to millions, but listening pleasure to seated audiences and serious musicians as well, cannot be denied. And in 1954 the *New York Times* announced a new use for jazz, as reported at the National Association for Music Therapy. From experiments conducted at the Veterans Administration Hospital at Albany, by doctors in charge of clinical psychology and psychiatric services there, the conclusion was drawn that jazz was especially effective in aiding schizophrenic patients in recovering from shock treatments. It is also helpful in cases of melancholia and violent states. The director of special projects for the Hospitalized Veterans Service reported that "Jazz has a beneficial effect upon psychiatric patients awakening from electrical shock treatment." He further stated that not only "the use of music enhanced the speed of awakening, but the patients who heard jazz music recovered more speedily than those who heard quieter music."

Today a large number of high schools and many colleges now have their own jazz bands. Because of the widespread interest of young America in jazz, these school bands often serve the good purpose of bringing together into musical units the youth of many different racial and religious backgrounds, and as such have provided a democratic activity in the school and the community. How an interest in jazz may lead to an increased interest in other more academic cultural pursuits is shown by the letter which a fifteen-year-old high school girl in El Paso, Texas, wrote to a poet in 1955. In part she said, "Our assembly manager at school heard of a group of Negro soldiers stationed at Biggs Field who have a very good jazz band. They call themselves *The Biggsters,* and the entire student body went wild over them when they played at an assembly. So popular were *The Biggsters* that, in the school elections, the candidate who promised to bring them back for another assembly won! They have been back to entertain us, and we hope they come again. As I sat in assembly and heard them, I decided to read some Negro poetry. . . . Now I shall probably have to pay a fine on the books when I return them to the public library because I am going to keep them for several weeks and read over all the poems again and again." So jazz led one young girl from listening to reading, from music to poetry, and—in a state which still has many legal color lines—perhaps to an interest in bettering race relations.

The first jazz band to be recorded was the Original Dixieland Jass Band, in 1917, a white group from New Orleans that had learned their music from Negroes. Jelly Roll Morton's Red Hot Peppers, Bessie Smith's blues, and Louis Armstrong's first records with various groups were among the early best sellers of Negro jazz. Since jazz began being recorded it has made a fortune for recording companies and juke box combines, and has been the main contributor to the vast incomes of the radio chains. Today it supports thousands of disc jockeys. It has become the mainstay of the dance band and night club businesses. Jazz has contributed its rhythms to most Hollywood musicals. It nourishes Tin Pan Alley. Billions of dollars have been made from jazz. Not much of this money went to the musicians themselves, and very little indeed to its pioneer creators. Except for a handful of outstanding stars like Louis Armstrong, the old-timers of jazz are not well off. Juke boxes reap nickels, dimes, and quarters, but nothing of this harvest goes to the music makers. Current copyright laws, sadly in need of amending, have not protected recorded performances in the past from being used *solely* for the profit of juke box owners. Once the performers have been paid for the original recording session, that is usually the end for them, no matter how big a hit a record may become on the mechanical machines—and there are hundreds of thousands of juke boxes in the world.

Since the days of the troubadours, musicians of whatever race have seemingly never known how to gather gold and songs at the same time.

Bland, who wrote *Oh, Dem Golden Slippers,* died a pauper, and Stephen Foster of *Swanee River* fame passed away in the charity ward of Bellevue Hospital. Most musicians remain poor. But the music that they make, even if it does not bring them millions, gives millions of people happiness. The jazz musicians and composers of the United States have contributed to the delight of the whole world, and America's own music, jazz—of Negro origin—has gone everywhere. Negro music has been one of our great cultural contributions, and Negro musicians have been among the most joyous of our ambassadors.

Famous Negro Heroes of America

(1958)

To my namesake cousin, Langston

Contents

Esteban
Discoverer of Arizona

Early 16th Century

Among the many fabulous stories concerning the New World that were circulating in Europe during the 16th Century, none had more appeal to adventurous explorers than the fascinating tales of a group of seven wonderful cities rumored to be built of gold. No white man had ever seen these cities, said to be somewhere to the north of Mexico, and inhabited entirely by richly dressed Red Men. These fabled Seven Cities of Cibola, beyond the rim of the northern desert, were declared to be rich in treasure, but no one knew exactly where to find them. The hardy Spaniards then penetrating American shores certainly hoped to find them for, by the time Cortés had conquered Mexico, the existence of these cities had come to be accepted as gospel truth. Among the Aztecs in Mexico the Spaniards had unearthed an amazing civilization, but they found no cities built of gold. These rich centers remained undiscovered, although various expeditions had set out in search of them. In 1539 another such expedition left Mexico City, headed by a Franciscan monk, Fray Marcos de Niza. It included in its party a Negro called Esteban.

Esteban, whose nickname, Estebanico, meant Little Stephen, was from Morocco where mixtures of African and Arab blood had produced a population ranging in color from ivory white to ebony black. The bearded Esteban must have been very dark because, in the records that have come down to us, he is described as *negro,* and in Spanish the word *negro* means black. Esteban was an amazing man who had traveled all across the North American continent from what is now the coast of Florida to the west coast of Mexico. In his travels, he had learned to speak a number of Indian languages. This knowledge made him invaluable as a translator and guide for the Spaniards. Besides, Esteban, over a time span of more than eight years in his pathless journey from the Atlantic to the Pacific, had lived for long periods among the Indians, so he was not afraid of them, nor were the Indians afraid of him. He thus became a valuable addition to any group of European explorers strange to American shores.

In both Spain and Portugal in the 15th and 16th centuries, Negroes were not uncommon. Some had crossed the Mediterranean from Africa as seamen, others had been brought to Europe in bondage. Esteban was by no means the first Negro to come to the New World. Pedro Alonso Niño, one of the pilots with Columbus on his first crossing, is recorded as a man of color. In the years that followed, Negroes frequently were found among the crews of sailing vessels navigating the Atlantic, and the early logs of the Conquistadores record the names of a number who made the long crossing to the shores of North or South America. In 1513 some thirty Negroes helped Balboa chop his way through the tropical jungles of the Isthmus to discover the Pacific Ocean. That same year with Ponce de León in his search for the Fountain of Youth in Florida, there were black men. Others accompanied Menéndez at the founding of St. Augustine in 1565. When Hernando Cortés invaded Mexico in 1519, one of the Negroes in his army of 700 found in his ration of rice one day some grains of wheat. These he planted, and so is credited with introducing the first wheat onto the mainland of the New World. And by 1523 there were so many Negroes in Mexico that it was decided to limit their entrance, since it was thought they might try to seize the ruling powers from the Spaniards—as indeed some in 1537 were accused of plotting to do, and were killed.

But the Spaniards often used Negroes to help them in subduing native peoples. Some two hundred men of color aided Alvarado to conquer the Indians of Central and South America. And black soldiers of fortune in Peru carried the body of Pizarro, the founder of the city of Lima, into the Cathedral there after he was killed in 1541. A Negro priest was officiating at Quivira in 1540, and at Guamanga in 1542 a considerable number of colored members participated in the Brotherhood of the True Cross. Black men accompanied the Jesuit missionaries to the Americas, and many of them had settled with the French in the Mississippi Valley in the 17th century. Some forged ahead to California, and among the forty-four settlers who in 1781 established the town of Los Angeles, there were 26 Negroes. But, perhaps because of the written records kept by Cabeza de Vaca and Marcos de Niza, the name of and an account of the exploits of Esteban have been handed down in more detail than those of other early Negro explorers.

Written history confirms that more than four hundred years ago now, as a part of the ill-fated expedition of Pánfilo de Narváez sponsored by King Charles the Fifth, Esteban set sail from Spain in 1527 with some six hundred other men seeking their fortunes in that New World which Columbus had discovered. Five Franciscan monks were among the sailors, and by royal warrant, Álvar Núñez Cabeza de Vaca—whose name, Cabeza de Vaca, meant Cow's Head—was treasurer of the expedition whose fleet consisted of five caravels with billowing sails on tall masts. It was a long journey then across the Western Ocean, and when the galleons eventually reached the shores of Santo Domingo, the men lingered there for more than a month, savoring the fruits of the West Indies and refreshing themselves with the waters of the mountain springs. Meanwhile, they provisioned the ships for the onward voyage to the mainland, leaving behind a number of deserters who found this first lush island to their liking.

In Cuba a great tropical hurricane destroyed some of the ships and blew completely away some sixty men and many horses. There Cabeza de Vaca took over command of the remains of the fleet, and in the Spring of 1528 set sail for Florida, coming up the western coast to the point where the peninsula curves around the gulf. Here unfriendly Indians greeted them with war cries rather than open arms. Pitched battles developed. The heat was terrific, mosquitoes and sand flies bothersome, and fevers and other illnesses broke out. In less than three months in Florida more than half of the white men died from sickness, or at the hands of the Indians. Since they found only a hostile welcome along the sandy beaches where they had landed, and no riches, they decided to go further. But, as they sailed along the coast, a storm came up. The crafts of the Spaniards were blown on the reefs and were quickly battered to pieces by the high seas. Narváez, leader of the expedition, drowned. Only four men managed to swim ashore. Among these four was Estebanico. The other three were Spaniards, including Cabeza de Vaca.

Possibly because of the hostile Indians, the four survivors did not tarry on the coast. They headed inland through the Florida palmettos, living on game, wild oranges and the food that more friendly Indians to the North gave them. Since, with no boats, they could not escape from the mainland, they decided to explore it—to follow the setting sun and see what lay beyond the horizon. Estebanico and his three companions were true adventurers, facing they knew not what unseen dangers, but curious to travel ever forward, wondering what they would see. At times they were held captive by Indians and made to serve as slaves until able to escape. It took them eight years to cross on foot, along the Gulf Coast and over part of what is now Texas, into Mexico and southward as far as the great city at its center where a Spanish Viceroy held sway. There they were again among numerous Europeans who, under Cortés, in the name of Spain had lately conquered the Indian peoples of Mexico.

In Mexico City, Esteban served under the Viceroy of Spain and at the capital he remained for three years. But, having no liking for a sedentary life, in 1539 he agreed to become one of the members under Fray Marcos de Niza of the newly organized party which intended to explore the lands to the North where, maybe, the seven storied cities of Cibola might be located, and vast fortunes of silver, gold, emeralds and turquoise were to be hoped for as a reward for discovery. With such visions of riches and fame in mind, with government supplies and Indian guides, over the mountains and through the Sonora Valley they set out toward the deserts of the North. Under the blistering summer sun, the Spaniards in the party eventually gave out. The trek over seemingly endless sands, with only parched plains ahead as far as the eye could see, became enough to discourage even the most stouthearted—and there had been no gold, no treasure, no fabulous cities anywhere along the way. But there *might be*—just over the land's rim.

"Estebanico, you go ahead and see," said Brother Marcos.

The others agreed. The Spaniards prevailed upon the seemingly tireless Negro to forge forward with a group of Indian guides to see what lay across the barren wilderness. Esteban set out on foot toward the North until he reached the San Pedro River which he followed as it ran toward the Gila. Since communication between the Spaniards and the Indians was limited, Esteban had worked out with Fray Marcos a simple system by which he might send messages back to the encampment as to what he had discovered. If Esteban discovered nothing of value, he would send back by an Indian runner each day a very tiny cross—about the size of a hand—made of two twigs. If things looked promising, he would send a larger one—a sturdy branch crossed and tied with thongs to a larger branch. If he made a really important discovery, he would send to the Spanish encampment a very big cross made from the trunks of saplings. Then they would know Esteban had come across gold, treasure, or large settlements of rich interest. With this understanding, the Negro departed.

The sun was blazing, the pathless plains and sandy desert were hot underfoot. There were rattlesnakes and scorpions, coyotes, prairie dogs that barked, buzzards that circled overhead and mountain lions that howled at night. The Indian runners wondered where Esteban wanted to go as he urged them on and on into a seeming nowhere. Of the Seven

Cities of Cibola, the Indians themselves knew nothing, and certainly they had no idea where to look for them. The first crosses that Esteban sent back to the Spaniards were very small crosses indeed, no larger than the palm of a hand. But, after a number of days, what seemed at first like distant mesas rising from the desert turned out to be in reality houses— a whole pueblo of houses. The strangers distinguished, as they drew near, that some of the houses towered as high as four stories and were beautiful to behold.

Esteban had come into the land of the Zuñis, a tribe of Pueblo Indians of advanced civilization, who lived not in tepees, but in well-constructed buildings of adobe or of stone. And, though their houses were not built of gold, above many doorways were embedded turquoise and other semi-precious jewels. The Zuñis ate from gracefully designed pottery, slept on brightly woven blankets, and lived in a manner that denoted comfort and well-being. That day, from a stout sapling Esteban cut a pair of sturdy poles, made them into a cross as tall as a man, and sent a band of Indian runners bearing this cross as his signal to the Spaniards that he had made a discovery of great importance.

As soon as the Indians panted into the distant camp with the cross, the Spaniards prepared to follow them northward to see what manner of riches Esteban had found. Their hopeful crossing of what is now the southeastern part of Arizona did not carry them as far as the Zuñi villages and they never saw Esteban again. Three battle-scarred and frightened Indians met them somewhere in the desert with the news that Esteban was dead and that they themselves were the only survivors of the Zuñi arrows that had massacred their companions. Suspicious of his mission, the Zuñi chiefs had ordered their warriors to set upon Esteban and all his band outside the walls of Hawikuh. And it was there that an arrow pierced him through, and his body was cut into pieces as a lesson to other intruders.

Wishing at least to see these beautiful Indian cities, Fray Marcos approached as near to them as his fear permitted. From a mountain summit he looked down at their gleaming adobe houses in the distance and termed the countryside that he saw "the greatest and the best that has hitherto been discovered." Then he went back to Mexico to spread the news to others in the name of the King of Spain. Soon a host of European explorers surged into the West. Larger and better armed expeditions penetrated the lands of the Zuñi and eventually the invaders built there settlements, religious missions, trading posts, and military presidios to protect their interests. But for the initial penetration of the Europeans into this new land of gold and copper, sunshine and flowers—what is now Arizona—the intrepid Negro, Esteban, is credited with opening the way.

Crispus Attucks
Martyr for American Independence

About 1723–1770

Before the American Independence, when the Thirteen Colonies were ruled by Great Britain, governors and tax collectors were sent out from England to siphon off their wealth for the sake of the Mother Country. However, three thousand miles of ocean between the New World and the Old made it difficult for the British always to control such distant possessions with a strong hand. And as the colonial population multiplied and the sturdy New Englanders began to feel quite self-sustaining through agriculture, seafaring and small industries, their aspirations toward independence grew. But the more the colonists wanted freedom, the harsher became the restrictions which the British put upon them, and the more taxes they wished to collect from their American subjects. Customs collectors were granted broad search warrants permitting them to enter anybody's house or shop to look for smuggled goods, and the use of these warrants was often abused. Good citizens were harassed on the slightest pretext and their privacy invaded. The colonists were not free to conduct their own foreign trade. And under the English Navigation Laws most colonial products could be sold only to Great Britain, and they had to be shipped in English boats.

Then in 1765 a form of taxation called the Stamp Act was passed in London. This act was designed to place on the colonists the burden of support for the upkeep of British troops quartered among them. It was also required that they furnish lodgings for English soldiers when barracks were not available. But the indignant colonists declared that, in their opinion, no taxes should be imposed upon them except by their own consent, and many merchants refused to sell taxable goods in their stores. Soon angry boycotts and protests beset the British, and women refused to wear dresses made of English goods, making instead their own homespun cloth. Nevertheless, in 1767 England imposed a series of new taxes on colonial imports. These included tea—which they felt the people could not get along without. When riots took place because of the new taxes, the British gunboat *Romney* mounted with fifty-four guns was dispatched to Boston Harbor. Also two additional regiments of soldiers were landed on Massachusetts soil and cannon were set up in King Street, Boston, pointing toward the Town House. It was then that Samuel Adams, a distinguished leader, immediately declared that this quartering of troops in the colonies without the consent of the people was a gross violation of basic freedoms, and that these soldiers were looked upon as intruders. Meanwhile, the soldiers behaved very badly, fighting in the streets and racing horses on the Sabbath on Boston Common. Between the soldiers and the citizens ill feeling grew. Minor clashes took place and gradually tension mounted throughout New England.

Then in Boston on the night of March 5, 1770, a serious clash of citizenry and soldiers occurred. A few days before there had been various fist fights between the townspeople and the soldiers and responsible persons had complained to the Council that the only way to avoid bloodshed would be to request the removal of the troops from the city. It was widely reported that the soldiers had openly threatened to wet their bayonets in New England blood. After working hours angry crowds gathered on street corners to discuss the situation. Such a crowd had gathered in front of the British barracks on Brattle Street on the evening of March 5. In response to irritating taunts from the soldiers, the citizens replied not only with harsh words, but with very hard snowballs. Whereupon sentries tried to drive them away, striking at the people with the butt ends of their rifles or attacking them with their fists. Noses were bloodied and there might have been a battle royal had not one of the captains of the Red Coats ordered all of his men inside the barracks. But by that time, someone had rung the great bell in the Old Brick Meeting House and, taking it as some sort of alarm, hundreds of Bostonians poured into the moonlit streets and rumors of all sorts began to fly thick and fast through the night.

Near the waterfront, in the crowd milling about between Dock Square and Long Wharf, a gigantic man of color stood out above almost everyone's head. A mulatto of light complexion then in his forties, his name was Crispus Attucks. He was a seaman but lately discharged from a whaling vessel, and little is known about his life except that in his youth Attucks had been a runaway slave. Twenty years before that fateful night of moonlight and blood this advertisement had thrice appeared in the *Boston Gazette:*

> Ran away from his Master, *William Brown* of Framingham, on the 30th of Sept. last, a Mulatto Fellow, about 27 Years of Age, named Crispus, 6 Feet

two inches high, short curl'd hair, his Knees nearer together than common; had on a light colour'd Bearskin Coat, plain brown fustian Jacket, or brown all-Wool one, new Buckskin Breeches, blue Yarn Stocking, and a check'd woolen Shirt. Whoever shall take up said Run-away, and convey him to his abovesaid Master, shall have ten pounds, old Tenor Reward, and all necessary Charges paid. And all Masters of Vessels and others are hereby caution'd against concealing or carrying off said Servant on Penalty of the Law.

Boston, October 2, 1750.

But, so far as is known, in spite of the repetitions of this ad, William Brown of Framingham never recovered his runaway slave. Crispus Attucks had taken to the high seas as a sailor. So on that night of March 5, 1770, with snow on the ground and a bright moon in the sky, he felt himself a free man allied with the citizens of Boston in their indignation that freedom to run their own affairs should be denied them by the English.

About nine o'clock that night, taunted by youngsters, a sentinel had knocked a boy down in front of the Custom House. Whereupon, other boys began to throw snowballs at the Red Coat as a crowd of men came running to the scene. Crying for help, the sentinel ran up the steps of the Custom House while someone else of his company rushed to call out the guard. A group of British privates officered by Captain Preston trotted double-quick up King Street and were met by a crowd of citizens that included the towering Crispus Attucks, and these were armed with sticks and stones. As the soldiers ran with drawn bayonets through the street, they were pelted by chunks of ice and handfuls of snow. Then the Red Coats encountered this group of men with stones and sticks in their hands. Crispus Attucks cried, "The way to get rid of these soldiers is to attack the main guard! Strike at the root! This is the nest!" And the men began to use their crude weapons against the well armed British.

Then the guns went off. An order to fire had been given. The very first shot killed Crispus Attucks. Maybe, being tall and Negro, he was the most conspicuous person in the crowd. At any rate, Attucks was the first man to lose his life in the cause of American freedom, pierced by a British bullet in the streets of Boston.

To his aid came Samuel Gray, a white man. And Gray, too, on the instant was shot dead. The next to fall was a sailor, James Caldwell. Then Patrick Carr and a boy of only seventeen, Samuel Maverick, gravely wounded, tumbled to the cobblestones. The boy died the next morning and Carr nine days later. A half dozen others were shot, but not fatally.

When the soldiers passed, there was blood on the snow. The moon looked down on an ever-growing crowd of rebellious Bostonians thronging the streets. Before midnight the entire Twenty-ninth Regiment was called out to preserve order. But by sundown the next day these same soldiers had been removed from Boston. Three thousand irate citizens in town meeting—first at Faneuil Hall and then to a larger place, Old South Meeting House—had that day demanded the removal of the British lieutenant-governor and the members of the King's Council. That afternoon two regiments of soldiers were sent to Castle William outside the confines of Boston.

This preliminary victory in the first stages of the American Revolution, said the historian, John Fiske, came about through "the sacrifice of the lives of Crispus Attucks, Samuel Gray, James Caldwell, Samuel Maverick, and Patrick Carr. . . . Their deaths effected in a moment what seventeen months of petition and discussion had failed to accomplish. Instead of the king's representatives intimidating the people of Boston, it was the people of Boston that had intimidated the king's representatives . . . and for achieving this particular result the lives of those five men were forfeit. It is, therefore, historically correct to regard them as the first martyrs to the cause of American independence."

Concerning the Boston Massacre in which they died, years later Daniel Webster said, "From that moment we may date the severance of the British Empire"—although it was not until 1775 that the War for American Independence actually began, and it was 1783 before it ended in victory. During all that time of turmoil, the citizens of Boston did not forget Crispus Attucks and the men who died with him. Each 5th of March after their death, their martyrdom was remembered by an oration in the Old South Meeting House. But when Independence came, the date for this oration was changed to the 4th of July.

The day after their deaths—while Gray and Maverick were mourned in their homes—the homeless seamen, Attucks and Caldwell, were laid in state in Faneuil Hall, and hundreds of people passed to look at these fallen heroes. Then all four men, the Negro and the whites, were buried in a single grave as thousands joined the final ceremonies.

Today there stands on Boston Common a monument to Crispus Attucks, Samuel Maverick, James Caldwell, Samuel Gray and Patrick Carr, erected by joint action of the Commonwealth of Massachusetts and the city of Boston. At the unveiling of this memorial in 1888 William H. Dupree, the Chairman of the Citizens' Committee, said, "On the 4th day of March the British troops seemed to be immovably entrenched in

Boston, and the enactments of their superiors were supposed to be the paramount law of the land. On the 5th, by the death of Attucks and his comrades, submission to English law gave place to active opposition. . . . The people were masters. The real authority had been wrested from the king, and assumed by his subjects. The death of these men made the republic secure." And, long before the dedication of the monument, John Adams had declared, "On that night, the foundation of American independence was laid."

As the monument was unveiled before the large crowd gathered in Boston Common, the poet John Boyle O'Reilly read a poem entitled *Crispus Attucks,* dedicated to the "Negro Patriot—Killed in Boston, March 5, 1770," which said in part:

Honor to Crispus Attucks, who was leader and voice that day—
The first to defy, and the first to die, with Maverick, Carr and Gray.
Call it riot or revolution, his hand first clenched at the crown;
His feet were the first in perilous place to pull the King's flag down;
His breast was the first one rent apart that liberty's stream might flow;
For our freedom now and forever, his head was the first laid low.
Call it riot or revolution, or mob or crowd, as you may,
Such deaths have been seed of nations, such lives shall be honored for aye.

Jean Baptiste Pointe Du Sable
Founder of Chicago

About 1745–1818

About thirty years before the Declaration of Independence was signed, in St. Marc, Haiti, Jean Baptiste Pointe Du Sable was born of mixed French and Negro parentage. His father was a pirate, the mate of a sailing vessel called the *Black Sea Gull* flying the skull and crossbones from its mainmast and raiding ships throughout the Caribbean. In those days all the waters of the West Indies were plagued by pirates who often sacked and burned coastal towns, sailing away with what riches they could find and sometimes carrying off beautiful women as well. Jean Baptiste's father had stolen his wife, Suzanne, from slavery on a Danish plantation on St. Croix. He carried her off to Haiti as a prize of piracy, and in Haiti she was free.

When Jean Baptiste was about ten years old, his mother was killed in a Spanish raid on St. Marc, and their house was burned. Shortly thereafter his father took him to France and put him into a boarding school for boys not far from Paris. There little Jean made friends with another youngster from the West Indies, Jacques Clemorgan, of Martinique. Their friendship lasted a lifetime and, as young men on their return to the New World, they had many adventures together.

Perhaps for the sake of his son, the elder Pointe Du Sable decided to quit being a pirate. In Haiti where he bought land and set up a shop, he became a dealer in coffee, hard woods, and other products of the island. Soon he acquired a schooner, the *Suzanne,* named after his deceased wife. When Jean returned from school in France, he worked a few years in his father's business. Then it was thought wise that he seek his fortune in the New France of the mainland, Louisiana, a virgin field for exploitation. With his father's blessing, and in the company of his Martinique friend, Jacques, young Jean, when he was about twenty, sailed away toward the Gulf of Mexico in the little ship *Suzanne*. But he never reached Louisiana under his own sail. Off the western coast of Florida, a hurricane came up and the *Suzanne* was blown to pieces. Only with difficulty did the young men save their lives. Fortunately a Danish vessel picked them up and carried them into the port of New Orleans.

Being a Negro who had never known slavery, Jean Baptiste suddenly found himself in a city where to be colored was to be suspected on sight of being a slave. Without identification of any sort, since all his papers had been lost in the wreck of the *Suzanne,* Jean might at any time be falsely claimed by someone as an escaped slave. Fearful of this, he took refuge with a group of Jesuit monks, where he was given employment until he decided to venture further into the interior. Having in mind trading with the Indians for furs and other things which he could sell for profit, he began to make plans for travel. But first he applied for work with one of the large trading companies in New Orleans. He was turned down because of his color. This caused him to make a little boat of his own and head up the Mississippi. With his friend, Jacques, and Choctaw, an Indian who knew several languages, he set out paddling his way upstream, intending to hunt and trap fur-bearing animals, and bargain for goods with the Indians along the river banks. Eventually they got as far as St. Louis, and for a time Du Sable lived with the Illinois Indians, learned to speak their tongue, to use the bow and arrow, and to hunt buffalo on the great plains. Later he went on to the shores of the Great Lakes and as far as Detroit where he worked for the British governor of the region for a time.

Jean Baptiste Pointe Du Sable was about twenty-five when a beautiful Indian girl of the Potawatomi tribe captured his fancy and he married her. Kittihawa—Fleet-of-Foot—was her name, and to marry her Du Sable had to become a member of her tribe, taking the eagle as his tribal symbol. Together they settled down near Fort Peoria where he purchased land, and soon a son was born. But the young man did not linger long at home. About a year later, in 1772, at a point of portage between the southern end of Lake Michigan and the river where many travellers passed on their way to or from Canada, Du Sable decided to build a trading post. Then an unsettled wilderness, the area was called by the Indians *Eschikagou,* or sometimes simply *Chikagou.* This new trading post prospered, and two years later in 1774 Du Sable moved his family and all the Indians of his wife's clan there from Peoria. He built for his wife a house of five rooms with a large fireplace. This house became the first permanent home, and the beginnings of the first settlement, on the site of what is now the city of Chicago. And the first child whose birth was recorded in the new settlement was Suzanne, Du Sable's daughter, whose African-Indian heritage made her a beautiful nut-brown baby, named after her Haitian grandmother, but accepted by the Potawatomis as one of their tribe. Later the Indians, in speaking of Du Sable, often said, "The first white man in Chicago was a Negro."

Through Du Sable's efforts, surrounding his trading post and home, soon a little city grew. Kittihawa's relatives and tribesmen built houses for themselves and their families and began to cultivate gardens. As a part of his business, Du Sable himself erected several new buildings: barns and poultry houses, a dairy, a bakehouse, a smokehouse, a workshop, a mill, and a forge. Traders called Du Sable's the best trading post between St. Louis and Montreal. Soon the community became a busy center and the trading post a place to house passing travellers and supply the needs of pioneer hunters, trappers, and explorers. Thus it was that this unsettled tract of land Eschikagou gradually grew into the city of Chicago—its first citizen having been Jean Baptiste Pointe Du Sable.

Described in the old chronicles as "of commanding appearance," some six feet tall, stalwart, bearded and handsome, Du Sable was a man of business acumen and intelligence as well as good-looking. To these qualities must be added that of bravery—plus curiosity—for all his life Jean Baptiste had the urge to push on to new frontiers, to explore the possibilities of lands beyond whatever might be, at the time, his own horizon. This adventuresome spirit eventually caused his arrest by the British who were then in control of the Great Lakes region. A black man who spoke both French and the Indian tongues, and who moved about freely among the Indians hostile to the British, they could not but consider an enemy. The English commander of the area who ordered Du Sable's arrest described him as a "handsome Negro, well educated and settled at Eschikagou, but was much in the interest of the French." And at that time, after all, the British and French were enemies. Du Sable was interned at Fort Mackinac in 1778, arrested "in the name of the king." Although held in custody, he was treated kindly, and was free to hunt and fish in the woods surrounding the fort. Since there were no actual charges against the man, he was after a number of months released to return to his family.

Du Sable's relations with the Indians grew ever closer and at one time he was proposed as the chief of the tribe. His businesses prospered. His children grew up, married, and grandchildren came. In 1800, as old age approached, Du Sable sold his Chicago interests to a St. Joseph firm, the bill of sale and the amounts received being recorded in the Wayne County Building in Detroit. Eventually he settled down in semi-retirement in St. Charles, Missouri, where his son, Jean Baptiste, Jr., lived. But, since through this small frontier town almost daily came groups of horsemen and strings of covered wagons heading westward, the ever venturesome Du Sable soon began to dream of the wide open territories beyond the Missouri River. His son, however, dissuaded him of further pioneering at his age. So he contented himself with exchanging stories with the frontiersmen who passed his way. He sometimes translated for them when they needed to bargain with the Indians. And he loved the masses at a nearby Catholic church, and the conversations of the priests.

In the late summer of 1818 Jean Baptiste Pointe Du Sable died and was buried in St. Charles Borromeo Cemetery among the graves of numerous other pioneers of the West. As the founder of America's second largest city, his memory is kept alive today in the archives of the Chicago Historical Society. And a beautiful book has been written about him by another Negro American—Shirley Graham's *Jean Baptiste Pointe Du Sable.*

Paul Cuffe
Seaman and Colonizer

1759–1817

Paul Cuffe spent all of his life on or near the sea. When he was sixteen he signed on a whaling vessel out of New Bedford heading for the Bay of Mexico. When he was twenty he himself built a boat for coastal trading in New England waters. When he was twenty-five he bought a fishing schooner and sailed it to St. George's Banks in search of cod. At thirty-five Cuffe owned his own whaling boats. And by the time he was forty he was the captain of vessels sailing to the West Indies and across the Atlantic. Through the tropical hurricanes of the Caribbean and the lashing winter storms of the Western Ocean, Cuffe sailed his vessels and never lost a ship.

Paul was born in 1759 on the southernmost of the Elizabeth Islands, Cuttyhunk, off New Bedford, a decade and a half before George Washington gathered his armies to free New England from the British. Paul's father had been brought from Africa as a slave, but had purchased his own freedom. He married an Indian woman of the Wampanoag Tribe and, among their ten children, Paul was the youngest of the sons. When Paul was in his early teens his father died, then the boys in the family had to provide for their sisters and mother. Young Paul became a sailor on a whaling vessel, and learned to man the mainmast and harpoon the monsters of the sea. Down around the tip of Florida into the Bay of Mexico and to the various islands of the West Indies he sailed. During the Revolutionary War he was captured by the British and held prisoner in New York for some time.

During the War seagoing became dangerous for Americans, so for a while Paul settled down on a farm near Westport, Connecticut, tilling the soil by day and studying navigation at night. By candlelight or the light of an open fireplace, he pored over charts of the seven seas and worked with compass and navigator's rules. His limited schooling made books hard for him, but he persevered.

Together with his brother, David, he built a small open boat and went into the business of coastal trading for himself. But David did not like the water, so both went back to farming again. Paul, however, soon built himself another boat and set out for the Elizabeth Islands with a store of goods to sell. Within sight of the coast, pirates seized his boat, robbed him of all his goods, and left him in the sea to swim ashore as best he could. Undeterred, Paul built a third boat, purchased cargo on credit, and sailed for Nantucket. Again he was chased by pirates and he wrecked his boat on the rocks trying to escape. But he managed to get back to the harbor of Westport, repaired the boat, and made a round trip to Nantucket. More than once he was robbed and beaten by the sea bandits infesting coastal waters. But Paul preferred the dangers of the ocean, even in a little boat, to the safety of the soil and the plow. And from some of his voyages he managed to make a small profit. This he saved and shortly he was able to purchase a covered boat, employ a deckhand, and make more extended trips up and down the coast.

By the time Paul got married at the age of twenty-five, he was the owner of a larger boat, one of eighteen tons, equipped for cod fishing off the St. Georges Banks. Several of his wife's brothers were seamen, and together they established a profitable business in the Westport River. The same year in which Paul Cuffe married, the State of Massachusetts granted to its Negro citizens all the rights of full citizenship. And this development came about largely through Cuffe. He and his brother John had petitioned the legislature for the right to vote and other civil rights, but their petition was unsuccessful. "Taxation without representation" had been the rallying cry of the Americans in the Revolutionary War against the British which had just ended. Taking this slogan to heart, free Negro Americans like the Cuffes saw no reason why this maxim should not apply to them also. Yet they were asked to pay taxes without having the right to elect representatives. Paul and John Cuffe refused to pay their taxes and a suit ensued. The attention which this attracted to the problems of free Negroes in the new Republic, just after a war for freedom, so moved the liberal lawmakers of Massachusetts that they granted the ballot to the Cuffes and all other colored citizens within the Commonwealth.

Not only was Paul Cuffe a good seaman, but he was an active citizen in all the affairs of his community. When his children were small there was no school in the vicinity of his farm on the Westport River, so Cuffe proposed a community school to be built in cooperation with his neighbors. Numerous meetings were held concerning the proposal, but it finally came to naught, possibly because some of the people did not wish to go into a cooperative project with a colored man. Paul Cuffe then, with his own funds and on his own land, built a school, employed a teacher, and invited all the parents who wished to send their children there to do so without charge.

Meanwhile, as seaman and boatbuilder Cuffe's activities continued to expand. With his brothers-in-law he constructed a twenty-five-ton vessel and made a number of successful voyages to Belle Isle and Newfoundland. With the profits from these trips they jointly bought a ship "of 42 tons burthen" that made several more trips up the coast. Then in 1793 Cuffe went back to whaling, setting out with two boats of his own ownership on an expedition that netted seven whales, two of which he himself harpooned. This voyage was a most profitable one. At the port of Philadelphia Cuffe sold his cargo of sperm oil and whale bone for sufficient money to purchase the materials for a third ship, the keel of which he laid on his return to Westport. This schooner of upright masts and billowing sails was called the *Ranger* and was "of 69 tons burthen" when completed. Loading it with a $2,000 cargo, Cuffe headed for Norfolk.

On the return trip, Cuffe heard of a plentiful harvest of Indian corn on the Eastern Shore of Maryland, so he steered his vessel into the mouth of the Nanticoke River with the intention of purchasing a cargo. The Maryland whites were so amazed at seeing a large beautiful ship manned entirely by Negro sailors, that they did not want to allow Captain Cuffe and his men to come ashore. Indeed, they asked him to withdraw at once from the river. In a land of slavery, whites were not accustomed to associations with free Negroes, and many did not dream that any black man alive had enough money to purchase a shipload of corn, let alone claiming ownership of an ocean going vessel. Captain Cuffe was required to produce all his papers of ownership, as well as proof of his captaincy and capabilities as a navigator. Finally his papers were declared in order and he and his men were permitted ashore. The members of the crew of the *Ranger* were all intelligent young Negroes, polite and well behaved, and so remained in Maryland several days without incident. But the whites tried to prevent them from in any way associating with their slaves, for fear the sailors would fill their heads with ideas of freedom, or incite them to revolt. From the sale of the 3,000 bushels of corn which Cuffe loaded aboard his vessel, he made sufficient profit on his return to Westport to purchase a new house and farm, the running of which he turned over to one of his brothers. Cuffe himself continued at sea, bringing back from the South corn, molasses, gypsum, and other profitable products for resale in New England.

By the early 1800's Cuffe had become the owner of several ships, one a brig of 162 tons commanded by a nephew, Thomas Wainer, while Cuffe himself sailed the *Alpha,* a larger vessel of 268 tons. Then he acquired a half-interest in a handsome two-mast square rigger called the *Traveller* with a lower fore-and-aft sail. This sturdy vessel made a crossing from New England to Sierra Leone, West Africa, in two months under Wainer's charge, but with Cuffe aboard as financial backer. This voyage to Africa, and Cuffe's subsequent interest in that continent as homeland for the Negro people, eventually caused him to become one of the important figures of his times, with the record of his activities duly inscribed in history.

Paul Cuffe had been born free. But it was not until more than a hundred years later that Abraham Lincoln signed the Emancipation Proclamation granting freedom to the majority of the Negroes in the United States. Under slavery some Negroes bought or worked out their freedom, as Cuffe's father did; others ran away into the free states or Canada and some were born of free parents. But all over the United States the position of the free Negro gradually became more and more precarious so long as slavery existed. There was danger that any free person of color might falsely be claimed as a slave and carried off into servitude, with the courts loath to interfere. Also, Southern slave owners greatly resented any large body of free blacks being at large, agitating for freedom for their brothers still in bondage, and setting a living example of the values of belonging to one's self alone, not to any master.

In the Northern communities where free Negroes were tolerated, prejudice against them often made it difficult for them to find work. In hard times, white laborers resented employment being given to blacks, and race riots ensued. Nevertheless, free Negroes continued to strive for equal rights both as workers and citizens. In some tolerant communities such as the New England coastal cities which Paul Cuffe knew, a colored man, *with great industry,* might manage to get ahead in the world as Cuffe did. But some Negroes felt that with so many pressures against them, it would be better to look for a home elsewhere than in the United States. A few turned to Canada. Others dreamed of far-away Africa, their ancestral homeland. But Cuffe, on behalf of his oppressed brothers, did more than dream. He went to Africa to investigate the possibilities of colonizing there.

Cuffe's first trip convinced him that there were interesting opportunities in Africa for the free Negroes of America, since he saw with his own eyes the riches of the Dark Continent. The English in 1787 had taken over, as their colony, Sierra Leone. There on New Year's Day, 1811, the *Traveller* arrived in port, and Paul Cuffe immediately arranged for a series of conferences with the governor and other high officials relative to settling American families of color in that land. The Friendly Society of Sierra Leone was then created for such a purpose. After a brief sojourn, Cuffe set sail for London to pursue the matter further at the seat of British power. In England he secured the goodwill of such men as the English abolitionist William Wilberforce. Meanwhile he loaded his ship with a cargo of goods for the Friendly Society and returned to Sierra Leone with British permission to transport from the United States a group of Negroes to instruct the natives in agriculture and manual arts, the immigrants in turn to be provided with land and farming implements. From Sierra Leone Cuffe returned home to Westport greatly heartened at the prospect of eventually aiding large numbers of American Negroes to migrate to West Africa.

He planned to make at least one voyage a year to Africa. But soon after Cuffe's return to New England the War of 1812 against the English began, and intercourse with Britain or British colonies was considered treasonable. Meanwhile, Cuffe travelled to most of the large cities of the East rallying free colored men to the cause of African colonization. In New York and Philadelphia two large societies were formed for this purpose. But it was not until the War was over that any further practical steps could be taken. Just before Christmas in 1815 Paul Cuffe again sailed on the *Traveller* headed for Sierra Leone. This time he transported to Africa nine families—in all thirty-eight free persons of color—himself bearing all the expenses.

This was the first effort at African colonization by Americans and, as such, it attracted wide attention. Great debates sprang up all over the country among both whites and Negroes as to its value. Southern whites particularly, being slave holders, approved of Cuffe's plans, for they saw in their extension a way to get rid of all free Negroes whom they felt were a menace to the practice of slavery—as indeed they were. Soon the American Colonization Society was organized with most of its officers Southerners, and such slave holders as the Kentuckian Henry Clay and John Randolph of Virginia among its prominent members. Federal aid for the establishment of an American Negro colony in Africa was solicited, and shortly the territory of Liberia in West Africa was purchased by the government for that express purpose. At once white abolitionists and free Negroes attacked the Liberian project as one designed to deprive free colored citizens of what few rights they had in the United

States, and to leave slavery triumphant everywhere. Said the free colored people of Hartford, "Why should we leave this land so dearly bought by the blood, groans and tears of our fathers? This is our home."

Most American Negroes did not want to go to Africa at all, and Cuffe's well meaning scheme also began to be bitterly attacked. In Philadelphia three thousand colored people led by Bishop Allen branded African colonization "an outrage" and refused to endorse emigration to Liberia, Sierra Leone, or any other land outside the United States. In spite of the hardships Negroes suffered, they declared their intention to remain in "the land of the free and the home of the brave" and attempt to bring to realization the Declaration that all men are endowed "with certain unalienable rights; that among these are life, liberty, and the pursuit of happiness." Such rights, they thought, should belong to Negroes, too.

Paul Cuffe made no more voyages to Africa. The youngster who had begun his travels as a whaler and ended them as an international figure in the affairs of his country (and, indirectly one of the creators of the Republic of Liberia) died on a bright September day in 1817 just before the leaves of New England began to turn the ruddy colors of autumn. To his family he left what was, for that time, a large estate. To seamen he left memories of his skill and heroism as captain and navigator of ships of sail. To Negro Americans he left a new awareness of their one-time homeland, Africa. Even if few in the United States wanted to migrate there, Paul Cuffe saw Africa as a land of great beauty, great possibilities, and a great tomorrow. He himself had been there and knew.

Cuffe was a Quaker. Over his grave behind the Westport Meeting House, the Society of Friends have dedicated a monument to his memory. The brief inscription reads:

> In Memory Of
> CAPTAIN PAUL CUFFE
> A Self-Made Man
> Patriot, Navigator, Educator,
> Philanthropist, Friend
> A Noble Character

Gabriel Prosser
Freedom Seeker

About 1775–1800

Freedom is a mighty word—and a word best understood perhaps by those who do not possess it. When at Jamestown, Virginia, in 1619 a Dutch man-of-war put ashore into bondage twenty Africans, the roots of slavery were planted in our soil. For two hundred and fifty years those roots were to grow, gnarled and twisted and ugly, until every foot of American soil eventually became infected by them. And, after Emancipation, for generations in one form or another, the evil aftermaths of slavery lingered in our national life. Nobody ever enjoyed being anybody else's slave, so means of escape were always being devised. In the slave ships of the 17th and 18th centuries many captive Africans died of their own will, suicides. Some chained in groups leapt into the sea, pulling others after them. And hardly had slavery begun on American soil than slaves began to run away—into the woods, into the swamps, into the sea, anywhere to be free. Some took refuge with the Indians, many fled to Canada. Some organized revolts and attempted to fight their way to freedom. Freedom is a very powerful word indeed.

Slavery meant more than being forced to work without pay. Slavery meant no freedom of movement, no visiting of friends, no travelling without permission. Slavery meant being struck or beaten at the whim of a master or a mistress. It meant seldom if ever marrying whomever one might love. It meant seeing sons and daughters sold away, families separated, friends divided. It meant no right to assemble freely, even for religious services, without special permission. It meant eating whatever was given you, sleeping in whatever shacks were provided and doing whatever one was commanded to do, no matter how hard or distasteful the tasks. In short, it meant that a slave was entirely at the will of the master. That some masters treated their slaves well, there is no question. But that many treated them badly is also clear, particularly on the great plantations managed by overseers whose job it was to get as much work from a slave as possible with as little expenditure of money needful for food or clothing. An old slave song said:

We raise de wheat,
Dey give us de corn.
We bake de bread,
Dey give us de crust.
We sift de meal,
Dey give us de huss.
We peel de meat,
Dey give us de skin.
And dat's de way
Dey take us in.

Who could possibly want to be a slave under such conditions?

Historical records and advertisements for fugitive Negroes indicate that there were thousands of runaways. The records indicate, too, that hundreds of slave revolts took place in both the North and the South in colonial days as well as after Independence. As early as 1663 in Virginia slave uprisings are reported. In New York in 1712 nine persons were killed in a rebellion. In 1741 in that same city nineteen slaves were hanged for plotting an uprising, thirteen were burned at the stake, many publicly whipped, and a large number sold in chains into the deep South. The punishments meted out by slaveholders to rebels were usually excessive, inspired both by terror and a practical determination to keep their human property in bondage at any cost. In spite of almost certain death if discovered, slaves continued to rebel right up to the end of the War Between the States in 1865. Of the great slave rebellions, four stand out in history as having attracted wide attention: that in 1739 at Stono in South Carolina in which more than seventy persons, white and black, lost their lives; that of Gabriel Prosser in 1800 near Richmond; of Denmark Vesey in 1822 at Charleston; and of Nat Turner in 1831 in the Virginia countryside. These revolts were all unsuccessful in so far as freeing the blacks involved went, but they shook the institution of slavery to its foundations.

In the year 1800 Gabriel Prosser was a dreamy-eyed young coachman of twenty-four. He was a man of few words and his dark impassive face looked as if it were carved from ebony. He belonged to Thomas Prosser of Henrico County from whom he had taken his second name. But mostly folks called him just Gabriel, and the revolt which he organized became known as "the great Gabriel conspiracy." Of all the slave uprisings in the South, some historians consider Gabriel's the most significant in its effects upon the ever tightening codes of slavery. Certainly it spread fear of the slaves in an ever-widening circle from Richmond throughout the entire white South. And there might have been a most frightful massacre in the city of Richmond had it not been that the elements intervened on the night set for slaughter.

Gabriel had planned his revolt very carefully, and he must have been a man of great persuasive powers to be able to swear so many people to secrecy in so dangerous an enterprise. But his Negro followers were said to number well over a thousand. There were in Virginia in 1800 about 347,000 slaves, of whom some 32,000 were in the city of Richmond and its surroundings. But the white population of Richmond was only about 8,000 persons. Some of these were French and some were Quakers—minorities, to be sure, but of liberal tendencies. These groups, Gabriel felt, would be sympathetic to his cause—the French because of the ideals of their Revolution, *Liberté, Egalité, Fraternité,* and the Quakers for their known opposition to slavery and all for which it stood.

As early as April Gabriel began to make active plans for a slave uprising at the time of harvest when the grain would be ripe, the gardens full, and fruit hanging from the trees. Then, he reasoned, for Negroes who would be no longer dependent on their masters, there would be plenty to eat. In his own mind he set the date of the revolt for the very end of August, and on the first of September he planned to occupy Richmond, killing all of the slave owning whites, but sparing the French, the Quakers, and poor old women who owned no slaves. Throughout the summer he met secretly with groups of his fellow slaves, never gathering twice in the same place or at the same time. Sometimes groups would meet in a smokehouse, again in a tannery, sometimes in a cabin, other times in a grove, sometimes at a crossroads late at night. Gradually Gabriel had several hundred men and women of bondage sworn to uphold him in a mighty bid for freedom for all.

Gabriel thought that if enough Negroes could be united to seize Richmond from the whites, other slaves in all the surrounding countryside would join them in taking over the houses and lands of the masters throughout Virginia. Then he would set up an empire of newly freed slaves with himself at the head. Behind those wide eyes in his impassive face there was a very great dream—*freedom for all* within the entire area with which he was acquainted. Gabriel was illiterate, but he had heard about France, and he had heard the slogans of the American Revolution. He had heard, too, of the Declaration of Independence. And if he had never heard of any of these things, Gabriel was still the kind of man who would have wanted to belong to himself, not to any other man. Even if he bore his master's name, he did not love his master.

Gabriel was a giant of a man, six-feet-two in height, and he had a friend, Jack Bowler, equally tall and powerful physically. Together with Gabriel's brother, Martin, they planned to lead a three-way invasion of Richmond between midnight and dawn on the first of September, each to conduct a group of slaves by a different route into the city. From any sharp tool available that they could find, or steal away from white tool houses, they made weapons. They cut the blades of scythes in half and made from each blade a pair of cutting irons capable of severing a man in two. They made bayonets of kitchen knives. They fashioned clubs, stole firearms, tied slingshots to forked branches. For Gabriel and his lieutenants, it was a summer of feverish activity. When they would be ready to march, every man would be armed with something, at best a gun, at worst a club or a stone. With their crude arms, they planned to take the government arsenal in Richmond.

Whenever Martin was present at a secret meeting of slaves, he expounded on the Scriptures, and quoted that part of the Bible that declared that God would strengthen a hundred to overthrow a thousand. And the assembled slaves would shout, "Amen!" for they believed that God was on their side. Meanwhile another of Gabriel's brothers, Solomon, busied himself with the making of cutlasses. Of the crude weapons of these Virginia slaves a white witness later said, "I have never seen arms so murderous." In reality they had very little with which to fight for freedom—by the end of summer only a few muskets, a peck of bullets, ten pounds of ammunition, some pikes, and twelve dozen scythe-swords. Clubs and stones did not count much. And what were fists and bare hands to subdue an arsenal? But of audacity and courage they had a very great deal.

On the last night in August, a Saturday, the slaves agreed to meet in Old Brook Swamp at a point six miles outside of Richmond, there to receive their orders from the young leader, Gabriel, and by sundown those who could get away so early had started for the appointed place from plantation and mansion, country cabin and city shop. According to an account written later by Thomas Wentworth Higginson, these were Gabriel's plans for the meeting in the swamp: "Eleven hundred men were to assemble there, and were to be divided into three columns, their officers having been designated in advance. All were to march on Richmond under cover of night. The right wing was instantly to seize upon the penitentiary building, just converted into an arsenal; while the left wing was to take possession of the powder-house. These two columns were to be armed chiefly with clubs, as their undertaking depended for success upon surprise, and was expected to prevail without hard fighting. But it was the central force armed with muskets, cutlasses, knives, and pikes, upon which the chief responsibility rested; these men were to enter the town at both ends simultaneously and begin a general carnage. . . . In a very few hours, it was thought, they would have entire control of the metropolis. . . . For the insurgents, if successful, the penitentiary held several thousand stand of arms; the powder-house was well stocked; the capitol contained the State treasury; the mills would give them bread; the control of the bridge across the James River would keep off enemies from beyond. Thus secured and provided . . . in a week it was estimated they would have fifty thousand men on their side, with which force they could easily possess themselves of other towns."

But none of this ever happened. Instead, on the Saturday night of the planned rendezvous in the swamp, "the most furious tempest ever known in Virginia burst upon the land. . . . Roads and plantations were submerged. Bridges were carried away. The fords . . . were rendered wholly impassable. The Brook Swamp, one of the most important strategic points of the insurgents, was entirely inundated, hopelessly dividing Prosser's farm from Richmond; the country Negroes could not get in, nor those from the city get out." The fields turned to bogs, the roads to rivers. From early evening on the rain came down in torrents, the wind howled and lashed the rain into stinging blades of water. In the stormy dark, pitch black and water-filled, it was impossible for the slaves even to see the roads, and short cuts across meadows or paths through forests were utterly indecipherable. Only a few hundred men were able to slosh through water or wade through mud up to their ankles to get to the appointed meeting place in the swamp. Gabriel's expected thousand dwindled to a miserable soaked group of faces that he could not even see in the dark and the rain. For any of them to reach Richmond that night would have been impossible. There was nothing for him to do but dismiss them, and before they could reassemble, they were betrayed.

The slaves who betrayed them were named Tom and Pharaoh, and they belonged to a Mr. Moseby Sheppard whom they considered a kind master. Tom and Pharaoh did not wish their master to be killed, so on the very day that Gabriel's great meeting was planned, they told Sheppard all about it. Sheppard in turn notified the authorities, and Governor James Monroe, of Revolutionary fame, late that afternoon called for a troop of United States cavalry to guard the city, appointed three military aides to conduct the defense of Richmond, and ordered cannon

wheeled into place around the capitol building. Even as Gabriel's followers that evening were hurrying through the dusk toward the swamps,
the city was prepared to blow them to bits should their plan be carried out.

But it was only the next day when the full scope of Gabriel's plot
became known that panic swept the city and martial law was declared.
The whites were aghast at the unsuspected danger that had threatened
them. As the news spread the whole state of Virginia became alarmed.
Plantations turned into armed camps and in all the cities military patrols
were doubled. Everyone realized that had it not been for the unusually
terrible storm of the night before, a great deal of blood might have
been shed and many lives taken. In the white churches of Richmond
that Sunday God was thanked for having spared their lives from Negro
slaughter. Providence had protected Richmond by tempest, by thunder,
lightning and rain. God, the whites felt, was on their side.

Quickly the authorities proceeded to take vengeance on the helpless
Negroes. From Tom and Pharaoh and other docile frightened slaves,
mostly house servants, they extracted all the names they could of those
implicated in Gabriel's plans. Some slaves were hanged without trial no
sooner than they were caught. But to expose in full "the conspiracy"
the governor ordered a series of trials for the hundreds of suspected
slaves who were rounded up. For Gabriel himself, who had escaped,
a reward of $300 was posted. Jack Bowler surrendered. Other leaders
were captured. But nobody would tell where Gabriel had gone. And the
soldiers could not find him in the bog of Old Brook Swamp.

When the trials began in Richmond, Higginson writes that, "Men
were convicted on one day, and hanged on the next—five, six, ten, fifteen at a time, almost without evidence." So many slaves were put to
death until various masters began to complain at the loss of so much
expensive property. Able plantation hands and good servants were not
always easy to come by, even through purchase; and among the followers of Gabriel had been some of the most intelligent and hard working
slaves of the region. Finally the courts were urged to give fewer death
sentences, lest they decimate the best of the slave population of Henrico County. In mid-October, as the excitement began to die down, the
New York *Commercial Advertiser* reported from Richmond, "The trials
of the Negroes concerned in the late insurrection are suspended until
the opinions of the Legislature can be had on the subject. This measure is said to be owing to the immense numbers who are interested
in the plot, whose death, should they all be found guilty and be exe-

cuted, will nearly produce the annihilation of the blacks in this part of the country." Jail sentences, chains, public whippings and other punishments were meted out to many. Innocent and guilty alike suffered, for slaves had to be taught the lesson that freedom was not meant for black men and women, only for whites. But the two slaves who betrayed Gabriel—Pharaoh and Tom—were quickly pardoned for their loyalty to their master.

As to Gabriel, he too was eventually captured. They found him in the hold of the schooner *Mary* when it docked at Norfolk after a trip from Richmond. They brought him back to Richmond in chains. And so important did they consider this prisoner that the governor himself interrogated him. But Monroe reported that Gabriel "seemed to have made up his mind to die, and to have resolved to say but little on the subject of the conspiracy." It had been Gabriel's plan to make a flag for his army of freedom and to inscribe on this flag Patrick Henry's famous slogan, "Liberty or Death." But Gabriel never had a chance to make the flag. However, he must have remembered, as he sat on trial in Richmond, what would have been emblazoned on his flag had the rebellion succeeded and the slaves taken Richmond.

Except for the informers—and there were only three whose names are remembered, Sheppard's two slaves and another called Ben Woolfolk—little information could be gotten from the men brought to trial. Indeed, some refused to talk at all in court. Their very silence frightened the slave masters, astonished the prosecutors, and shook the composure of the judges. Said one slave calmly when ordered to testify, "I have nothing more to offer than what General Washington would have had to offer, had he been taken by the British officers and put to trial by them. I have ventured my life in endeavoring to obtain the liberty of my countrymen, and am a willing sacrifice to their cause; and I beg, as a favor, that I may be immediately led to execution. I know that you have predetermined to shed my blood. Why then all this mockery of a trial?"

Gabriel's process took more time than any of the others, but from him, so newspaper accounts of the time indicate, the court learned almost nothing. The Norfolk *Epitome* reported, "The behavior of Gabriel under his misfortunes was such as might be expected from a mind capable of forming the daring project which he had conceived." Another account declared, "When he was apprehended, he manifested the greatest marks of firmness and confidence, showing not the least disposition to equivocate, or screen himself from justice." The *United States Gazette* added that the man displayed "the utmost composure, and with the true spirit of heroism seems ready to resign his high office, and even his life." Gabriel went to his death without naming anyone implicated in his plans. On October 7, 1800, he was hanged. In the wind that blew about his gallows that day, those living who were still slaves must have heard the whisper of a word—*freedom . . . freedom . . . freedom.*

James P. Beckwourth
Frontiersman

About 1798–about 1865

Around the time that James Beckwourth was born in Virginia, the first Yankee clipper sailed around the Horn to California. From New England in 1776 this American merchantman rounded the tip of South America into the rolling Pacific and with billowing sails continued up the coasts of two continents into the Bay of Monterey. California was at that time governed by Mexico, so Monterey was largely a Spanish-speaking city. But this ship returned to New England with such tales of California riches that, from then on in ever increasing numbers, Easterners began to head West. "Westward, ho!" was their cry. The West was a land where young men might make their fortunes, adventurers find adventure, women find husbands, and pioneers discover new wealth. In spite of the length of the trips, some sea captains made enormous fortunes in the Pacific trade. But by sea the voyage west was long and expensive. Many migrants could not afford it, so they took the overland routes, and the going was rough. Nevertheless, by 1826 many fur trappers were heading overland to California, and a few years later a regular trade route was opened through Santa Fe. By the early 1840's the federal government was sending official expeditions to the West Coast while American merchants and dealers in raw furs had become well established in most of California's Mexican-owned communities.

The northern routes across country led through high and windy passes and over snow covered mountains. The southern routes lay across parching deserts, waterless and sunbaked. Either way hostile Indians threatened the guiding horsemen and the covered wagon trains of the pioneers as they sought their way through uncharted territory toward the Pacific. In 1841 John Bidwell's party, starting out from Missouri, was almost driven crazy by the heat and thirst of the desert. When they reached the mountains, weak, and with supplies almost exhausted, they nearly died of hunger. A few years later, when winter came surprisingly early that year, the Donner pioneers were caught by swirling snows in the mountains. Unable to forge ahead in the zero weather, in quickly built huts, with food exhausted, many of them died. After the flesh of their horses and oxen had been eaten, the survivors made soup from the hide of these animals and from their bones.

In 1848 the Gold Rush began. When John W. Sutter found in the stream that propelled his saw mill something that glittered—and that was gold—from all over the land excited thousands of men and women began the long trek to California, leaving jobs, homes, families, everything in a pioneer search for wealth.

> *Oh, Susanna,*
> *Don't you cry for me!*
> *I'm goin' to Californy*
> *With my banjo on my knee.*

Across dusty plains and over rocky mountain trails went the wagon trains, often inadequately supplied and without guides. Eventually the skeletons of many a man and horse lined the way, and new graves from the Missouri to the Coast indicated that only the hardiest of travellers had managed to go on. By sailing ship from New York to the Coast was a trip of usually more than six months. Every old unseaworthy boat that could be secured was pressed into service. Many sank before they reached the Pacific, and the voyagers were never heard of again. Yet the wave of Westward migration continued. In 1850 California had only 92,000 inhabitants. Ten years later there were 380,000. And among those who reached the Coast in that decade was the Negro pioneer, James Beckwourth.

Beckwourth's father had been an officer in the Revolutionary War. He moved Westward when Jim was a child and settled his family on a farm near a point where the Missouri River flows into the Mississippi. With his numerous offspring and even more numerous slaves, for little Jim's father was a white man and his mother a slave, a whole community was created known as Beckwourth Settlement. Although a son of his master's, young Beckwourth was officially a slave. So, at the age of about twelve, he was apprenticed by his father to a blacksmith in St. Louis under whom he worked for several years. But as Jim grew older and began to court girls, attend dances, and stay out all night, trouble brewed. The result was that he often showed up at the blacksmith's forge after dawn, late for work. Frequent reprimands did no good. One morning after a severe scolding by the blacksmith, a quarrel broke out around the glowing forge between the young man and the old, and angry words split the air. Young Beckwourth was stubborn and impudent. In anger, the blacksmith picked up a hammer and threw it at Jim, but missed. Jim in turn grabbed the hammer and threw it at his boss. Then the two men fought it out with fists, and the young man won. But he was sent packing from the blacksmith shop, his apprenticeship cancelled.

The older man, however, followed the boy to his lodgings, had him put into the street, and gave orders that he should no longer be housed or fed at his expense. In the street a second fight broke out, and the constables were called. Jim fled into hiding. That night he got onto a boat, and went down the river to seek work in the mines. Shortly he became a hunter in the southern Illinois area, supplying wild game as meat to the workers in the mines. At this he did well. Soon he had saved some money with which he took a trip by boat to New Orleans—just for fun. But Jim did not like that city. Perhaps being colored had something to do with it, for in New Orleans there was a great deal of segregation, and so a Negro could not enjoy himself in as lively a fashion as could a white man. Young Jim began to dream of going West, to the far West, as far as the Rockies. Beckwourth attached himself to an expedition of the Rocky Mountain Fur Company in charge of General Henry Ashley, heading by horse and mule train westward from St. Louis. His duties ranged from shoeing horses to Indian fighting, trapping beavers and skinning furs to hunting game for food. Provisioning of the expedition was a most important operation. Years later he dictated in his memoirs, "No company could possibly carry provisions sufficient to last beyond the most remote white settlements. Our food, therefore, consisted of deer, wild turkeys, bear meat, and even, in times of scarcity, dead horses." Sometimes an enormous buffalo provided a campfire feast for the men. At other times they might have to eat the stringy unpalatable meat of a coyote, or depend on tiny prairie dogs for a meal. Fortunately, Beckwourth's months of experience as a hunter for the Illinois mining camps stood him in good stead. He was a crack shot, and wasted few bullets aimlessly.

He was also, by his own admission, good at horse stealing. Travelling fur expeditions were always in need of horses, particularly since the Indians were good at horse stealing, too, and frequently raided white men's encampments. Horses were the cause of many skirmishes with the Indians who cared little for furs, since they were plentiful, but they loved horses. Since Beckwourth had picked up a smattering of various Indian languages, he could sometimes bargain with an Indian for a horse. If he could not bargain, he could threaten with a loaded rifle. Or he could lasso and steal a mount in a pinch, riding swiftly away, perhaps with an arrow whistling toward him. In his memoirs, Beckwourth recounts some pretty tall tales. But serious historians believe that there is a basis of truth in most of his stories. Certainly he did turn up in many places throughout the Wild West, and he did pass a long and active life as frontiersman. Physical danger became a part of daily living and unknown hazards in mapless places gave zest to his keen spirit of adventure. Beckwourth loved the rugged life he lived and, after a half century of intensive pioneering years, he was still alive to tell about it in *The Life and Adventures of James P. Beckwourth,* transcribed by T. D. Bonner in San Francisco in 1854 and published two years later by Harper & Brothers.

Beckwourth in his book did not mention his Negro heritage. Being a mulatto, he was light in complexion, and on the frontier color did not matter much anyway. There a man was a man, and that was that. Frontiersmen had to be rough and ready fighters, quick on the draw, and able to defend themselves not only against Indians, but against each other. The men who went West in those days were not milksops. They were the toughest and most rugged of characters, and self reliance was a basic quality. If hungry, they would take food. If horseless, they would steal horses. If challenged, they would fight back. Good men were so mixed up with bad men, that there was often adequate cause for even a pacifist to fight, if for no other reason than self-protection. The historian, Charles A. Beard, reports that in the rough and tumble years following the Gold Rush there was in Los Angeles an average of a murder a day. And the city was full of horse thieves, gamblers, and rogues.

From the date of his first decisive fight with the blacksmith to whom he was apprenticed as a youth, Jim Beckwourth appears always to have been able to protect himself. In skirmishes with the Indians, he was so successful that—never being felled by their bows and arrows—in time he began to believe he could not be killed by an Indian. He never was. And he was no respecter of persons when it came to a fight. Once he challenged General Ashley himself, his employer, to a fight because of a name the general called him which he did not like. Even after the general apologized, Beckwourth still wanted to battle it out. But being of a cooler head, General Ashley felt that, after all their months together, they had been through too much in common to raise their hands one against the other. Indeed, on two occasions, as the general later made public, Beckwourth had saved his life—once from a charging buffalo bull, and again when the General had fallen into the current of a swirling river and was about to go under. Beckwourth, a powerful swimmer, had pulled him out. And together they had both fought the Indians. Having been associated in matters of life and death, why fight over a word?

General Ashley's expedition returned to St. Louis with a fortune in furs, and through the streets the bearded Beckwourth himself led a grizzly bear—the unshaven man, back from long months in the wilderness, being himself almost as grizzly as the animal. Everyone was paid off in full, and for days they enjoyed the gaieties of the town. But after about a week, General Ashley called Jim Beckwourth into conference. As one of his most trusted aides, he decided to send him on an important mission to Bill Sublett, the captain of his trappers in the region of the Great Salt Lake, weeks away, as travel was in those days. Beckwourth, meanwhile, had practically gotten himself engaged to be married in St. Louis. But he decided to postpone that event until his return. The urge to travel overcame the call of love. Off he went again into the wilderness that lay beyond the plains. With a companion, on horseback both, and a pack mule, Beckwourth headed once more toward the West. It was fourteen years before he returned to resume his romance with the girl in St. Louis. And every one of those fourteen years had their share of danger and adventure—for they were spent almost entirely in the wilds among Indians and frontiersmen.

When after months of travel, Beckwourth finally reached Bill Sublett, Ashley's western agent, Sublett proposed to him another mission—to help establish a trading post among the Blackfeet Indians. He warned that whoever undertook this task might be scalped, but Beckwourth was willing to try it. In appearance, being light brown, he himself looked like an Indian, so he could move among them without attracting too much attention. In fact, until he opened his mouth to speak, the Indians often took him for a tribal member. At any rate, Jim's stay with the Blackfeet was so successful that he married an Indian woman. Indeed, he says he married two, first one sister, then the other, but this may be exaggeration. At any rate, with the Blackfeet, he lived as they lived, ate what they ate, and danced their tribal dances.

Later, for a time, among the Crow Indians, Beckwourth passed as a Crow, causing them to believe that as a child he had been captured in battle by the Cheyennes, and so had forgotten the Crow language. So convincingly did this fiction work, that an old Crow woman actually claimed him as a long missing son. Suddenly he found himself part of a family he never knew he had, consisting of father, mother, four daughters, and several boys. And in honor of this lost son found, his "father" went in search of the finest young women of the tribe he could find that Beckwourth might choose from among them a wife. The bride he chose was called Still Water. But, while she remained at home, her new husband went off with the other braves to fight the neighboring tribes. He fought so well that eventually he was raised, so he says, to the rank of chief and given the proud name of Bull's Robe. As a warrior, Jim could scalp with the best of them. On his return from battle he would, as did the other Indians, paint his wife's face with beautiful colors. But one day he decided to go back to St. Louis—after almost fifteen years had gone by. When he got there, he found that the girl he left behind him had become tired of waiting for his return. She was married to another man.

For a time Beckwourth worked as a guide to wagon trains crossing the mountains to California. From coast to coast he wandered in one activity or another, Florida to Mexico, Louisiana to the Rockies. Hunter, trapper, guide, interpreter among the Indians, advisor to travellers, fur trader, go-between in the problems of whites and Indians, as a man of many abilities, James Beckwourth took advantage of almost all the opportunities his pioneer age offered—except the advantage of staying in one place and getting rich. This he never did, preferring to leave the acquisition of wealth to less restless and less adventurous men. Time after time Jim came to the big cities, and time after time he left them for the plains, the mountains and the wide open prairies—those trailless spaces of Red Men and buffaloes, vast skies and beckoning horizons.

Finally, Beckwourth bought a ranch in the Feather River Valley. But when the Gold Rush came, he headed for California. There it seems he became involved in a ring of horse thieves, so he had to get away from possible prosecution. In Denver he operated a general store and found a new wife, this being about his fifth marriage. But running a shop was too tame an existence for him. At the request of the government, he undertook a mission to his old friends, the Crow Indians, whose liking for the warpath disturbed the federal authorities. Washington seemed to feel that Jim Beckwourth might be able to show them the beauties of peace. He was well received by the Crows, but his visit had little effect on their war-like proclivities. Already in his sixties, perhaps by then Beckwourth's powers of persuasion were weak. Indeed, he himself must have been pretty well worn down by this time. The year was about 1865 when, shortly after a great outdoor feast which the Crows tendered him, Jim Beckwourth fell ill at Absaroka, and there among the Indians he died. His contribution, that of a great pioneer in the opening of the West, is now a part of history.

Frederick Douglass
Abolitionist

About 1817–1895

The state of Maryland is divided by the Chesapeake Bay into two parts known as the Western Shore and the Eastern Shore. Frederick Douglass was born on the Eastern Shore on a remote plantation near the Choptank River, where he lived with his grandmother. His mother was a slave, Harriet Bailey, and as a child Frederick went by the name of Bailey, too. His father was an unknown white man whom he never saw. Frederick knew only that he had a master who worked for Colonel Lloyd, and that his master would someday take him away from his grandmother and put him to work as soon as he was big enough. Frederick scarcely knew his mother for she had been hired out as a field hand twelve miles away from her home plantation. To see her child, Harriet Bailey had to walk that distance after sundown, then be back in the fields again by morning. Slavery had no regard for the love of mothers and children. They were often separated early, or sold away from each other entirely. Little Frederick was fortunate if he saw his mother a few times during the year. When he was eight years old, she died.

By that time Frederick had been taken from his grandmother and sent to live miles away with a group of other slave children in a cabin presided over by a mean old hag named Aunt Katy who did not like youngsters and treated them very badly. Starvation was one of her forms of punishment. Little Fred was often so hungry, he recalled later, that he would "dispute with old Hep, the dog, for the crumbs which fell from the kitchen table." "Many times," he said, "have I followed with eager step the waiting-girl when she shook the table cloth, to get the crumbs and small bones flung out for the dogs and cats. It was a great thing to have the privilege of dipping a piece of bread into the water in which meat had been boiled, and the skin taken from the rusty bacon was a positive luxury."

So fared this little slave boy who belonged to Captain Anthony, chief overseer on the great plantation of Colonel Edward Lloyd who was a rich man. Colonel Lloyd owned more than a thousand slaves, as well as a number of plantations besides the one on which he and Anthony lived. His Great House was white with large wings on three sides and a park all about, neatly tended by the slaves. Then there were barns, poultry houses, tobacco sheds, blacksmith shops, wash-houses, greenhouses and arbors. "Over the way from the stable was a house built expressly for the hounds, a pack of twenty-five or thirty, the fare for which would have made glad the hearts of a dozen slaves." And there was also a private cemetery of stately tombs where the dead Lloyds rested beneath firs and weeping willows. From all this family wealth, Frederick and the black children received little. As clothing until he was a very big boy, Fred wore only a single cotton shirt to his knees. Of schooling he had none, but for Colonel Lloyd's children there was a private tutor from New England. As soon as they were old enough, the slave children were given such tasks as carrying water to the fields for the hands, or they were organized in "trash gangs" to keep the yards and quarters tidy. When they were ten or eleven years old, they began to work in the fields themselves, or about the stables. By the time slaves were in their early teens, they were considered grown and ready for any sort of labor the master might require of them.

While still a child, the cruelty and helplessness of being a slave was deeply impressed upon Frederick by the whipping which a girl who was his cousin received from a cruel, drunken overseer to whom she had been hired out on a remote farm. This man had beaten her so badly that she fled for protection to Captain Anthony, her original master and still her owner. She reached the Lloyd plantation with a severely scarred back and streaks of blood on her face from a gash in her forehead. But the girl got no protection from Captain Anthony. She was told only that she probably deserved the beating she had received, and that she must return at once to the man who had given it to her. Little Frederick did not understand how her master could be so cruel to a girl. But many years later he wrote, "I think I now understand it. This treatment was a part of the system, rather than a part of the man. To have encouraged appeals of this kind would have occasioned much loss of time and would have left the overseer powerless to enforce obedience. Nevertheless, for some cause or other the slaves, no matter how often they were repulsed by their masters, were ever disposed to regard them with less abhorrence than the overseer. Yet these masters would often go beyond their overseers in wanton cruelty. They wielded the lash without any sense of responsibility. They could cripple or kill without fear of consequences."

Little Frederick saw his master whip a young woman just outside the hut where he was sleeping. Condensed from his telling of it in his memoirs, he said, "It was early in the morning when all was still, I was awakened by the heart-rendering shrieks and piteous cries of poor Esther. Esther's wrists were firmly tied, her arms tightly drawn above her head. Her back and shoulders were perfectly bare. Behind her stood old master, cowhide in hand. Again and again he drew the hateful scourge through his hand, adjusting it with a view of dealing the most pain-giving blow his strength and skill could inflict. Each blow, vigorously laid on, brought screams from her as well as blood. But her piercing cries seemed only to increase his fury. After laying on I dare not say how many stripes, old master untied his suffering victim. When let down she could scarcely stand. From my heart, I pitied her. I was terrified, hushed, stunned, and bewildered."

No wonder Frederick, even as a child, asked himself, "Why am I a slave? Why are some people slaves and others masters? These were perplexing questions and very troublesome to my childhood. I was very early told by some one that God up in the sky had made all things, and had made black people to be slaves and white people to be masters. I could not tell how anybody could know that God made black people to be slaves. Then I found, too, that there were puzzling exceptions to this theory of slavery, in fact that all black people were not slaves, and all white people were not masters."

Little Frederick learned, too, that not all white people, even in the slave country, were cruel and unkind. One of Colonel Lloyd's daughters, Miss Lucretia, took a liking to him, gave him little errands to do, and treated him with friendliness. When she knew he was hungry, she would sometimes give him a slice of bread and butter. And once when another child struck him in the forehead with a cinder, she herself washed away the blood and put a bandage about his wound. It was Miss Lucretia who first told him that it had been arranged to send him to Baltimore as a slave boy in the household of her brother-in-law, Hugh Auld. Frederick was ordered to soak himself in the creek for days until all the plantation dirt had come off his skin, then he would be given his first pair of trousers especially for the trip to Baltimore. It was the first time in his life that he had been promised anything to which to look forward— a pair of pants. These, and the trip, excited him greatly. Frederick was being sent to little Tommy Auld as a present from Captain Anthony. The voyage to Baltimore was made on one of the boats belonging to Colonel Lloyd, carrying a cargo of sheep to market there. Frederick was a part of the cargo, too. When he was delivered to Mr. and Mrs. Auld, he was presented to a bright eyed little white boy who was told that here was his "little Freddy, who will take care of you." Thus he became this little boy's slave.

Mrs. Auld was a kindly woman who had never herself owned slaves, and she treated Frederick almost as a member of the family. His duties were not arduous—running errands and looking after Master Tommy. His mistress often read the Bible aloud to both the boys. Frederick's listening to her read kindled in him a desire to learn to read, as Tommy had already done. Finally the Negro boy became so bold as to ask Mrs. Auld if she would teach him.

In spite of the fact that it was against all law and custom in Maryland to teach a slave to read, she began to do so. But, being proud of his progress, Mrs. Auld made the mistake of telling her husband how rapidly little Fred had mastered the alphabet. Instantly he ordered his wife to discontinue her teachings. "If you teach him to read," Mr. Auld said, "he'll want to know how to write—and this accomplished, he'll be running away with himself." Being an obedient wife, Mrs. Auld gave the little slave no further lessons.

But the seed of learning had been sown, and Frederick determined to carry on alone. He learned from the little white boys with whom he and Tommy played in the streets. He learned from copying the words he saw scrawled on fences, the advertisements on store signs, the mastheads of newspapers. And then, as he tells it, "By this time my little Master Tommy had grown to be a big boy, and had written over a number of copybooks and brought them home. When my mistress left me in charge of the house I had a grand time. I got Master Tommy's copy-books and a pen and ink, and in the ample spaces between the lines I wrote other lines as nearly like his as possible. The process was a tedious one, and I ran the risk of getting a flogging for marking the highly-prized copybooks of the oldest son. In addition to these opportunities, sleeping as I did in the kitchen loft, a room seldom visited by any of the family, I contrived to get a flour-barrel up there and a chair, and upon the head of that barrel I have written, or endeavored to write, copying from the Bible and the Methodist hymn-book and other books which I had accumulated, till late at night, and when all the family were in bed and asleep."

Why, Frederick wondered, should he have to learn alone in secret while little white boys learned openly? Why should his master forbid him to be taught? He could not feel badly toward the kindly Mrs. Auld, for even then he realized, as he later wrote, "We were both victims to the same overshadowing evil, she as mistress, I as slave." It was all a part of the same pattern, the beatings on the plantations, the denials in the city, the refusal of learning. "To make a contented slave, you must make a thoughtless one. It was *slavery,* not its mere *incidents* that I hated. I had been cheated. I saw through the attempt to keep me in ignorance. I saw that slaveholders would have gladly made me believe that in making a slave of me, they were merely acting under the authority of God, and I felt to them as to robbers and deceivers." The helpless youngster dreamed of a way out. "I wished myself a beast, a bird, anything rather than a slave."

Meanwhile, he had come across a book with words in it like *freedom.* It was a book of speeches, noble speeches, called *The Columbian Orator,* and in it were the orations of the great William Pitt, Sheridan on the Catholic Emancipation, and Lord Chatham's speech on the American Revolution. It was not a good book to fall into the hands of a slave be-cause it was filled with ideas of liberty and freedom. Frederick purchased it himself with a half dollar that he had earned in his spare time shining shoes. At night in his garret he poured over *The Columbian Orator* and copied from it words he did not know. Later he would slyly ask someone what they meant. Frederick had determined to learn to read, and he did. And then, "with play-mates for my teachers, fences and pavements for my copy-books, and chalk for my pen and ink, I learned to write."

Growing now to be a big boy, he was sometimes sent to work in Master Hugh's shipyard, keeping a fire under the steam-box, and watching the tools while the carpenters went to dinner. About that time Frederick learned that he had not been given outright to the Aulds in Baltimore. He was there on loan. When his old master, Captain Anthony, died, Frederick was still considered a part of his estate. As such, he was ordered returned to the plantation on the Eastern Shore where a division was to be made of Anthony's property. Young Frederick had no way of knowing what might happen to him then, to whom he might be sold, or where his ultimate destination would be. His heart was heavy as he left Baltimore and the Aulds, who had treated him kindly compared to his former state of being in the country. Then, too, Frederick knew that Captain Anthony had a relative, Master Andrew, who drank heavily and was known for excessive cruelty toward his slaves. All slaves were frightened at the prospect of falling into the hands of an irrational, drunken owner. Frederick thought, suppose this should happen to him! Being a spendthrift, Master Andrew might run through his inheritance in no time, then sell him South into the cotton country, Georgia or

Alabama, where he had heard that slaves were often worked to death in the blazing sun. When Frederick left the Aulds' house, not only did he weep, but his mistress wept, and little Tommy, too.

Fortunately, in the settling of the estate, it was decided to send Frederick back to the Aulds in Baltimore. But he remained long enough on the plantation to see what happened to most of the other slaves, including his relatives, who were scattered hither and yon as purchasers chose. For none did Captain Anthony's will provide freedom. Concerning this disregard of humanity, years later in his autobiography, Frederick wrote, "Now all the property of my old master, slaves included, was in the hands of strangers. All remained slaves, from the youngest to the oldest. If any one thing served to deepen my conviction of the infernal character of slavery and fill me with unutterable loathing of slaveholders, it was their base ingratitude to my poor old grandmother. She had served my old master faithfully from youth to old age. She had peopled his plantation with slaves; she had become a great-grandmother in his service. She had rocked him in his infancy, attended him in his childhood, served him through life, and at death closed his eyes forever. She was nevertheless a slave—a slave for life—a slave in the hands of strangers; and in their hands she saw her children, her grandchildren, and her great-grandchildren divided like so many sheep; and this without being gratified with the small privilege of a single word as to their, or her own, destiny." Thought again her teen-age grandson, Frederick, as he was sent back to Baltimore, "Oh, to be a beast, a bird—anything, anything but a slave!"

This time Frederick's stay in Baltimore was short for, with him, from the Anthony estate the Aulds had also been sent a badly crippled slave girl named Henny. Finding her of no use, they soon returned her to the plantation. This so angered the other heirs that they demanded that the Aulds also return Frederick. So he, too, was shipped back to the desolate Eastern Shore. Then about sixteen years old, Fred found himself in the service of a third master, another Auld named Thomas, in the village of St. Michaels. This man and his wife had been among the poorer relations in the family and so were not used to having slaves. To show their authority they treated them with a cold and distant sort of meanness which they thought indicated aristocracy. They also starved them. To get enough to eat, Frederick had to learn to steal. In St. Michaels he lived a miserable life indeed. His only pleasure came in being asked to conduct a Sunday School in the home of a free Negro, James Mitchell, who had a Bible and a few old spelling-books. The pupils wanted to learn to *read* the Testament as well as understand it. Of the former objective the whites of the village soon became aware—Negroes being taught to read! On the second Sunday of Frederick's class, in rushed his master, heading a mob of other irate whites armed with sticks and stones. The Sunday School was broken up and the slaves were driven away with the command never to assemble again for such a purpose. As for Frederick, he was threatened with shooting if he attempted any further teaching in St. Michaels.

Thomas Auld did not like Frederick, and the tall young slave, on his side, found it difficult to hide his contempt for his master, especially after repeatedly having witnessed the cruel lashings which Auld gave the poor crippled girl who also had become his property. Thomas Auld frequently whipped Frederick, but there was something about the stubborn silence with which the young slave received his beatings that irritated Auld no end. Frederick bore these whippings stoically, but it hurt him deeply to see this girl, a cripple, beaten. Finally the master accused Frederick of allowing his favorite horse to run away once too often. As punishment he announced that he intended to send the young slave to the farm of a man named Edward Covey, famous in the region for his ability to tame obstreperous blacks. Other slave owners often sent their Negroes there "to be broken" and after a twelve-month period they were returned to their masters so cowed and docile that no more trouble was had from them ever.

Covey's farm was located on a wild and desolate point jutting out into Chesapeake Bay. Down the bleak road to this farm on New Years Day of 1834 Frederick trudged, his worldly belongings in a bundle at the end of a stick across his shoulder. His heart was heavy. Although he was glad to be leaving the hunger of his master's house, he feared the brutality of his new abode, for Covey was known to be free with the lash, the club, or any other object of punishment at hand with which to abuse a slave. Shivering in the bitter cold as he hurried along, Fred thought that now, "I am given to understand, like a wild young working animal, I am to be broken to the yoke of a bitter life-long bondage." Then he heard in his mind again the word *freedom,* and the word *liberty*—those words that ran all through *The Columbian Orator.* But shortly before his eyes loomed the unpainted wooden house of the slave-breaker, Covey, and beyond that the barren sands and foam-white waters of the icy Bay. Through the scraggly pines at the road's end howled a bitter winter wind. This was no happy New Year for Fred.

After only three days with Covey, Fred was beaten so severely that he could hardly walk. He had lost control of a yoke of oxen hitched to a load of wood he had been sent to gather in the pine forest. Frederick had never driven oxen before and had had no instructions from Covey on how to manage them. The beasts ran away, smashed into the entrance of the farm with the load of wood, and broke the gate to splinters. Covey immediately ordered Frederick back to the woods, but this time without the oxen. The big white man walked behind the frightened boy. There in the woods on the freezing cold day, he ordered the boy to take off his clothes. Meanwhile he cut from a strong sapling a number of long stout branches commonly used as ox-goads. Then he looked at Frederick who had not taken off a single garment.

"If you will beat me," Fred thought, "you shall do so over my clothes." He made no move, in spite of threats and curses from Covey, to remove them. Then it happened. The enraged slave-breaker, he said, "rushed at me with something of the savage fierceness of a wolf, tore off the few clothes I had on, and proceeded to wear out on my back the heavy goads which he had cut from the gum tree. . . . This flogging was the first of a series of floggings. During the first six months that I was there I was whipped, either with sticks or cowskins, every week. Aching bones and a sore back were my constant companions. I was made to drink the bitterest dregs of slavery during the first six months of my stay with this man Covey. We worked all weathers. It was never too hot or too cold; it could never rain, blow, snow, or hail too hard for us to work in the field. I was somewhat unmanageable at first, but a few months of this discipline tamed me. Covey succeeded in breaking me—in body, soul, and spirit." Or so, in his despondency, Fred thought as spring turned into summer, the sun grew hotter, and the work in the fields became even harder.

But there was in this young Negro—in spite of what he thought—something that refused to be broken. One day in August Covey beat him almost to death, kicking him, then striking him in the head with a hickory slab as he lay half-fainting on the ground. Fred's offense had been unintentional. He had become ill from a long day in the heat of the treading-yard where wheel-horses trampled the straw from the grain. In the blazing sun, his head grew dizzy, ached violently, and his strength left him. He could not keep from sinking to the ground in the dusty yard, the world whirling, his stomach heaving, his breath short. Covey ordered Fred to rise, and when he could not, began to kick him with his heavy boots. Finally Fred staggered to his feet, only to fall again. It was then that Covey split his head with the hickory slab and left him bleeding on the ground. When Fred came to his senses, he resolved to go back to his real master and plead most humbly to be removed from Covey's farm, lest he die there. Battered and bruised as he was, he managed to steal away across the fields without being detected and walk the seven miles to St. Michaels.

Thomas Auld at first seemed moved by Fred's bloody and woe-begone appearance. But true to the slaver's code, that night he ordered the boy back to Covey's place to serve out the rest of his year. And Fred was commanded never to come to him again with such complaints. Auld did let the wretched boy spend the night in St. Michaels before returning to Covey for a second punishment as a runaway. On his way into the farm on Sunday morning, Fred passed Mr. and Mrs. Covey on their way to church. That day the slave-breaker did not molest him— for Covey did not think it right to whip slaves on the Sabbath. But the next morning when he approached Fred to beat him once more, something happened of which Covey never dreamed. The young Negro had resolved in his own mind not to allow any man to so mistreat him again.

At dawn as Fred was tending the horses in the stable, Covey sprung at him from behind and flung him to the floor, intending to tie his legs, so that he might then whip him without difficulty. But young Fred was too quick for the older man. He leapt to his feet, and each time Covey came toward him, he flung the slave-master to the ground. Fred did not wish to injure the man, but he did intend to defend himself. Covey was so taken aback by this show of defiance that he trembled in every limb.

"Are you going to resist, you scoundrel?" he shouted at the lad.

"Yes, sir," Fred replied, his hands raised to repel another attack.

Covey tried again to strike or to tackle Fred. But each time the white man came forward, the young Negro parried his blows, or flung him back when he tried to grab him. Finally in a rage Covey cried for help, and other slaves came running into the barn. But none of them, in spite of sure punishment to come, would take the slaver's side against Fred. Covey's cousin, a young man, did attempt to aid the slave-breaker, but Fred dealt this relative such a blow there in the stable that he "went off, bending over with pain," and left Covey to battle it out alone. The match spilled through the door into the barnyard where, determined not to be bested, for more than two hours Covey tried to get hold of Fred to whip him, panting and battling all the while. It was long after sunrise when he finally gave up.

"Now, you scoundrel, go to your work," Covey cried, making a pretense at having won. "I would not have whipped you half so hard if you had not resisted."

But, in reality, Covey had not whipped Frederick at all. And for the young slave, that memorable morning was a turning point in his life. "I was a changed being after that fight. I was nothing before; I *was a man* now. I had reached the point at which I was not afraid to die. . . . When a slave cannot be flogged, he is more than half free."

Probably because Covey did not want to let anyone know he had been bested by a black boy of sixteen, he never reported the incident to Frederick's master, or to the authorities. And he never attempted to whip the boy again. He tried only to work him to death.

When his term with Covey was up, Frederick was transferred on a yearly contract to a new master, a William Freeland, on a small farm near St. Michaels. Freeland was a kindly man and although Fred's work as a field hand was hard, the change was heaven compared to life at Covey's. But, kind master or not, by now Fred's hatred of slavery was so strong that he could not help but think of ways of escaping. He had heard of the North where men were not slaves, and of Canada where slavery had been abolished. Meanwhile, Fred commenced to conduct Sunday School classes again, this time in the open air under the trees during the summer. In the woods out of sight of the whites, with more spelling books than Bibles, he began to teach those who could not read. At one time he had more than forty pupils, all in danger of lashes on their backs if caught. "We might have met to drink whiskey, to wrestle, fight, and to do other unseemly things with no interruption from the saints or sinners of St. Michaels. But to meet for the purpose of improving the mind and heart, by learning to read the sacred scriptures, was a nuisance to be instantly stopped."

During his second year with Mr. Freeland, Frederick made up his mind to run away, and he persuaded five other young men in the neighborhood to make the break for freedom with him. The very thought of attempting escape made them so happy that as they worked they began to sing such spirituals as:

I thought I heard them say
There were lions in the way—
I don't expect to stay
Here much longer . . .

And another even more explicit one disguised in Biblical phrases:

> *O Canaan! Sweet Canaan!*
> *I am bound for the land of Canaan.*

Every Sunday Frederick and the five other young men met to discuss their plans—not of rebellion and the harming of their masters, but simply escaping from them and making their way North into a free state. For such plans, however, slaves could be put to death, and this they knew. On any road any white man might stop a Negro suspected of running away and hold him for arrest, or slave-catchers might seize them and sell them into the far South. Nevertheless, just before the Easter holiday they determined to start. Frederick wrote out temporary passes for each of them, such as a master might give a slave when granting permission for a visit at a distance. On the appointed morning they gathered for work in the fields as usual, "but with hearts that beat quickly and anxiously." Somehow Fred had a premonition that they had been betrayed. Sure enough they were. Shortly three constables appeared, Fred's master with them, and the six young men were quickly bound with ropes and taken into Easton for investigation. They were "drawn along the public highway—firmly bound together, tramping through dust and heat, barefooted and bareheaded—fastened to three strong horses whose riders were armed with pistols and daggers." Before the youths were taken away, the master's mother pointed a bony finger at Frederick and cried, "You devil! You yellow devil! But for you, you long-legged yellow devil, Henry and John would never have thought of running away." And it was true—Fred had put into *other* minds the thought of freedom.

Fortunately the passes Fred had forged were not found. Some of the fellows succeeded in throwing them away, others ate theirs as they were dragged panting and stumbling behind the horses fifteen miles to jail. In Easton the slave-traders crowded around them, inspecting them, and hoping to buy the husky youths for resale in the Deep South. But after several days in prison, the masters of the others came to get them, leaving Fred there alone. Finally his master came too, but trusting him no longer, Mr. Freeland sent Fred back to Baltimore where he could no longer "contaminate" his other slaves. Being a Negro with "book-learning" Fred was considered dangerous.

This narrow escape from severe punishment did not deter Fred from continuing to dream of escape. In Baltimore he was hired out to a shipyard contractor who placed him as a helper at the beck and call of all the white carpenters and calkers in the yard. These white workers gave the young slave a hard time, a half-dozen voices at once calling him to different tasks, with threats and curses coming from every direction if he did not move fast enough to satisfy them all. And *all* of Fred's wages went to his master. Everywhere white workmen were resentful of slave labor, believing that such competition helped reduce jobs for them. This resentment they took out on helpless Negroes like Fred who were placed in the Baltimore shipyards through no will of their own. Sometimes the white workers spat at him, while vile names and curses accompanied almost all their orders. One day one of them struck Fred. When the boy attempted to defend himself, he was set upon from all sides and beaten until he could hardly stand. Finally someone dealt him a blow from behind with a hand-spike, while another worker kicked him squarely in the eye as he lay on the dock. Meanwhile, more than fifty other white shipbuilders stood around and did nothing to help the lone colored boy.

Fred's master, Hugh Auld, was outraged when the blood-covered youngster dragged himself home. Auld was angry, not so much that Fred had been injured, but that a piece of "property" belonging to him had been so badly damaged without his permission. He took Fred to the magistrate, but this representative of the law refused to arrest anyone on the mere word of a colored boy, even though his swollen face and bruised body testified as to what had happened to him. "The laws and morals of the Christian city of Baltimore afforded no protection to the sable denizens of that city," Fred later wrote as he reflected that, "Nothing was done, and probably would not have been done, had I been killed in the affray."

But Master Hugh did remove Fred from that particular shipyard. He permitted him to hire himself out, providing he turned over to his master each week all of his wages. Why, Frederick asked himself, should every cent of his hard earned money be taken from him by Master Hugh? "He did not earn it; he had no hand in earning it; why then should he have it?" So more than ever Frederick thought of again running away. One day, when he was twenty-one years old, he did. Disguised as a sailor, and with a borrowed Seaman's Certificate, Frederick boldly boarded a train in Baltimore station headed for Wilmington. He changed there to the Philadelphia boat, and that night caught a train to New York. The journey covered about twenty-four hours, without mishap. And in New York Frederick was free—at last he belonged only to himself!

Frederick got married in New York and, with his bride, he set out for New Bedford where he found work on the docks. There, as a protection against being traced, he dropped his slave name, Bailey. From a character in Scott's "The Lady of the Lake" he took a new name, Douglass—Frederick Douglass—and by the end of the next decade, that name was known all over America. Brave enough as a teenager to defy the slave-breaker, Covey; later brave enough to make an unsuccessful attempt to escape from slavery; then at twenty-one to succeed in gaining his freedom—Douglass shortly became brave enough to defy the *whole* institution of slavery by becoming one of the leading forces for abolition in the country. This took a great deal of not only moral, but physical courage. To be a *white* Abolitionist in those days was dangerous enough, reviled as they were, stoned by mobs, and even killed. But to be a *black* Abolitionist was to run greater and more frequent risks than whites ever could know. All the Abolitionists were under continual attacks by the press, accused of being in league with the devil and trying to overturn the government. Because they believed in freedom for all slaves everywhere, Douglass paid no attention to the barrage of charges against them. He thought, "Abolition—whatever else it might be—was not unfriendly to the slave." In 1841 at Nantucket, Douglass made his first speech before an Anti-Slavery Society, and from that time on he grew into one of the greatest forces against slavery in the United States.

Frederick Douglass at twenty-four was six feet tall. He had warm deep set eyes, a shaggy head of hair like a lion, a rich voice and a powerful personality. In telling his personal story of bondage and escape, he could move an audience to tears, then with logic verbally demolish the whole slave system, and cause thinking people to want to aid in its actual abolition. The unthinking, of course, would not listen to Douglass, and mobs attempted more than once to break up his meetings. In Indiana a group of pro-slavers tore down the outdoor platform on which Douglass was speaking, beat him into unconsciousness, and left him on the ground with a broken hand which never fully recovered its usefulness. Kind-hearted Quakers nursed him back to health and strength and Douglass continued his speaking tours, collecting large sums of money everywhere to aid the Abolitionists in their fight to free America of slavery.

As the eve of the War Between the States approached, and the issue of slavery more and more divided the nation, passions on both sides became ever more heated; the division grew between North and South, between political parties, and even between families and friends. Then old John Brown, a white man, began to plan his raid on Harpers Ferry in Virginia, where he intended to seize the government arsenal and free all the slaves in the surrounding area, hoping thus to start slave insurrections throughout the South. John Brown invited Frederick Douglass to join him in this enterprise. It took great courage for anyone then in any way to associate himself with John Brown, or correspond with him, or be seen in his company. Douglass did not approve of Brown's plans, thinking them impossible of fruition, but nevertheless he sheltered Brown upon occasion, and he went to confer with him at Chambersburg shortly before the eventful raid. The authorities so strongly believed that Douglass was involved in the bloody uprising at Harpers Ferry, that he had to flee to England for a time to escape unjust prosecution.

When, over the issue of slavery, the Southern states seceded and set up the Confederacy, and the War Between the States began, the Union Army would not at first recruit Negroes. Douglass urged Lincoln to do so. He reproached the North "that they fought the rebels with only one hand, when they might strike effectually with two—that they fought with their soft white hand, while they kept their black iron hand chained helpless behind them." When enlistments were opened, Douglass urged every Negro "to get an eagle on his button, a musket on his shoulder, and the star spangled banner over his head." He said, "Liberty won by white men would lose half its luster. . . . Who would be free themselves must strike the first blow. . . . I urge you to fly to arms, and smite with death the power that would bury the government and your liberty in the same hopeless grave." Among the first colored men to join the Union Army were Douglass' two sons; and thousands of other Negroes, free and slave, flocked to the colors.

At the close of the War, when freedom was won, Douglass devoted himself to the cause of complete citizenship for colored men and women under democracy. The right to vote, the right to work, the right to be treated as decently as others in public places, all these things Douglass desired for the Negro people. Not only did he speak about them and write about them, but he actively tried to achieve them. Once when a railroad conductor attempted to segregate him on a train in the North by trying to move him to a coach for colored people only, Douglass held on to the arms of his seat and refused to be ejected, even by force. Determined to make him move, several strong white bullies were called. But so tightly did Douglass grip the seat, that the seat and all had to be torn from the floor before he would be carried from the coach. Only in this way did they move this man who would not change places to please the segregationists.

All of the broad social problems of the day came within the scope of the interests of Frederick Douglass. When very few men stood up for woman's suffrage, Douglass contended that women were human beings and citizens just as men, and should therefore have the right to vote. He was associated with such famous feminists of the day as Lucretia Mott, Lydia Maria Child, and Abby Kelley. And at some votes-for-women conventions, Douglass was the only male speaker on the platform. Temperance was also one of his interests, as well as the unionization of workers, and the participation of Negroes in workers' leagues. Through his newspaper in Washington, "The National Era," Douglass often presented strongly worded views on liberal causes then opposed by most of the nation's press. A courageous crusader of the written and spoken word, Douglass so remained until his death at the age of seventy-eight.

On February 20, 1895, in Washington, Frederick Douglass had just given stirring support to the feminist cause before a large gathering. With applause still ringing in his ears, on his return home that night he paused in the hallway to tell his family what had happened at the meeting. With a gesture as if he were reenacting his speech, the old man fell to his knees. For a moment those around thought this merely a dramatic way of telling the story. But when he quietly sank to the floor and did not rise again, they knew something was wrong. Frederick Douglass was dead.

In the long summations of his life that appeared the next day in newspapers all over the country, some of them repeated a story that had often been told about his very first speech—that before the Anti-Slavery Convention in Nantucket more than fifty years before when the tall young man just out of bondage stood before an audience composed largely of whites and quite simply poured out his heart to them. When Douglass had finished speaking the great abolitionist, William Lloyd Garrison, arose and cried to the crowd, "What I want to know is: Have we been listening to a thing, a piece of property, or a man?"

As one voice the audience shouted back, *"A man!"*

Harriet Tubman
Liberator

About 1823–1913

Some forty years before Abraham Lincoln signed the Emancipation Proclamation, Harriet Tubman was born on the Eastern Shore of Maryland, a slave, the property of the Brodas Plantation. One of eleven brothers and sisters, she was a homely child, moody and wilful as well. Harriet was not cut out at all for slavery. Very dark, and of pure African ancestry, for her grandparents had been brought from that land in chains, Harriet was said to be a descendant of the Ashanti people, among the most rebellious and warlike of Africans.

When Harriet was nine or ten years old, she was ordered into the Big House to assist the servants there. On her very first day in this capacity her mistress whipped her four times. Soon the white lady grew utterly impatient with the sulky and seemingly stupid girl so she sent her to work in the fields. This Harriet liked better than washing pots, emptying garbage and making kitchen fires. Even a slave out under the sky could look up at the sun and sometimes listen to birds singing in the bright air. But in her early teens a cruel thing happened to Harriet, and from the slavemaster's point of view, it was her own fault.

One evening about dusk a slave boy wandered away from the corn husking to which he had been assigned and went down the road to a country store. An overseer pursued him, intending to whip him for leaving the place without permission. When he grabbed the boy in the store, the youth resisted. The white man then called upon other slaves standing about to help him. No one moved to do so. Then the boy started to run and the overseer called to Harriet who was standing in the door to stop him. Harriet did not stop him nor did she move out of the door so that the overseer could get by. This made the white man so angry that he picked up an iron weight used on the scales and threw it at Harriet. The weight struck her in the head making a deep gash and knocking her unconscious in the doorway. As she lay there bleeding, everyone thought she was dead, and she did not come to her senses again for days. Tossing and turning on a pallet on the floor of her mother's cabin, talking strange talk, Harriet's delirium caused the others in the family to conclude that she might be demented for life. Indeed, when she finally recovered, her master believed her to be half-crazy. Harriet did nothing to change his opinion—but she was not crazy. From the blow on her head there did result, though, an unusual condition. From that time on, all her life, Harriet could not prevent herself at times from unexpectedly blacking out, going suddenly sound asleep no matter where she was. Then, after a spell, just as suddenly, she would come to herself again. And the deep dent which the iron weight made in her head remained until her death.

When Harriet grew to be a young woman she determined to escape from slavery. She had never learned to read or write, she had never seen a map, and she had no idea where the North—that place of freedom—was. But, nevertheless, she made up her mind to find it. Meanwhile, she had married. She urged her husband to come North with her but he refused. She also asked some of her brothers and sisters if they would go with her but only two of them, Henry and Robert, agreed, and at the last moment, they turned back. But with company or without, Harriet had made up her mind to risk the dangerous trek to freedom.

Before dawn one morning the young slave girl gathered her necessities into a bundle and started out. For fear that her mother and others would be greatly worried upon finding her missing, perhaps even thinking that slave-catchers had kidnapped her to sell into the Deep South, Harriet wanted in some way to tell them goodbye. But to do this was dangerous, both to them and to herself. So instead, in the early evening of the night she planned to leave, Harriet walked slowly through the slave quarters singing, and she knew that all the slaves would understand her song—if not then, soon:

> *When dat old chariot comes,*
> *I's gwine to leave you.*
> *I's bound for de Promised Land.*
> *Friends, I's gwine to leave you.*
> *Farewell! Oh, farewell!*
> *I's sorry friends to leave you.*
> *Farewell! Oh, farewell!*
> *But I'll meet you in de mornin'*
> *On de other side of Jordan. . . .*
> *Farewell! Oh, farewell!*

That night Harriet stole away across the dark fields and through the woods, guided only by the North Star, heading for freedom. When she reached the Choptank River, she trudged hour after hour upstream, for by walking in water, bloodhounds trained to scent runaways could not trail her. Eventually she found a sheltering place with kindly Quakers whom she knew to be friendly to escaping slaves. There she was rested and fed and given directions for crossing into Delaware. If the night was cloudy, she felt the trunks of trees to find on which side the moss grew, for moss indicated the northern side. Sometimes, tree by tree, Harriet headed for freedom. Sometimes she hid in caves, sometimes in graveyards, and she had many narrow escapes from the constant slave patrols that rode the highways, and from suspicious strangers who looked at the young black woman and wondered where she came from and whose slave she might be. But finally Harriet reached Philadelphia where she found work, and was no longer anybody's slave.

She said, "I looked at my hands to see if I was de same person now I was free. Dere was such a glory over everything! De sun come like gold through de trees and over de fields, and I felt like I was in heaven." But to Harriet, the North was not heaven so long as her friends and kinfolks remained in the slave country. Almost immediately she began to make plans to go back South to lead others along the hazardous road to freedom. In the years to come, it was as a liberator of slaves that Harriet Tubman became famous—a work which demanded anonymity and yet which, against her will, turned the spotlight of a nation upon her. She became one of the most successful conductors in the Underground Railroad, noted for her courage and her cunning, with at one time a reward of $40,000 offered for her capture.

The term *Underground Railroad* was applied to a widespread system of aiding escaped slaves which the Quakers and other friends of freedom had established. Eventually, such friends set up way stations along several routes from South to North at which runaways could be sure of assistance. One such route ran from the coastal states of the South up to Philadelphia, New York and Boston; another from the mid-South by way of Cincinnati to the Great Lakes and Canada. Along these routes slaves were hidden in barns, corncribs, attics, cellars, sometimes even churches. They were provided with hot food, warm clothing, perhaps a little money, and information as to where to find the next friendly family. Passwords, or the correct number of raps on a door in the night, were given; and above all from such friends came the knowledge that not all whites were out to harass and endanger those who sought escape from bondage. Sometimes when the going was rough and slave-catchers were known to be infesting the highways, workers in the Underground Railroad might transport fugitives from one station to another hidden under a load of corn in a wagon with a false bottom; or a male runaway might be disguised as a coachman and put to driving a fine carriage in which a white man sat as if he were the master. When the "coachman" had gotten to a safe hiding place, the white rider would drive his carriage back home, having aided another slave to freedom.

It was dangerous, and eventually illegal, for whites to engage in such activities. But it was doubly dangerous for a Negro to do so, and especially for an escaped slave such as Harriet Tubman. But Harriet did not let fear stand in her way. Most former slaves, once having escaped, never ventured back into slave territory again. But Harriet returned to the South more than nineteen times, and each time she brought back with her to the North a band of fugitives. None were ever captured. As a conductor on the Underground Railroad she once said, "I never run my train off de track, and I never lost a passenger." It is estimated that she brought more than three hundred slaves to freedom in the decade between 1850 and 1860. First she conducted her sister and her two children North from Baltimore, then on subsequent trips she penetrated the Eastern Shore and brought out various relatives and friends brave enough to attempt the Northward journey. But it was not until 1857 that Harriet was able to get her aging parents out of the South. Since they could not walk the long miles to freedom, it took great ingenuity to transport them through slave territory by two-wheel cart. It took money, too, for train fare once they had crossed the border but eventually Harriet got them to Canada.

To earn money for her forays, Harriet worked between trips as a domestic servant or hotel maid in Pennsylvania and New Jersey. After the cruel Fugitive Slave Law was passed in 1850, which permitted escaped slaves (and even free Negroes falsely charged as slaves) to be seized in the North and sent back in chains to the South, Harriet had to accumulate enough money to buy train tickets for her fugitives all the way through the Free States to Canada. In Canada slave catchers did not operate. But from Maryland to the Canadian border was almost five hundred miles—a long journey for a man or a woman with nothing. However, as the fame of Harriet's desperate missions spread, Abolitionists of means came to her aid, funds were supplied her, food and hiding places provided, and prayer meetings held for her safety. The white abolitionists marvelled at her bravery. The New England minister, Thomas Wentworth Higginson, termed her, "the greatest heroine of the age. . . . Harriet Tubman, a black woman and a fugitive slave, who has been back eight times secretly and brought out in all sixty slaves with her, including all her own family, besides aiding many more in other ways to escape. Her tales of adventure are beyond anything in fiction and her generalship is extraordinary. . . . The slaves call her Moses."

Angered by the callous application of the Fugitive Slave Law, and determined to help as many slaves as possible escape, the leading abolitionists of the times, white and Negro, aided Harriet Tubman in her objectives. In Wilmington, Delaware, a Quaker business man, Thomas Garrett, gave her money for train fare, food and winter coats. In Philadelphia the Negro William Still, who kept a record of all the escaped slaves passing through his station, stood ready to help. In New York City the editors of the *National Anti-Slavery Standard,* one Negro and one white, David Ruggles and Oliver Johnson, aided Harriet in pushing on to Albany with her band of runaways. Near Albany the wealthy Gerrit Smith gave counsel and funds as well as secret shelter. At Syracuse the former slave Rev. Jermain Loguen found ways of forwarding his black brethren to the Abolitionist center of Auburn where Senator William H. Seward gave them sustenance and a place to sleep. Then at Rochester, the great Negro leader, Frederick Douglass, provided aid for the last jump to Canada. Sometimes, before a group departed on that last lap to freedom, remembering the South, they might sing:

> *Farewell, old master,*
> *Don't think hard of me.*
> *I'm on my way to Canada*
> *Where all the slaves are free.*
> *I'm now embarked for yonder shore*
> *Where a man's a man by law.*
> *The iron horse will bear me o'er*
> *To shake the lion's paw.*
> *Oh, righteous Father,*
> *Wilt thou not pity me,*
> *And aid me on to Canada*
> *Where all the slaves are free!*

One runaway, Josiah Bailey, for whom a large reward had been offered, was so frightened of being captured at the last moment that he would not even look out of the window to see Niagara Falls as the train crossed into Canada. But when Harriet Tubman and her party of eleven men and women left the coach on safe soil, Bailey then began to sing loudly and shout and no one could stop him, "Heaven! Heaven! Heaven!" Harriet, who was a plain spoken woman who did not go in for demonstrations, barked, "Well, you old fool, you! You might at least have looked at Niagara Falls on the way to heaven."

Numerous examples of Harriet Tubman's heroism have been recorded and one example is commemorated on a bronze tablet in Troy, New York. There, one day in 1869 while on her way to an anti-slavery meeting in New England, she heard that a runaway slave named Charles Nalle was that very afternoon being arraigned in Federal Court for return to slavery. Immediately Harriet sprang into action, organized a rescue party of free Negroes and whites and arranged to have a boat in readiness to take Nalle across the river to Albany as soon as he could be kidnapped from the Court. She had no difficulty in getting followers for this daring attempt for the abolitionists believed that whether a rescue attempt failed or not, it got headlines in all the papers, served to keep anti-slavery sentiment alive and was worth a hundred speeches.

By pretending to be a crippled old woman of no importance, Harriet hobbled into the courtroom to watch the process and to wait for the proper moment to give a signal to the crowd outside. When the bailiffs prepared to move the prisoner, Harriet seized the astonished slave and the crowd in the street immediately thronged about them. Harriet and Nalle made for the river but officers overtook them. A pitched battle went on for hours between officers and abolitionists that day and both Harriet and Nalle were injured in the struggle. But finally the police were bested and the boat with the fugitive started for Albany, his supporters following on a ferry. There, another battle with the authorities took place but eventually Nalle got away. That night he was safely hidden in a wagon bound for Canada. But Harriet Tubman had to go into hiding for the next day her name made headlines throughout the nation. She had taken a prisoner away from government marshalls.

Most of Harriet's rescues from slavery, however, were made without the help of crowds. They began in slave territory itself and were therefore fraught with danger. One of these dangers was betrayal. All who went North with her were, of course, sworn to secrecy but some grew weak and weary on the way. Frightened, cold and tired, they wanted to turn back. Once back on the plantation they could be beaten until they disclosed all they knew and the names of the other runaways as well as their leader. This Harriet could not permit. For weak-kneed freedom seekers she had a remedy. That remedy was a pistol which she carried in the folds of her dress. And weary ones who wanted to turn back were faced with this pistol and advised that they would either go on or be shot. They always found the strength to go on. In this way no one who started out for freedom with Harriet Tubman ever failed to become free. Her bands of runaways were never betrayed.

Because of her qualities as a leader, when the slave issue split the nation asunder and the war between the North and South broke out, Harriet Tubman went into the service of the Union Army. She became the only woman in American military history ever to plan and conduct an armed expedition against enemy forces. But before this happened Harriet served the Union cause in numerous other capacities, her basic work being as an organizer among the Southern Negroes of a branch of the government Intelligence Service at the direction of the General Staff. Newly liberated slaves in battle areas could be most useful as scouts and spies for they knew the terrain, the location of stores of food and often where rebel ammunition dumps were located. And Harriet could teach them the secret of moving quietly through enemy lines without creating suspicion. She herself often went with scouting groups and did active work as a government spy against the slaveholding forces. With this objective for her in mind, Governor Andrew of Massachusetts arranged for Harriet's transportation to South Carolina aboard the government transport *Atlantic*. At Port Royal Harriet was given army rations but when she noticed that other Negroes, hungry and ragged and just out of slavery, grew jealous of this, she relinquished her special privileges, began to make pies and cakes to sell the soldiers and thus earn her own keep. She moved among the refugees of war—contrabands, as such liberated or escaped slaves were called in Union camps—and taught them how to keep their quarters clean, wash, sew and find ways of making a living. When epidemics broke out in the camps, Harriet served as a nurse, not only tending the sick but keeping hospital barracks clean, shooing flies and acting as friend and counselor. In fact, wherever and whenever she was needed, she would go. She became a kind of trouble shooter for the Union forces from the Carolinas to Florida.

But Harriet's most famous exploit during the war was the leading of a raid from Port Royal inland up the Combahee River. A group of her Negro scouts had prepared the way and had learned from slaves on the plantations along its banks the locations of torpedoes in the river. With a picked detachment of some 150 Negro troops led by Harriet herself on a fleet of three small gunboats and with the assistance of Colonel James Montgomery, on the night of June 2, 1863, she started up the river.

As the Federal gunboats approached, most rebel outposts fled, but first sent word to inland headquarters of the presence of the Union fleet. At each plantation Harriet ordered groups of soldiers ashore to burn houses, burn crops that could not be salvaged for Union stores and alert slaves to join the liberating forces. At Combahee Ferry the bridge was destroyed and a large detachment landed to set fire to the four rich plantations. By this time it was dawn and all the plantations on both sides of the river had been aroused. In vain did overseers try to keep their slaves from fleeing through rice fields and marshes toward "Mr. Lincoln's gunboats" and the freedom they promised. Confederate soldiers went into action against the fleet, but with little effect. As Harriet and her men steamed back toward the coast, all along the way they picked up slaves who, now under Federal protection, were slaves no more. Once again Harriet Tubman functioned as a liberator—although only incidentally now within the larger framework of the war which would eventually free all the slaves. Her work did much to prove how invaluable Negro troops, and even untrained slaves, could be toward the winning of that war. Eventually Harriet Tubman was credited with freeing more than seven hundred bondsmen in the regions where she and her scouts were active. Her song to them went:

> *Of all the whole creation*
> *In the East or in the West,*
> *The glorious Yankee nation*
> *Is the greatest and the best.*
> *Come along! Come along!*
> *And don't you be alarmed—*
> *Uncle Sam is rich enough*
> *To give us all a farm.*

Concerning the Combahee River raid, rebel reports blamed the inadequacy of their own command for allowing "a parcel of Negro wretches calling themselves soldiers, with a few degraded whites, to march unmolested with the incendiary torch to rob, destroy and burn a large section of the country." But the Boston *Commonwealth* reported otherwise and gave full credit to Harriet Tubman's leadership for this successful military foray. It said in part:

"Colonel Montgomery and his gallant band of 300 black soldiers under the guidance of a black woman, dashed into the enemy's country, struck a bold and effective blow, destroying millions of dollars' worth of commissary stores, cotton and lordly dwellings and striking terror into the hearts of rebeldom, brought off near 800 slaves and thousands of dollars' worth of property without losing a man or receiving a scratch. It was a glorious consummation."

Reporting the celebration which was held in Beaufort after the raid, it said:

"The Colonel was followed by a speech from the black woman who led the raid and under whose inspiration it was originated and conducted . . . Many and many times she has penetrated the enemy's lines and discovered their situation and condition and escaped without injury but not without extreme hazard."

Colonel Montgomery had already termed Harriet "a most remarkable woman and invaluable as a scout," while General Saxton said she displayed "remarkable courage, zeal and fidelity." And in his memoirs of the War, Samuel J. May declared, "She deserves to be placed first on the list of American heroines."

One of the simplest and most beautiful word pictures of a battle is Harriet Tubman's description of that at Fort Wagner at which she was present and where to Colonel Robert Gould Shaw, the Union commander, she served his last meal before he led his black troops into action and was himself killed. Of this battle, one of the Union's most bitter defeats in which more than 1500 men were lost and the ocean beach was crowded with dead and dying, Harriet Tubman said, "Then we saw de lightening, and that was de guns; and then we heard de thunder, and that was de big guns; and then we heard de rain falling, and that was de drops of blood falling; and when we came to get in de crops, it was dead men that we reaped."

Harriet Tubman lived for a half-century after the Emancipation Proclamation was signed by President Lincoln and those for whom she cared so greatly were freed. Eventually the government granted her a meager pension of $20 a month. And from the book, *Harriet, the Moses of Her People,* which Sarah H. Bradford wrote, came a little money. But, ever generous to a fault, Harriet Tubman died poor at the age of nearly a hundred. Poor but remembered—for the whole city of Auburn, New York, where she died went into mourning. And quite appropriately, her last rites, as befitting a soldier of liberation, were military. At her funeral the local post of the Grand Army of the Republic presented the colors.

One of the most beautiful of tributes ever paid her came, however, from that other great fighter for the freedom of the slave, Frederick Douglass. In a letter to her some years before she died, he wrote:

"The difference between us is very marked. Most that I have done and suffered in the service of our cause has been in public and I have received much encouragement at every step of the way. You, on the other hand, have labored in a private way. I have wrought in the day—you in the night. I have had the applause of the crowd and the satisfaction that comes of being approved by the multitude, while the most that you have done has been witnessed by a few trembling, scared and footsore bondsmen and women whom you have led out of the house of bondage and whose heartfelt, *God bless you,* has been your only reward. The midnight sky and the silent stars have been the witnesses of your devotion to freedom and of your heroism."

Robert Smalls
Patriot

1839–1915

When Robert Smalls became famous as a Civil War hero, he was only twenty-three years old and a slave, the father of three children. They were little children, hardly aware as yet as to what slavery was. But Smalls did not want his offspring to remain slaves a moment longer than necessary, so he stole a Confederate gunboat and transported them into the waters of freedom. This daring exploit earned for him national recognition. And eventually Smalls became a Congressman from the very state in which he had been a slave.

Robert Smalls was born in Beaufort, South Carolina, in the Spring of 1839. His parents, Robert and Lydia, belonged to the McKee family there, a family with the reputation of treating their slaves well. They even allowed slave children to acquire a little education, so by the time young Robert was in his teens, he knew how to read and write. When his master moved to Charleston, Robert was hired out as a hotel waiter. But, having grown up near the sea, he was attracted to ships, and shortly he was permitted to work at the dockyards where he became a rigger. Sometimes, to his delight, he was allowed to take short trips outside Charleston Harbor. At seventeen Robert was allowed to marry a girl of his choice—a privilege not granted many slaves. And his life was a happy one in comparison to that of most other men in bondage.

But in spite of a lenient master, there was something about slavery that irked young Robert. For one thing, when Fort Sumter was fired on by the batteries of the new Confederacy and Charleston became its fortress, with no freedom of choice on his own part, Robert was impressed into the rebel service and forcibly assigned without pay to the crew of the *Planter,* a cotton transport hastily converted into an armed frigate by the Confederate Navy. The ship's commander, Captain Relay, and its two mates were, of course, white. But the sailors, firemen, and all the rest of the crew were Negro slaves. Robert Smalls became a fireman, stoking the boilers whenever the *Planter* ventured outside Charleston's waterways. Meanwhile, by watching the officers in charge of the ship, he learned all he could about navigation. Being a bright young man, Robert soon knew how to run the vessel himself and, if need be, could pilot it out of Charleston Harbor to the open sea.

The proud city of Charleston, a center of Southern wealth and culture, was one of the chief harbors during the war through which ammunition and supplies from abroad found their way to the Confederate rebels. This happened in spite of a Union blockade of the Eastern seaboard from Maryland to Florida. The North looked forward to capturing Charleston, although this was not easy. But the Union armies had early managed to take control of the nearby Sea Islands off the South Carolina and Georgia coasts, and to these islands flocked thousands of runaway slaves, or those liberated by the government forces. Hilton Head, Beaufort, and Port Royal were crowded with destitute freedmen—contrabands—who found even a hungry freedom preferable to bondage. Throughout the Union camps they sang:

> *Slavery chain done broke at last,*
> *Broke at last, broke at last!*
> *I'm gonna praise God till I die!*

Or another song that they made up themselves often filled the air:

> *No more auction block for me,*
> *No more, no more. . . .*
> *No more driver's lash for me,*
> *No more, no more.*

Robert Smalls had heard of these centers of freedom only a short distance from Charleston, but to get to them through the rebel lines with his wife and children would be a dangerous and difficult thing to attempt. In normal times runaway slaves might be beaten within an inch of their lives. Now, in war time, they might be killed. In his mind Smalls began to conceive a plan of escape so bold that he hardly dared think about it. If the plan which he kept in the back of his head were successful, it would benefit not only himself and his family, but the Union cause as well. The scheme was simply to take charge of the *Planter* if and when such an opportunity came, place his family aboard and with himself at the helm, sail out of Charleston Harbor into the off-shore waters of the Union blockade fleet. This required not only great daring, but careful thinking as well.

Smalls knew that some nights when the ship was at dock, one or two of the white officers went to their homes in the city to sleep. If only some evening *all three* of them would go ashore for the night—the captain and both of his mates! For this eventuality, Smalls waited. Finally such a night came in the Spring of the second year of the War. On Monday, May 12, 1862, all three of the white officers of the *Planter* decided to go ashore to their families for the night. It was on this night that Smalls quietly rounded up his own family, his sister, and his brother John's wife and child. John himself was an engineer on the *Planter* and had already been taken into Robert's confidence. Together the two brothers decided to make their dash for freedom, taking not only their closest relatives, but the entire crew of Negro seamen with them. They made a group of sixteen in all.

They realized that by using the property of the Confederate government for escape—a vessel of the rebel navy—the penalties if captured would be severe. So these sixteen slaves agreed that if they were pursued and overtaken by Confederate gunboats, they would blow the *Planter* and themselves to bits. Failing in this, they would link their hands together and jump into the sea. All of them were willing to die attempting to be free. None meant to be taken alive. Charleston Harbor was full of ships and ringed by guardposts, so they were under no illusions as to the dangers involved. But their hopes were high, and the very audacity of Robert's plans gave them all courage. To sail away to freedom on a Confederate gunboat! They had to laugh at the idea of slaves doing such a thing. But that is just what they did.

While Captain Relay and his mates were at home that Monday sound asleep in their beds, soon after midnight by devious routes through darkened streets, the Negro women and children made their way to the wharf where the *Planter* lay. One by one they crept aboard and hid themselves in the hold. A few hours before dawn, Robert Smalls fired the boilers and soon the steam was up. Then he mounted the bridge and gave orders for the crewmen to cast off the ropes mooring the vessel to the dock, and to haul up the anchor. In the starry darkness Smalls raised the Confederate flag on the tallest mast and, with himself in charge, gave orders to sail. Everything was done as Captain Relay would do—for Smalls's plan was to make it appear that the *Planter* was leaving the harbor for early morning reconnoitering in the waters outside Charleston. And indeed, this is what the sentries on the docks must have thought as they saw the ship glide away from shore and steam slowly down the harbor through its ring of fortifications.

Deliberately, so as not to excite suspicion, the ship slid through the water. And, at each harbor post, Smalls gave the proper signal with a pull of the whistle cord. He had put on the captain's clothes and donned the same wide-brimmed straw hat that Relay wore when on deck. In the dark from a distance anyone might think it was Captain Relay himself on the bridge. The night was kind to Robert Smalls. He was short, stocky, brownskin, and looked nothing at all like the Confederate officer whose vessel he was so audaciously sailing away under the very noses of the harbor guns. But this young Negro's heart must have been in his mouth as the ship approached Fort Sumter, the heavily armed bastion at the mouth of the harbor. Suppose, for some unusual reason, orders came from the Fort to halt the vessel for inspection? What would happen then? Would the batteries of the Fort open fire on one of its own boats, if the ship did not stop? Smalls did not know. But fortunately such an eventuality did not come to pass. Calmly, as the *Planter* passed the Fort, Robert Smalls gave the accustomed signal on the whistle. The sentries, after what seemed like a very long time, called back, "Pass the *Planter!*" And the runaway ship went on to the open sea.

Manned by Negroes and carrying sixteen slaves dreaming of freedom, the *Planter* now sailed full steam ahead into the Atlantic. About the same time in the East the sky began to lighten as dawn came. Now out of range of the harbor guns, and well out of sight of the shore patrols, Robert Smalls hauled down the flag of the Confederacy and hoisted in its place a sheet taken from one of the bunks—a white flag of truce—and everyone aboard breathed easier. In the first gray light of morning, they sighted one of the Union vessels that was blockading the coast. The captain of the *Onward* recognized their flag of truce. And by the time the sun rose, Robert Smalls had turned over to the Union Navy the Confederate gunboat, *Planter.*

The Flag Officer of the Union Blockading Squadron, S. F. DuPont, sent at once to the Secretary of the Navy in Washington a report on the receipt of this prize of war, and in his report he praised Robert Smalls to the highest. He also recommended that Smalls and the members of his crew be awarded prize money for having delivered the *Planter.* Upon its passage, President Lincoln signed the measure. Money and honor. But greater than all to Smalls and his crewmen was the freedom that they found beneath the Union Jack.

Of his freedom Smalls made good use. Information which he supplied Union naval officers was described as "of the utmost importance." Apparently it was, since he is cited in an official report of the Secretary of the Navy to President Lincoln. According to this report, "From information derived chiefly from the contraband pilot, Robert Smalls, who has escaped from Charleston," the Union forces were able to occupy Stono and thus secure what the document describes as "an important base for military operations." Because of his general seamanship and his knowledge of the buoys and fortifications of Charleston Harbor, Smalls was appointed a pilot in the Quartermaster's Department of the United States Navy and, on the monitor *Keokuk,* he took part in an attack on Fort Sumter. Later he was transferred to the *Planter* and, in December, 1863, when the commander of that vessel under Confederate fire deserted his post, Smalls took charge of the ship and steered it out of danger. For this, besides being cited for gallant and meritorious action, he was shortly promoted to the rank of Captain, and remained in the naval service for the duration of the War.

Meanwhile, Smalls's fame had spread throughout the state of South Carolina, and when the post-war reconstruction commenced, he became active in the political life of the region. In 1868 he was one of the members of the State Constitutional Convention convened to propose a new civil code and to rehabilitate the state's administration. For the former slave owners, including his own master, Smalls preached leniency, not vindication. In his heart there was no malice toward the past, only high hopes for the future of all, white and black, and the desire that they might work together for the good of the South. As a speaker Robert Smalls was fluent, self-possessed and convincing, commanding the respect of all who heard him. People of both races often referred to him as "the smartest colored man in South Carolina."

On January 1, 1863, as a war measure, Abraham Lincoln had signed the Emancipation Proclamation granting freedom to "all persons held as slaves within any State, or designated part of a State, the people whereof shall then be in rebellion against the United States." And in 1865 Congress, by the addition to the Constitution of the 13th Amendment, ended slavery everywhere in the United States. Some three and a half million bondsmen had then become free men, at a loss to the slave owners of over two billion dollars in human property values. In 1868 the 14th Amendment to the Constitution was passed granting the Negro full citizenship and declaring that no state should "deprive any person of life, liberty, or property without due process of law, nor deny to any person within its jurisdiction the equal protection of the laws." Lastly, in 1870 the 15th Amendment concerning suffrage was added to the Constitution. This stated that "The right of the citizens of the United

States to vote shall not be denied or abridged by the United States or by any State on account of race, color, or previous condition of servitude."

These edicts were great steps forward in the processes of American democracy. But the former slave-holding states immediately sought ways of circumventing them. In some localities "Black Codes" were formulated which permitted Negroes to be indentured or apprenticed for long periods to white employers under conditions amounting to slavery. Curfew laws were instituted. Jury service was denied to blacks. And the Ku Klux Klan and other terrorist organizations came into being to prevent men of color from exercising their citizenship rights, particularly the right of the ballot. It became necessary for Federal troops to protect the polling places of the South. But, under such protection, for a while freedmen took an active part in Southern politics. It was during this period that Robert Smalls was elected to the South Carolina legislature, where for a time Negroes held the majority of the seats, since they constituted more than fifty per cent of the population. Since most freed Negroes were uneducated, they wanted education, and so they voted for free public schools for all. They wished protection for their own civil rights, so they sought such protection for all. In general colored office holders were influential in bringing about liberal and advanced legislation in many fields in the South.

For a number of years after the War, Robert Smalls was an officer of the South Carolina State Militia in which he held various commissions. Being a staunch Republican, he became a delegate to several of that party's national conventions. And in 1875 he was sent as an elected representative from South Carolina to Washington where he served several terms, in all, a longer period in Congress than any other representative of color. After his congressional service, Smalls was appointed Collector of the Port of Beaufort, a post which he held for many years. After his retirement he lived in Beaufort until his death in 1913 at the age of seventy-four.

Of all the things that happened to Robert Smalls in his long and interesting life, perhaps none remained more vivid in his memory than a day when at the end of the War Between the States, as captain of the *Planter*—the ship on which he had escaped to freedom—he took part in the ceremony attending the raising of the Stars and Stripes once more over Fort Sumter. That day Captain Robert Smalls steered the *Planter* into Charleston Harbor, his mind and heart full of memories of the time when, a few years before, he had first taken command of the ship as a slave. Now on April 13, 1865, as the harbor guns boomed their salutes to victory, Smalls transported into Charleston a crowded shipload of jubilant Negroes from the Sea Islands, including the distinguished colored officer, Major Martin R. Delany, and his soldier son of the famous 54th Massachusetts.

Boatloads of distinguished people from the North had come down for the victory ceremonies, including a number of famous abolitionists and almost the entire congregation of Henry Beecher's church in Brooklyn. Thousands of Negroes had gathered in Charleston, too. On the eve of the celebration at Michelville near Hilton Head outside the harbor of Charleston, in a crowded Negro church, William Lloyd Garrison, who had spent long years in the cause of freedom, rose to speak. The stirring Negro spirituals in wave after wave of joyous singing had already swept the congregation, and there were tears and cries of jubilation from the newly freed men and women packed into the building. And when they rose as one to greet Garrison, they were rising in salute to all the men and women, white and black, who had contributed to their freedom—from Lincoln and Garrison and Beecher to black Harriet Tubman, Frederick Douglass, and Charleston's own Robert Smalls whom they all knew so well. When the singing and crying had subsided, with a majestic passage from the Bible Garrison began his speech, "And Moses said unto the people, Remember this day in which ye came out from Egypt, out of the house of bondage . . . And it shall be when thy son asketh thee in time to come, saying, *What is this?* that thou shalt say unto him, By strength of hand the Lord brought us out of Egypt from the house of bondage . . . And it shall be for a token upon thine hand, and for frontlets between thine eyes: for by strength of hand the Lord brought us forth out of Egypt."

Robert Smalls and the steamship *Planter* are a part of the story of the Negro's heroic escape from the house of bondage.

Charles Young
West Pointer

1864–1922

Charles Young attained the highest rank accorded a Negro up to his time in the United States Army, that of colonel. Previously there had been a number of Negro officers of lesser rank, and in every war since the colonial period colored soldiers had taken part. Many were slaves impressed by their masters; others were runaways. Some were free men. They fought at Lexington and Concord, Ticonderoga, and the Battle of Bunker Hill in 1775. In 1776 when George Washington crossed the Delaware, Oliver Cromwell and Prince Whipple were with him, the latter in Washington's own boat. Tack Sisson took part in the raid on British headquarters at Newport in 1777. And that same year, history reports that at the height of the battle, "In the fight at Brandywine, Black Samson, a giant Negro armed with a scythe," swept through the ranks of the Redcoats. Paul Laurence Dunbar's poem about Samson asks:

> *Was he a freeman or bondsman?*
> *Was he a man or a thing?*
> *What does it matter? His brav'ry*
> *Renders him royal—a king.*

In some states slaves who served in the armed forces were granted their freedom at the war's end by legislative action, like those in Virginia after the revolution who had "contributed towards the establishment of American liberty and independence." It was during the Revolutionary War that the first American woman to wear a uniform saw official service as a soldier. She was a woman of color, Deborah Gannett, who disguised herself in a man's uniform and fought for a year and a half in the Fourth Massachusetts Regiment of the Continental Army under the name of Robert Shurtliff. For her courageous service, the State Legislature granted her a special monetary award with a citation that declared, "Deborah exhibited an extraordinary instance of female heroism."

In the War of 1812, after the Battle of New Orleans, General Andrew Jackson said of his Negro soldiers, "I expected much from you, but you have surpassed my hopes." And of the black sailors who then made up a sixth of the navy personnel on the Great Lakes, Commodore Perry said after the Battle of Lake Erie, "They seemed absolutely insensible to danger." And the commander of the *Governor Tompkins* declared that the name of one of his brave Negro seamen, John Johnson, deserved to be written high on the roll of fame.

In the War Between the States, fighting for their own liberty, almost two hundred thousand Negroes served in the Union Army or Navy. "The 62nd United States Colored Infantry," so it is recorded of the final skirmish in 1865 in Texas, "probably fired the last angry volley of the War, and Sergeant Crocket of that regiment received the last wound from a rebel hostile bullet, and hence shed the last fresh blood in the war resulting in the freedom of his race in the United States." All told, some 37,000 Negroes were killed in the service of the Union.

When the American battleship *Maine* in 1898 was sunk in Havana Harbor and the United States entered the war against Spain, the Twenty-Fourth and Twenty-Fifth Infantry and the Ninth and Tenth Cavalry were sent to Cuba. They saw action at San Juan, Las Guasimas, and El Caney, and other Negro units did occupation duty on the island after the war. At Santiago "for particularly meritorious service in the face of the enemy," four Negroes were commissioned lieutenants. And among the colored soldiers who are uniquely remembered in Cuba are thirty-five who volunteered to serve in experiments designed to check the yellow fever epidemics—and died as a result. It was in the Spanish-American War that Charles Young, then a major, took part.

Young was born on March 12, 1864, in the little village of Mayslick, Kentucky, but while still a youngster his parents moved to Ripley, Ohio. There Charles finished high school, and became a school teacher until, in 1884, he was appointed to the United States Military Academy at West Point. He was the ninth of his race to be admitted to this institution, but the large number of white Southern cadets made attendance there difficult for black students. Up to 1877 none had graduated. The first man of color to be graduated from West Point was Henry Ossian Flipper, born a slave in Georgia, who received his commission in that year; the next was John H. Alexander of Ohio in 1887; and in 1889 Charles Young was graduated. But in those days it was not easy for Negroes to get through West Point. Many fellow cadets would not speak to a colored classmate, and the usual indignities of hazings were doubled when it came to black plebes. But Young determined to stick it out, to perform his duties punctiliously, and to study hard. He came through successfully. At graduation

Charles Young was commissioned a second lieutenant in the all-Negro unit, the Tenth Cavalry. After various transfers, he was assigned in 1894 as an instructor in Military Science at Wilberforce University, a Negro institution in Ohio. Then when the Spanish-American War began, he became a major in charge of the Ninth Ohio Regiment which was transferred to Cuba.

Race prejudice in high army circles often made life difficult for all-Negro troops. For example the Twenty-Fifth Infantry embarked on a government transport for Havana. But in the port of Tampa, Florida, when other soldiers were given individual shore leave, the Negro troops were not allowed off the boat except as a marching unit under white officers. They were assigned to the very bottom of the hold in hot and airless quarters, and were not permitted to mingle on deck with their white comrades in arms. But in spite of such discriminatory treatment, once in action the Negro soldiers fought gallantly. And at San Juan Hill the Ninth and Tenth Cavalries especially distinguished themselves.

In June, 1898, two white battalions of the First Volunteer Cavalry under the command of Colonel Theodore Roosevelt (who was later to become President of the United States) began an attack against the Spaniards on Santiago Ridge at Las Guasimas. Known as the Rough Riders, these troops of Teddy Roosevelt's had previously distinguished themselves in battle, but this time they found the going rough, particularly at San Juan Hill. The garrison of El Caney there was well fortified, and the slopes below it were a tangle of bushes, vines, and stunted trees through which had been strung treacherous barbed wire. The approaches to the slopes were marshlands. Blockhouses guarded the hillside and Spanish sharpshooters were concealed in the jungle undergrowth. Unaware of the enemy's strength and strategic positions, the white Rough Riders soon found themselves under dangerous fire from all sides. When the colored Ninth and Tenth Cavalry units, stationed some distance away, heard of their plight, the Negro soldiers quickly mounted horses and galloped to their aid, arriving just in time, dismounting to join the battle.

"Firing as they marched," a New York paper reported, "their aim was splendid, their coolness was superb, and their courage aroused the admiration of their comrades. . . . The war has not shown greater heroism." One of the white corporals in the fight later stated, "If it had not been for the Negro cavalry, the Rough Riders would have been exterminated." And another soldier said, concerning the aid of these mounted fighters which turned a possible defeat into victory, "Every one of us, from

Colonel Roosevelt down, appreciates it." Certainly it was their strength that turned the tide of battle and contributed greatly to the battering into complete submission of the Spanish fort on the hilltop. Colonel Roosevelt himself added, "I don't think that any Rough Rider will ever forget the tie that binds us to the Ninth and Tenth Cavalry." And he repeated what one of the privates in his outfit had declared just after the battle, "They can drink out of our canteens."

After the Spanish-American War, Young served with military units in the Philippine Islands and in Haiti, then with General Pershing on the Mexican border. In 1915 in the punitive expeditions of American forces against Mexican guerrilla warriors across the border, a squadron of the Tenth Cavalry which Young commanded went to the rescue of Major Tompkins and his men when they were ambushed by the Mexicans near Parral. Young's bravery elicited wide newspaper comment. Shortly thereafter he was made a lieutenant colonel, and led numerous raids into the bandit-infested Mexican desert, seeking to dislodge the rebel leader, Pancho Villa.

But in spite of his military knowledge, his bravery, his experience and his rank, when in April, 1917, the first World War involved the United States, Colonel Young was not assigned to European service. As the highest ranking Negro officer in the armed forces, his failure to see active duty proved a great disappointment to Negro Americans. They felt that the then existing race prejudice in our defense system prevented Colonel Young from being given service commensurate with his rank. At any rate, the army placed him on its list of officers to be retired, giving the cause as high blood pressure. However, to prove his physical fitness, Colonel Young rode all the way on horseback from his home in Xenia, Ohio, to the capital at Washington where he laid his case before Newton D. Baker, Secretary of War, but to no avail. Despondent because he would not be permitted to fight in the European theatre of war, Young mounted his horse and rode back to Ohio where he prepared his mind for retirement. But the retirement papers never came. Young was kept on the active list, but given no assignment. Then, when the war was almost over—in fact, just five days before the Armistice—Colonel Young was ordered to Camp Grant in Illinois to be in charge of trainees.

When the installations at Camp Grant were disbanded, Young was sent to Monrovia, Liberia, as a military attaché, one of his assignments being to aid in the reorganization of the Liberian Army. Colonel Young had a deep interest in African life and culture, and he spent his leisure hours gathering material for a book he hoped to write. He was a quiet man of varied interests, not purely military, and fond of composing both poetry and music in his spare time. He wrote a play called "The Military Morale of Races" and a book about Toussaint L'Ouverture, the leader of the Haitian slave revolts against the French. For his church in Xenia he made beautiful new arrangements of old hymns, and for concert use he composed eight serenades. Young played the piano well, also the cornet, and had acquired fluency in Spanish, French, and German. His few public appearances as a speaker drew large audiences, and he became a greater popular figure with Negro Americans who had followed his career with interest from the days of the Spanish-American War to his death in Nigeria in 1922.

Colonel Young had gone from Liberia to Lagos, the capital of Nigeria, on furlough. Expecting to use this great African city on the Niger River as a center, he intended to explore the surrounding territory in search of material for his book. On the way to the walled city of Kano whose civilization dates back to before Christ, Colonel Young became ill of fever and had to return to Lagos. There, on the coast of the African continent that he loved (he himself was of almost pure African descent), he died, an American soldier in a far off land—which happened to be the land of his ancestors. With appropriate military ceremonies, Colonel Charles Young was buried in the National Cemetery at Arlington where today a tall marble shaft marks his resting place.

Matthew A. Henson
Explorer

1866–1955

The North Pole was discovered on April 6, 1909, by Rear Admiral Robert E. Peary of the United States Navy. With Admiral Peary at the North Pole was the Negro, Matthew Henson. In fact, Henson was the trail breaker for Peary's expedition and, as such, went ahead first to the Pole, reaching it some forty-five minutes before the Admiral himself. So Henson was actually the very *first* man to stand at the top of the world.

At the Pole the latitude is 90 degrees North and from there all directions are South. In Admiral Peary's Log Book his arrival at the North Pole is recorded thus: "Arrived here today, 27 marches from Cape Columbia, I have with me 5 men, Matthew Henson, colored, Ootah, Eginwah, Seegloo, and Ookeah, Eskimos; 5 sledges and 38 dogs. The expedition under my command has succeeded in reaching the POLE . . . for the honor and prestige of the United States of America." To Henson then, his only English speaking companion, Peary is reported to have said, "This scene my eyes will never see again. Plant the Stars and Stripes over there, Matt—at the North Pole." His brown face seeming even browner in his hood of white fur, in a world of white ice and white snow, the Negro, Henson, planted the American flag at the very top of the earth.

Born on a farm in Charles County, Maryland, the year after the close of the War Between the States, Matthew Alexander Henson had a harsh childhood. When he was two years old, his mother died and his father married again. But Matt was only eight when his father died, too. His stepmother was not kind to him. She made him work very hard, would not even allow him to go to school, and often whipped him severely. So when he was eleven years old, in the middle of the winter, Matt decided to run away. While everyone else was asleep in the house, in the dark of night he started out on foot, heading toward Washington, a city he had often heard of but was not sure of its location. Eventually the little boy got to Washington by himself. A kind colored woman who ran a small lunch room took him in, fed him, and gave him a job as her dishwasher at a dollar and a half a week. For a number of years he was happy, until the urge came over him to travel further. In Baltimore Matt had heard there were docks and great ships that sailed away into all the waters of the world. Young Henson wanted to become a sailor.

He was lucky. After walking from Washington to Baltimore, it was not long before the thirteen-year-old youth found a job on a boat, a square-rigger with tall white sails destined for Hong Kong, a port half way around the world. Matt was signed on as a cabin boy. Added to this good fortune was the fact that the *Katie Hines* was in command of a kind-hearted captain who took an interest in the brave Negro youngster who could hardly read or write. The captain decided to teach him to read and write well before the ship got back to Baltimore. In those days it was a voyage of many months to China. Every day the captain gave him a private class in his cabin, and in this way Matt acquired the groundwork of a good education on a windjammer rocking and rolling through the troughs of the sea.

For five years Matt Henson sailed on the *Katie Hines*, learning seamanship, learning from books, learning from people of all nationalities, and growing into a man. One entire winter the ship was locked in by ice at the Russian harbor of Murmansk, where Matt learned to speak Russian, hunt wolves, and drive sleighs. Later he saw the pagodas of Japan, the gypsies of Spain, the palm trees of the West Indies, and the great rivers of Africa. Matt picked up a smattering of many languages, and some he learned well. He acquired a knowledge and understanding of strange peoples and strange ways, and learned to take foreign customs in his stride and to mingle amiably with everybody. This ability to get along with strangers and live with folks whose language he did not speak stood him in good stead later in life, for it was his destiny to become an explorer. The good captain of the *Katie Hines,* who introduced the world to Matt, died when he was seventeen. His ship had just left Jamaica heading through the Caribbean for Baltimore. With the Captain in his cabin when he died was the boy he had guided toward manhood, young Matthew Henson. The master of the ship was buried at sea.

Matt did not sail on the *Katie Hines* again. He shipped instead on a fishing boat, but quit when it reached Newfoundland. In Boston and other cities along the coast as far as New York, young Henson worked at various jobs ashore—night-watchman, ditch digger, coachman. Then when he was nineteen he went back to Washington again. There, two years later, working as a stockroom clerk in a men's furnishing store, he met young Robert Peary, a civil engineer for the Navy, who came in to the store to buy a sun helmet for use in the tropics. Peary offered Matt Henson a job as his personal attendant on a surveying trip to Nicaragua for the government. Henson did not like the idea of being anyone's man-servant, but he felt intuitively that the job might lead to something better. Having adventure in his blood, he accepted it. In no time at all, Peary recognized in the young Negro qualities of value far beyond those of a personal servant, so he promoted him to his surveying crew as a field helper. For twenty-three years thereafter, Henson was associated with Peary in his work and his trips.

Peary was not a rich man so he could not always personally afford to pay Henson for his services. But on their return from Central America, a job was secured for Henson on government pay as a messenger in Peary's office at the Navy Yard in Philadelphia. About a year later, Peary told young Henson about a proposed expedition to Greenland. He intended to explore the northern icecaps, and he said he desired very much to take him along. But since the trip had very meager backing, there was no money to pay for Henson's services. Matt Henson volunteered to go without pay. In this he was joined by a number of adventuresome whites, all imbued with the spirit of exploration rather than gain. In 1888 they set out for Baffin Bay. In spite of the fact that Peary suffered a broken leg shortly after his arrival in Greenland, he and the whole party elected to allow their ship to depart, leaving them isolated for a year at the foot of a glacier they hoped to cross.

Matt built a house for Peary, his wife, and the rest of the party and aided in the construction of sledges for their inland trips. From the Eskimos, he learned how to handle a team of eight to sixteen dogs to pull sledges across the ice. Matt's light tan skin at first caused the Eskimos to think him one of them, but speaking another tongue. In short order he had established friendly relations with the native peoples and soon began to learn their language. That winter they taught him a great many things useful to know in the frozen North, especially how to hunt, trap, and fish for food. Since Henson put his newly acquired knowledge at the disposal of the entire party of explorers, he became a most valuable man to Peary's expedition. Lieutenant Peary realized his value and respected Henson accordingly. Matt, in turn, sympathized deeply with Peary's aims and marvelled at his determination. Soon between the two men there sprang up a relationship of mutual admiration and dependence. Finally, when the party set out in the face of stinging sleet through sub zero weather to conduct its explorations, Matt was considered one of the most important men in the group. By then, on the part of others, his race had been entirely forgotten. Here in the frozen North, no one thought of color lines. In the primitive Arctic, a man was a man—and that was that. When the expedition returned to New York in 1892, Peary told Matt Henson, "We are going back to the Arctic again—but next time, all the way to the North Pole."

At the turn of the century, no one knew what lay at either the North Pole or the South Pole. At the earth's axis would there be snow-covered land, or only drifting ice floes impossible of crossing? Nobody could tell. And how could a man reach the North Pole? By land or by sea? No one knew. In those days there were no radios to keep up communications with the rest of the world. There was no aviation to survey terrain from the air, or planes to drop food were explorers to be stranded, or to effect a quick rescue if men were isolated. To make an attempt to reach the North Pole, anyhow, was considered by most people to be a foolhardy adventure indeed. But Henson and Peary both wanted to attempt it. They did.

A party of eleven men and two women again headed for Greenland, with Peary intending to go further North this time. But, after a year of Arctic hardships and frustrations, all but two of the men returned to the United States. Only Matt Henson and one other stuck by Peary, electing to remain another year, sticking out a second winter that they might go forward in the spring. Peary's first attempt that year to reach the Pole had been unsuccessful, and their supplies were buried in a frozen drift of snow and ice. In April 1896, another attempt was made in the face of icy winds that bore down from the North under the cold but continuous glare of a twenty-four-hour sun on blindingly white snow. In their three dog-sledges, the men often lost contact in the swirling blizzards through which they travelled. It was slow and dangerous going over ice that might split and isolate one dog team from another. Finally the third man, Lee, was lost. Peary and Henson made camp trusting he would catch up to them but he did not. To keep warm while waiting and hoping, the two men slept huddled in furs as close together as they could, that their body heat might keep each other from freezing. After three days Henson went in search of the third man and luckily found him. But Lee was almost frozen on top of his dog sledge though still alive. Henson rescued him and treated him for frostbite and extreme exposure. When their food supply got so low the men could not share any of it with the dogs, they would each day kill a dog and feed that one to the other animals. Finally, the men were reduced to eating dogs themselves. After a month, however, the three pioneers had covered six hundred miles. But they were too exhausted by then and their supplies too low to hope to go any further and expect ever to make the long trek back to civilization alive. Besides, scurvy, the dreaded disease caused by malnutrition, set in. They had failed.

But they brought back to New York from the Greenland coast two large meteorites of scientific interest, leaving behind one of many tons that was too large to be loaded aboard their small ship. In 1896 Peary and Henson returned to Cape York to get this gigantic fallen meteor but again failed to dislodge it from the ice to haul it aboard ship, so they returned to the States without their prize. But in 1897 they secured a larger ship and stronger tackle, sailed again to Greenland and this time brought back to New York the largest meteorite in the world which gained Peary wide newspaper publicity as well as a profitable lecture tour. Matt, meanwhile, was employed by the American Museum of Natural History as an assistant in the mounting of Arctic animals and arranging true-to-nature panoramas of the beasts and backgrounds of the far North. In England Peary's lectures and interviews were so successful that a publisher presented him with a ship, the *Windward,* especially equipped for Arctic travel. On his return to America, he immediately began to plan another Polar search, this time working out details most carefully in advance, selecting a full complement of assistants to cover each lap and preparing to spend at least four years on the expedition. He alerted Matt to be ready to accompany him.

Off again in 1898, Peary and Henson steamed past the Statue of Liberty but ice prevented the *Windward* from penetrating as far north as Peary had hoped. They got only to Cape d'Urville on Ellesmere Island. From there Peary decided to go by sledge overland to Fort Conger, deserted fifteen years before by another exploring party which had left behind a large stock of supplies. This trip to Conger was one of two hundred and fifty miles through deep snowdrifts over mountains of ice but Matt and Peary, with a group of Eskimos, got there. On arrival, Peary's feet were frozen so badly that some of his toes snapped off as his shoes were removed. For three months at Conger, Matt cared for Peary, treating his frozen feet and trying to prevent gangrene from setting in. When they could travel again, they returned to Cape d'Urville where all of Peary's remaining toes, except one on either foot, had to be amputated. This great misfortune left him a partial cripple for life. Convalescence did not keep him from remaining for two years more in Greenland but again he failed on this trip to reach the Pole. At Etah, Matt and Peary passed many months alone, except for the Eskimos, and they were the first men finally to define for map makers the northern rim of Greenland. When they returned to New York in 1902, they had added to the geographical knowledge of the world by this major exploration.

Over a period of many years, from youth to middle-age, the still determined Robert Peary made a total of eight unsuccessful attempts to reach the Pole and on all but one Matt Henson accompanied him. Henson became an expert in his knowledge of the Arctic and its winds and weather. In the frozen North, far away from the centers of civilization, he developed into a sort of Jack-of-all-trades since there was nothing Matt would not do to be of value to himself or his party. He learned to harpoon walrus; to hunt reindeer, bear and musk-oxen; to skin and stuff animals; to cook over a hole in the ice and to build igloos as an ice shelter against zero gales. He could not only build a boat but navigate it. He could interpret for the white men and the Eskimos. He was so good at manipulating heavily loaded dog sledges even in blizzards of 50 degrees below that Peary once said of Henson, "He is a better dog driver and can handle a sledge better than any man living except some of the best Eskimo hunters themselves." With the Eskimos no one could form closer friendships or achieve their cooperation more quickly than could Henson. He not only learned to speak their language but to understand their jokes, eat their food and wear their clothes. He adopted an orphan Eskimo boy, Kudlooktoo. And once when Henson slipped on an ice floe and went into the freezing water, it was an Eskimo who pulled him out and saved his life.

On the expedition begun in 1905, they went by ship as far as Cape Sheridan, then by sledge and on foot across the ice of the Polar Sea. That year Peary and Matt Henson reached a new fartherest North, 87° 6", only 175 miles from the Pole. Here again they were stymied by all the conditions that make travel in the Land of the Midnight Sun excessively difficult—the breaking ice floes, the towering cliffs of frozen snow, the swirling blizzards and the terrors of complete isolation. With supplies gone, dogs emaciated and the Eskimos exhausted, for days they faced death on floating ice fields as they tried to make their way back to their base camp. Again defeated, Matt and Peary reached New York on Christmas Eve, 1906. The following year Henson got married.

But marriage did not keep Matt at home when the call came again to seek with the undaunted Peary a foothold at the top of the world. Two more determined men than Peary and Henson have never been known in the annals of exploration. One disappointment after another plus the ridicule of the press of the world at his continual failures only made Peary more adamant in his ambition to reach 90 degrees North where no man had ever stood before. On each expedition his accompanying members changed but Matt Henson remained with him. Henson was forty-two years old when again he left the United States on July 8, 1908, once more heading for familiar Cape Sheridan. This time President Roosevelt came aboard their ship in New York harbor to see the expedition off and to cheer its departure. Matt Henson's wife was at the pier, too, and he took her kiss with him to the Arctic.

Leaving the ship at Cape Sheridan, they travelled overland ninety-three miles across the snow to Cape Columbia where a base was established. From here across seas of ice it was four hundred uncharted miles to the Pole and the temperature was so cold that often the men's beards were frozen stiff from the moisture from their breath. Eighteen years of determination lay behind Peary when on February 28, 1909, he began another attempt to reach the Pole. Beyond the rim of the endless day that at that time of year lights the North, his goal lay. They got off to a good start. But in March a great lead of water that they could not cross—an Arctic river between the ice—stopped their progress and made it appear they might never get further. Fortunately, after a week of waiting, the weather went even further below zero. Then the lead froze permitting lightly loaded sledges to cross and re-cross conveying supplies to the other side. When they were a hundred and thirty miles from the Pole, the last of the supporting parties received orders to turn back. Now Peary and Henson were left alone with the Eskimos for their final dash Northward—one Negro man and one white man destined, if successful, to make history. They had with them four Eskimos, five sledges and a group of husky dogs. Matt was to blaze the trail, Peary to follow.

A gruelling trail it was over a white wilderness of snow and ice, but they pushed forward. "Day and night were the same," wrote Henson later in his autobiography, *A Negro at the North Pole*. "My thoughts were on the going and the getting forward and on nothing else. The wind was from the southeast and seemed to push us on and the sun was at our backs, a ball of livid fire rolling his way above the horizon in never ending day." But on this last lap, he continued, "As we looked at each other we realized . . . the time had come for us to demonstrate that we were the men who, it had been ordained, should unlock the door which held the mystery of the Arctic."

By April 5 they were thirty-five miles from the Pole. Peary with his mutilated feet was then fifty-three years old and Matt was no longer young either. Could it be that at last their dream of so many years would come true? That night only the Eskimos slept—uninterested in seeking a new spot of ice in this world of ice they had known all their lives. Henson and Peary could not sleep for the excitement of it. A part of Matt's job as trailblazer was to build an igloo of ice at each stopping point so that when Peary got there they could rest until time to start again. On the day when Henson, forging ahead, finally arrived at a point where North no longer existed, he knew he had reached the Pole. With Ootah's assistance, there he began to build an igloo. Forty-five minutes later, with Eskimos and a team of dogs, Peary arrived. To Matt Henson, Peary gave the honor of planting the American flag at the North Pole while he stood in salute. It was April 6, 1909.

Eleven years later Admiral Peary died, but Matt Henson lived to be eighty-eight years old. He passed away in New York City in 1955. In tribute to his long series of explorations, Matt Henson received a Congressional Medal, a gold medal from the Chicago Geographical Society, a loving cup from the Bronx Chamber of Commerce and a building has been named after him at Dillard University. On the occasion of the forty-fifth Anniversary of the Discovery of the North Pole, President Eisenhower honored Matt Henson at the White House.

Ida B. Wells
Crusader

1869–1931

Ida B. Wells was born in Holly Springs, Mississippi, a few years after the close of the War between the North and South. She grew to be a pretty little girl, slight, nut-brown, delicate of features. And she became a very beautiful young woman. To look at her, refined and ladylike in manner, lovely as a flower, no one would think that she was destined to become a defier of mobs and a vigorous crusader against all the brutalities that beset the Negro people in the Post-Reconstruction days in the South. But Ida B. Wells felt that all of the rights vouchsafed American citizens in the Constitution of the United States should belong to Negro citizens, too, particularly the right to the protection of life and liberty from mob violence. In Mississippi as a child little Ida saw the white-robed Ku Klux Klan ride through the night to frighten defenseless colored people away from the polls. She heard of the burning of Negro schools, and of Negro homes—if the owners happened to become too prosperous to suit the members of the Klan. These things Ida B. Wells thought wrong, undemocratic and uncivilized.

To better combat the evils of bigotry that she saw around her, even as a child Ida knew she had to acquire education. So when her parents were stricken with yellow fever and she found herself saddled early in life with the care of her younger brothers and sisters, she determined nevertheless to remain in school. First she attended Rust College in her home town, Holly Springs, then she went to Fisk University in Nashville where she wrote for the campus magazine. While still in her teens Ida became a country school teacher. Eventually she got an appointment in the public schools of Memphis and at the same time she began to write a column for a colored newspaper there. Intrigued by journalism and realizing the power of the printed word, she invested the money she earned from teaching in a paper called the *Memphis Free Speech* of which she became a co-owner and the editor.

In the South at that time there were still white people who wished to see Negroes back in slavery. Many who did not go so far as this in their desires still did not want, under any circumstances, to grant black men and women equal civil rights, or permit them to vote. Such persons had little use for Negro newspapers, especially if they spoke out against the abuses and illegalities forced upon the colored people. But as an editor Ida B. Wells could not keep silent in the face of the almost daily violence and intimidation then prevalent in Tennessee and surrounding states. For decades after the War, the Mississippi Delta was troubled by racial strife. Lynchings and violent incidents of the ugliest sort were commonplace, with the courts unwilling to convict their perpetrators when the victims of violence were colored. Under the editorship of the young Miss Wells, the pages of *Free Speech* blazed with indignation against such a state of affairs where not even the humblest and most subservient Negroes might feel reasonably safe as to life, liberty, or even the expectation of the pursuit of happiness.

More than once, because of her outspokenness in print, Ida B. Wells received threats against her life and against her newspaper. To continue to write and publish her editorials opposing bigotry and violence took a great deal of heroism on the part of this pretty young woman who looked too fragile to lift anything heavier than a pen in self-defense. But Joan of Arc in France had not been a big woman either, so Ida had read, but Joan had been brave, and she had stood up against armies for what she believed. Ida B. Wells was not afraid to stand up against mobs. But that any man or woman should have to do so in the United States was, she felt, the great shame of the times. To help wipe out this shame of racial prejudice, she decided to dedicate her life to stirring people into action against it. It was this dedication that eventually caused her to be driven out of Memphis.

When in 1877 at the end of the Reconstruction period, Federal troops were withdrawn from the South, the recently freed Negroes were left unprotected at the mercy of local prejudices. Their civil rights were violated at will, and in some communities black people were not even allowed to walk on the sidewalks. One petition in 1888 from Negroes in the Deep South which was printed in the Congressional Record declared that "unarmed and unable to offer resistance to an overpowering force which varies from a 'band of white' to a 'sheriff's posse' or the 'militia'," Negroes in the Delta were being "whipped and butchered when in a defenseless condition." Aside from the other forms of violence, there were in the South that year 137 recorded lynchings. The following year there were 170. And in the decade from 1890 to 1900, 1,217 Negroes met their deaths without trial through mob violence.

Just across the Mississippi River from Memphis where Ida B. Wells lived, conditions for Negroes in 1892 in Arkansas were so frightful that an appeal was sent to Northern newspapers for help. It read in part, "People all over the state are being lynched upon the slightest provocation; some being strung up to telegraph poles, others burnt at the stake and still others being shot like dogs. In the last thirty days there have been not less than eight colored persons lynched in this state. At Texarkana a few days ago, a man was burnt at the stake. In Pine Bluff a few days later two men were strung up and shot. . . . Over in Toneoke County a whole family, consisting of husband, wife and child, were shot down like dogs. Verily the situation is alarming in the extreme. . . . The white press of the South seems to be subsidized by this lawless element, the white pulpits seem to condone lynching. The colored press in the South is dared to take an aggressive stand against lynch law. The Northern press seems to care little about the condition of Negroes in the South. The pulpits of the North are passive. Will not some who are not in danger of their lives, speak out against . . . lynchings and mob violence? For God's sake, say or do something, for our condition is precarious in the extreme."

It was in a moral climate such as this that Ida B. Wells, then only twenty-three years old, published her paper and composed her editorials. Those men and women who, surrounded by decent people in their own communities, protest against evils in *far away* places, are not necessarily brave people. But men and women who stand *in the midst* of evil and fight it, especially in the face of physical danger, have within them the qualities of heroism. In Memphis Ida B. Wells knew that to protest mob violence was dangerous. But protest she must—and did. History remembers her heroism.

Early in the month of March in the year 1892 in Memphis, three young Negro businessmen were dragged from jail at night by a masked mob and riddled with bullets in a field just outside the city. Most of the members of the mob were well known to the community at large, but none were punished for these mass murders. The Negroes killed—Calvin McDowell, William Stewart, and Thomas Moss—were not hoodlums, but intelligent, clean-cut, ambitious young men, respected by all who knew them. Their violent and unwarranted deaths, said to have been instigated by white business competitors, almost touched off a race riot on the part of the Negro citizens of Memphis, so deeply hurt and angered were they by the lack of police protection which permitted this atrocious deed to happen. In her paper Ida B. Wells published a full account of the tragic affair, naming those said to have been among the mob, and pointing the finger of blame at lackadaisical city officials. Immediately her life was threatened. And the night after that week's edition of *Free Speech* appeared on the newsstands, a mob invaded its plant, destroyed its printing presses, and burnt the remaining papers. Then they went in search of the editor. But friends had spirited her from the city. Openly the whites threatened to lynch her if she returned. Ida B. Wells was forced out of Memphis.

She came North and secured work on a Negro newspaper in New York City, *The Age,* to which often she had sent dispatches before leaving Memphis. Its editor, T. Thomas Fortune, himself a distinguished journalist and good friend of Booker T. Washington, said of the new young writer on his staff, "She has plenty of nerve and is as sharp as a steel trap." In New York Miss Wells met the great Frederick Douglass, the Harvard graduate Monroe Trotter, a militant Boston editor, and other prominent colored men and women of that day. All of them took an interest in this daring young woman from the South. They encouraged her in her plans for bringing Southern conditions to the attention of the American public, aided her in getting lecture engagements, and donated funds for the collecting and publication of data on lynchings. In 1895 Ida B. Wells published the first carefully compiled statistical record of lynchings in the United States, a pamphlet entitled, *The Red Record.* And she became one of the leaders of a growing movement among liberals in the North to put an end to mob violence in America.

In 1898 she personally petitioned President McKinley at the White House to take action against mob law. She discussed with him the recent lynching of a United States postmaster in Florida. And respectfully the President listened as she added, "Nowhere in the civilized world save the United States of America do men, possessing all civil and political power, go out in bands of fifty to five thousand to hunt down, shoot, hang or burn to death a single individual, unarmed and absolutely powerless. Statistics show that nearly 10,000 American citizens have been lynched in the past twenty years. To our appeals for justice the stereotyped reply has been that the government could not interfere in a state matter. . . . We refuse to believe this country, so powerful to defend its citizens abroad, is unable to protect its citizens at home. Italy and China have been indemnified by this government for the lynching of their citizens. We ask that the government do as much for its own."

As a platform crusader against race prejudice and lynch law, Ida B. Wells became immensely popular not only in her own country but abroad. Of her lecture campaigns in Great Britain, a prominent churchman said, "Nothing since the days of *Uncle Tom's Cabin* has taken such a hold in England as the anti-lynching crusade." Quite correctly, Miss Wells did not entirely blame the South for mob evils. She once said, "Is not the North by its seeming acquiescence as responsible morally as the South is criminally for the awful lynching record of the past thirteen years? When I was first driven from Memphis, Tennessee, and sought a hearing in the North to tell what the Negro knew from actual experience of the lynching mania . . . not a newspaper to which I made application would print the Negro side of this question." And even in the North, free speech for Ida B. Wells was not always secure. She was not infrequently heckled from the audience, and sometimes physically threatened by bigots who did not like to see any colored person ask for the rights of democracy.

In 1895 Ida B. Wells married another crusader, a Chicago newspaper man, Ferdinand L. Barnett, and together they continued their campaign for equal rights for Negro Americans. They broadened the field of their activities, too, to include every social problem of importance in the Windy City where they lived. A great organizer of clubs, youth groups, and civic leagues, Ida Wells Barnett, as she was known in later life, continued active nationally, travelling throughout the Middle West and East, and sometimes into the South for speeches. She was among the six Negro signers of the initial call that resulted in a great national conference on Negro problems in New York in 1909, and out of which eventually grew the powerful National Association for the Advancement of Colored People, destined to play a most influential role in affairs relating to race in our country.

Active until the end, Ida Wells Barnett died in Chicago in the spring of 1931 after an illness of only two days. Now there stands in that city a large low-rent housing development bearing her name, and in many cities throughout the country there are women's clubs christened in her honor. At her death the *Chicago Defender* described her as the people of that city remembered her toward the end of her life: "Elegant, striking, always well groomed . . . regal." The work of keeping a statistical record of lynchings, which she began, was carried on by Tuskegee Institute. But, fortunately, that particular form of mob violence diminished so greatly in the United States until in 1951 there was only one lynching. And since the year 1951 none has been officially recorded. Many feel that Ida B. Wells' long life devoted to the eradication of lynching, no doubt, helped to put an end to that evil.

Hugh N. Mulzac
Master Mariner

1886–

Captain Hugh Nathaniel Mulzac is listed in "Who's Who in Colored America" as a master of ocean going steamships unlimited. He was born near the sea in Kingston on the island of St. Vincent in the British West Indies. There he attended the Church of England School. In his early twenties, looking forward to a career on the sea in Great Britain he enrolled at Swansea Nautical College in South Wales. In 1911 young Mulzac settled in the United States and shortly thereafter became an American citizen. He attended the Shipping Board School in New York. Between ocean voyages on which he gained his practical experience, Mulzac studied navigation and wireless techniques. By 1920 he was ready to take the examinations as a ship's master, and that year he received his papers. In 1922 he became the captain of the *S.S. Yarmouth* of the Black Star Line belonging to the Back-to-Africa organization of a famous Negro leader, Marcus Garvey. During his years at sea, Mulzac circled the globe fifteen times and visited nearly every major port on earth. But it was during World War II as the master of the Liberty Ship *Booker T. Washington* that Captain Mulzac became famous. Dodging submarines, his ship transported safely across the Atlantic 18,000 soldiers and prisoners, as well as thousands of tons of war material, without the loss of a single man.

Some 24,000 Negroes served in all capacities in the United States Merchant Marine during the War. The racial discrimination that had formerly prevailed on most American ships, both civilian and naval, when colored seamen were relegated largely to jobs as messmen, under wartime conditions gradually disappeared, partially in the navy and on merchant vessels almost entirely. The influential National Maritime Union, a large liberal organization, threw its weight against outmoded color lines in employment at sea, and President Roosevelt's Executive Order 8802 against discrimination in wartime contracts helped too. The result was that by the end of the war there were not only Negro seamen on deck but colored engineers in the engine room, wireless men in the radio cabin, and Negro officers on the bridge. Colored Americans of other minority groups were also employed in increasing numbers. In Captain Mulzac's crews there were whites, Negroes, Filipinos, and Chinese-Americans. Among the many new cargo vessels built especially for wartime voyages, fourteen were named after outstanding Negroes, and four for colored sailors who had sacrificed their lives in the service. Two such Liberty Ships, the *Frederick Douglass* and the *Robert L. Vann*, were sunk by the Germans.

As a teenager in the West Indies, Hugh Mulzac signed on a Norwegian sailing vessel for his first voyage, other than little trips from island to island on small boats in the Caribbean. The first foreign port at which he set foot ashore was Wilmington, North Carolina, and it was there that the Negro youth first experienced discrimination. With the Norwegian captain of his ship, Hugh went to church on Sunday morning. But because he was brown of skin, the ushers would not admit him to the church whose congregation was white. So the Captain refused to go into the services, also, declaring that Jesus Christ couldn't possibly be inside a church where all were not welcome.

From the United States the ship crossed to England, and there young Mulzac had a chance to see all the historic sites of London that he had read about in school. He had been a serious student who liked books as well as travel and adventure. He tried to read good books about all the countries he visited during his succeeding years at sea—from Europe to Australia, India and China, to South America. By the time he was twenty-five years old, Mulzac's knowledge of seamanship and harbors was sufficient for him to be granted a second mate's license for both sailing and steam vessels.

When the First World War began, Hugh Mulzac was shipping out of Baltimore, for in that city he had married and established a home. As a Second Mate he made a number of voyages to England and France on ships carrying war materials to the Allies, and in Baltimore he attended the War Shipping Board School for the training of officers desiring upgrading. Mulzac then took the examinations for Chief Mate and passed. Then in 1920 he appeared before the Merchant Marine Inspectors in Baltimore as a candidate for master's papers, and came through the examination with a very high rating. But, in those days, it was unheard of for a Negro to captain an American ship, so the young man was forced to continue to sail as a mate until after the war when Marcus Garvey made him captain of the Negro-owned *Yarmouth*, steaming between New York and the West Indies. During the Depression, however, this ship was docked, so for a time Captain Mulzac conducted a school for the training of seamen. Later he himself went back to sea, taking whatever positions his color would permit him to hold, from steward to mate to wireless operator. But he was blacklisted by ship-owners after taking part in a strike, and so was compelled again to seek work ashore, this time as a house painter.

When World War II broke out in Europe and all seamen were badly needed, Mulzac shipped on a boat carrying war materials to the British in Egypt. Nazi planes and subs forced the ship to go all the way around the tip of Africa, rather than through the Mediterranean. More than once Mulzac knew what it was to be bombed by the Germans. After two such trips for the British, when the United States entered the war Captain Mulzac applied to the War Shipping Administration to offer his services as master of one of the new vessels then being built by the government. He also placed applications as a ship's master with every steamship line in New York. But, even though they were crying for experienced officers, because of his color, no company would employ Mulzac as a master. Elderly white captains were being called out of retirement to take charge of vessels under dangerous wartime conditions of a sort such as many of them had never experienced. Mulzac had sailed through the First World War, but was being denied the chance of sailing in the Second.

Finally, after great pressure from Negro organizations, the National Maritime Union, other powerful labor groups, and the intervention of President Roosevelt's Committee on Fair Employment Practices, Mulzac was offered the captaincy of a new Liberty ship, the *Booker T. Washington,* then about to be launched in California. But he was told that he must gather an all-Negro crew for this boat. Not only would such a segregated crew have been against union policies, but it certainly was against Mulzac's own beliefs, since he felt that all seamen should work together, regardless of race. Therefore, Captain Mulzac refused to accept the ship under conditions which stipulated that his crew should be composed only of Negroes. He stuck to his point and in the end won the privilege of choosing the members of his crew from among any competent seamen who might apply for berths on the *Booker T. Washington.* When the ship took to the sea on October 15, 1942, almost half of the crewmen were white, the others colored. And all during the war years, there was no nationality barrier on Captain Mulzac's ship. So successfully did this vessel operate—the first in the American Merchant Marine to be captained by a Negro—that soon three other Liberty ships were commissioned with colored masters, commanding crews of their choice.

Southward through the Pacific to the Panama Canal and then into the Caribbean, Captain Mulzac took his new ship on her maiden voyage, then up the East Coast to New York. There the Greater New York Council of CIO Unions had prepared a banquet of welcome for this ship and its crew, and it was hailed as an inspiring example of the fact that whites and Negroes could easily work together without difficulties on an American vessel. The souvenir program of the banquet stated:

> The *Booker T. Washington* is more than a ship. Its crew heralds the people's unity which victory over the Axis will bring. These seamen, from 18 of the United Nations and 13 States of our Union, are America's answer to Jim Crow and Fascist race theories. On this new Liberty Ship, a floating symbol of our war aims, these brave sailors are proving that men of all races and colors can live and work together in harmony and concord and fight together for a world free from intolerance and oppression.

At this banquet, with the four stripes of gold of a Master Mariner on his shoulders, when Captain Mulzac rose to speak he was cheered.

After its New York reception, the *Booker T. Washington* headed for Halifax where it was to await convoy company through the submarine infested waters to Europe. From Nova Scotia on, the captain and his men would face all the dangers of modern warfare from both above and below the seas, at the mercy of planes as well as U-boats. And in winter the towering tons of water that compose the mighty waves of the North Atlantic, along with the thousand mile gales that blow, may be as dangerous in their impact as any man-made explosives. Just off the coast of Newfoundland, the *Booker T. Washington* encountered a terrific storm that battered her so badly she lost her place for a time in the convoy. Then, once back with the other ships, some of the cargo on the piled-high deck broke loose in a storm, endangering the entire boat, for shifting cargo can cause a vessel to sink. Again Mulzac had to drop behind the rest of the ships, and this time he lost them altogether. Quite alone now, through perilous waters, the *Booker T. Washington* had to make its own way into port. Mulzac steered for Ireland, and in spite of enemy wolf packs, he reached there safely. The only shot fired at his ship was from a patrol boat guarding the port of entry. The officers were not accustomed to sighting a lone vessel coming into harbor in wartime, so it was mistaken for a possible enemy ship off its course. So dramatic was this first voyage of the first merchant steamer captained by a colored man, that it was dramatized and broadcast nationally in the United States.

Between 1942 and 1947, the *S.S. Booker T. Washington* made twenty-two round trips between the United States and various ports of the battle areas, running the gauntlet of submarines and planes, gliding at night without lights through the Mediterranean blockade, and sometimes limping into port battered by waves, or with a part of its substructure shattered by a torpedo. Yet somehow this ship always managed to make it, even when the waters were shaken by explosives all about it. Some of its seamen said their boat led a charmed life—*just lucky*—while others credited the skill and judgment of their intrepid captain with keeping them out of the most serious jams. Certainly the officers and men on Captain Mulzac's ship had great faith in his ability and there was comparatively little turnover among the personnel of his ship. Mulzac took a deep personal interest in his crewmen, himself conducting a class in navigation for all who wanted to attend, and holding a ship meeting in the Officers Saloon every Sunday for licensed and unlicensed men alike. At such meetings anyone from the humblest messboy up to mates and engineers might have their say. And, once having been a ship's cook, on Christmas Captain Mulzac would himself make the plum pudding for all his complement. Small wonder that its mixed crew developed an *esprit de corps* second to none, and that the *Booker T. Washington* won the honor of being one of the cleanest and best disciplined ships in the American Merchant Marine.

For two years one of the members of the crew of Captain Mulzac's ship was the writer John Beecher, great-grandnephew of Harriet Beecher Stowe, author of *Uncle Tom's Cabin*. Beecher wrote a fascinating book called *All Brave Sailors,* subtitled, "The Story of the *S.S. Booker T. Washington.*" In it are pen portraits of the men of various nationalities making up the crew, and a warm and human word picture of their skipper, Mulzac, in his paint-smeared cap, never putting on airs or flaunting his authority, but nevertheless possessing the respect of all who came in contact with him. One of Beecher's chapters is called "Nazi Cargo" and concerns a group of five hundred German prisoners of war being transported to America on Mulzac's ship. Amusingly he writes about the astonishment of these "super-Nordics," filled as they were with contempt for Negroes, when they learn that the ship on which they are crossing to the United States is commanded by a colored man! And movingly Beecher reports the comment of one of the Germans as that voyage of the *Booker T. Washington* neared its end: "Our leaders told us that democracy in America was a fraud. They told us you were hypocritical when you said that all men were free and equal. They told us that

Negroes were no better than slaves in your country. But what we have seen on this ship, the happiness, the comradeship among all of you, your fairness to us when we had been told you would beat and abuse us, all that has made us think. At night, after the lights go out down in the hold we talk about it."

Henry Johnson
A Gallant Soldier

1897–1929

Of the 50,000 Negro soldiers who fought in the American armed forces during World War I, probably the most famous was Henry Johnson, a little Red Cap from Albany, New York, who became overnight a hero. In the United States some 400,000 Negroes were inducted into military service during the First World War. Of these about three-fourths were assigned to labor battalions, loading or unloading ships, salvaging war materials, detonating explosives, and burying the dead. Shortly after America's declaration of war in 1917, the first Negro stevedore battalion arrived in France. For the duration of the conflict colored soldiers on European docks handled an average of 25,000 tons of cargo a day, and were of vital importance in getting supplies to the various battle fronts. These Negro soldier-workers constituted more than one-third of the American forces on the Continent. But it was Henry Johnson's good fortune to belong to a combat unit, not a labor battalion. He was a member of the 15th National Guard of New York which became the 369th Infantry. This outfit developed into one of the foremost fighting forces in the American army. Also, it possessed the finest group of musicians in the army. The 369th Regiment Band conducted by James Reese Europe, assisted by Noble Sissle, is credited with introducing American jazz abroad. It gave concerts for all the fighting units, as well as for civilians in Paris and other cities. Of this band the soldiers often said, "They certainly have enough jazz in stock to last until the war is over."

The 369th Infantry was the first group of Negro combat troops to arrive in Europe, landing in December, 1917. That spring they withstood the Germans at Bois d'Hauza for more than two months. After a summer of training in open warfare, the outfit then went into action at Champagne, and did not cease fighting until they had reached the Rhine—the first Americans to cut through the German lines to that river. For more than six months they were continually under battle conditions. They held one trench ninety-one days without relief. They never retreated, and never was one of their men captured by the enemy. Of these fighters, their commander, Colonel William Hayward, said, "There is no better soldier material in the world." Upon the arrival of the 369th at the Rhine, the entire regiment was awarded the Croix de Guerre by the French government, having previously been cited for bravery eleven times. And two of its members, Needham Roberts and Henry Johnson, had been the first American soldiers in the war to receive individually the Croix de Guerre, awarded for unusual bravery in action.

One dark night these two privates were doing guard duty alone at an outpost not far from the enemy lines. About 2 a.m. a raiding party of some twenty Germans crept through the blackness and attacked their post with a volley of hand grenades. Both Johnson and Roberts were wounded. Roberts was hurt so badly he could not rise, but nevertheless, he was able to hand up grenades for Johnson to throw at the Germans, who by now had almost reached the post. Soon a full-scale battle was in progress between the two Negroes and the Germans. As Johnson later reported the action in conversation, he began modestly, "There isn't so much to tell. There wasn't anything so fine about it. Just fought for my life. A rabbit would have done that."

"Well, anyway, me and Needham Roberts were on patrol duty on May 15th. The corporal wanted to send out two new drafted men on the sentry post for the midnight-to-four job. I told him he was crazy to send untrained men out there and risk the rest of us. I said I'd tackle the job, though I needed sleep. German snipers had been shooting our way that night and I told the corporal he wanted men on the job who knew their rifles. He said it was imagination, but anyway he took those green men off and left Needham and me on the posts. I went on at midnight. Roberts was at the next post. At one o'clock a sniper took a crack at me from a bush fifty yards away. Pretty soon there was more firing and when Sgt. Roy Thompson came along I told him."

"What's the matter, men, you scared?" he asked.

"No, I ain't scared," I said, "I came over here to do my bit and I'll do it. But I was just lettin' you know there's liable to be some tall scrappin' around this post tonight."

"He laughed and went on, and I began to get ready. They'd a box of hand grenades there and I took them out of the box and laid them all in a row where they would be handy. There was about thirty grenades, I guess. I was goin' to bust that Dutch army in pieces if it bothered me."

"Somewhere around two o'clock I heard the Germans cutting our wire out in front and I called to Roberts. When he came I told him to pass the word to the lieutenant. He had just started off when the snippin' and clippin' of the wires sounded near, so I let go with a hand grenade. There was a yell from a lot of surprised Dutchmen and then they started firing. I hollered to Needham to come back. A German grenade got Needham in the arm and through the hip. He was too badly wounded to do any fighting, so I told him to lie in the trench and hand me up the grenades. Keep your nerve I told him. All the Dutchmen in the woods are at us, but keep cool and we'll lick 'em. Roberts crawled into the dugout, some of the shots got me, one clipped my head, another my lip, another my hand, some in my side, and one smashed my left foot."

"The Germans came from all sides. Roberts kept handing me the grenades and I kept throwing them and the Dutchmen kept squealing, but jes' the same they kept comin' on. When the grenades were all gone I started in with my rifle. That was all right until I shoved in an American cartridge clip—it was a French gun—and it jammed. There was nothing to do but use my rifle as a club and jump into them. I banged them on the dome, and the sides, and everywhere I could land until the butt of my rifle busted. One of the Germans hollered, 'Rush him! Rush him!' I decided to do some rushing myself. I grabbed my French bolo knife and slashed in a million directions. Each slash meant something, believe me. I wasn't doing exercise, let me tell you!"

By now other Germans had seized the wounded Needham Roberts and were dragging him off as a prisoner. Johnson ran after them, leaped on one of the men's shoulders, and stabbed him with a bolo knife he carried in his cartridge belt. "I picked out an officer, a lieutenant I guess he was. I got him and I got some more of them. They knocked me around considerable and whanged me on the head, but I always managed to get back on my feet. There was one guy that bothered me. He climbed on my back and I had some job shaking him off and pitching him over my head. Then I stuck him in the ribs with the bolo. I stuck one guy in the stomach and he yelled in good New York talk: 'That black so-and-so got me.' "

The Germans, as they saw one man after another fall, thought surely there must be a large number of American soldiers against them, so they turned to flee. As they scrambled through the barbed wire barricades, Johnson pelted them with hand grenades and brought down several more in pools of blood.

When this short pre-dawn encounter was over, four Germans lay dead and several more were wounded. The raiding-party had abandoned seven wire cutters, three Luegers, and forty hand grenades. Johnson had rescued his badly wounded companion, Roberts, too—thus sustaining the record of the 369th that not a single man of the regiment was ever captured. Reports of this encounter of May 15, 1918, between the two Negro Americans and some twenty Germans, with the Americans routing the enemy, received wide coverage in the press. The two men were hailed as heroes, particularly Johnson who had kept his comrade in arms from being dragged away to a German prison camp. The *New York "World"* called the affray the "Battle of Henry Johnson" and it became front page news in the American papers.

Henry Johnson, while he spent many weeks in a French hospital behind the lines, was promoted to the rank of sergeant. Most of the bones had to be removed from a shattered foot. In place of a shin bone in one leg, when he was released from the hospital, he had a silver tube. And on his body there were a half dozen permanent scars from less serious wounds. To him and to Roberts the Republic of France gave one of its proudest emblems, the Croix de Guerre with a star and golden palm. Of Roberts the citation said, "A good and brave soldier." And of Johnson, "a magnificent example of courage and energy." At war's end the French government gave to Johnson's regiment, the 369th, the signal honor of being the first Allied unit to march onto enemy soil. On November 17th, 1918, as the advance guard of the French Army of Occupation on the Rhine, the 369th took over three German towns. As one of its citations stated, this regiment had "fought with great bravery, stormed powerful enemy positions energetically defended, captured many machine guns, large numbers of prisoners, and six cannon." And among the bravest of its fighters was little Henry Johnson, a gallant soldier.

Dorie Miller
A Hero of Pearl Harbor

1919–1943

A hero, says the dictionary, is "a doer of great or brave deeds; a man of distinguished valor or intrepidity; a prominent or central personage in any remarkable action or event." In the very first few moments of conflict at Pearl Harbor, Dorie Miller became a hero—the first Negro hero of World War II.

The twenty-three-year-old Miller was a messman on the battleship *West Virginia*—the only rating he was permitted to hold as a colored man. Before Pearl Harbor Negroes could not serve in any branch of the Navy except the stewards department; in other words, they could serve only as servants. Dorie Miller was not supposed to fire a gun. But that is just what he did on that fateful morning when the Japanese planes attacked the Pacific fleet at Pearl Harbor. While firing, he brought down four Japanese bombers.

Dorie Miller was born on a farm near Waco, Texas, the son of share-croppers. He grew to be a big 200-pounder and the star fullback on the Moore High School football team in Waco as well as a very good boxer later. When he was nineteen Dorie enlisted in the Navy. He was nearing the end of his first stretch when the Japanese, without a declaration of war, attacked the United States Naval Base in Hawaii. Early on that peaceful Sunday morning of December 7, 1941, Dorie Miller was on breakfast duty below decks, serving as a mess attendant in the junior officers' wardroom of the *West Virginia*. The night before, at various naval officers' clubs there had been the usual Saturday night dances. Many officers who had been out late had not awakened as yet so were off duty. There was little to do that morning in the almost empty mess hall. Only two men were eating. The room was quiet when suddenly Dorie heard a distant explosion. But he was accustomed to such sounds and paid no attention to it. None of the men in the mess hall knew that Japanese pilots had just dropped a bomb on the seaplane hangars at the tip of Ford Island or that the following explosion was a torpedo landing on the battleship *Utah* across the island. No one dreamed that Pearl Harbor would be attacked that Sunday morning just when the entire Pacific

Fleet happened to be at anchor there. The Japanese had planned their sneak attack very carefully indeed. Four hundred of the planes swept in from the sea without interference by American aviation. Our great naval base was caught completely off-guard. For the first few moments no one knew what was happening. But within five minutes, Pearl Harbor was a shambles.

Suddenly aboard the *West Virginia* the public address system began broadcasting the alarm: "Air Raid! Air Raid! This is not a drill." In the room where Dorie Miller was waiting table, officers and messmen dropped whatever they had in hand as alarm bells rang and headed for the deck. By now the Sunday morning calm was shattered by ear-splitting detonations across the island and at that very moment a half-dozen Japanese torpedo planes were aiming at Battleship Row on the other side where, with eight more vessels, the *West Virginia* lay at anchor. A torpedo fell nearby and bullets from a strafing plane spattered the ship's deck. Then the *Oklahoma,* a few hundred yards away, was ripped by a torpedo. Two torpedoes fell on the nearby *Arizona;* then, suddenly, the *West Virginia* began to shudder from stem to stern as the first series of bombs hit her decks. Men were knocked down on their way up from quarters, others were hurled through space, lockers and tables overturned and heavy steel doors blown shut. The ship buckled and rolled beneath the impact of explosives hurtling from the skies. Just north of the *West Virginia,* the *Arizona,* squarely hit, burst into flames and exploded with an ear-splitting roar. Eleven hundred men went to their deaths aboard the ship or were blown into a harbor aflame with burning oil.

Meanwhile, Messman Dorie Miller reached the main deck of his ship just as a bomb tore away a part of the bridge and a slug of searing metal ripped into the Captain's stomach. Captain Mervyn Bennion fell to the deck, but still conscious and much concerned about what was happening to his ship. Miller lifted his captain up and carried him to a safer spot, where he died. An ensign called to Miller to come and help pass ammunition to two machine gunners on the forward deck. But by then Japanese torpedoes were falling thick and fast. Bombs bursting, ammunition from the supply stacks of burning American ships flying through the air as it exploded and anti-aircraft shells falling caused general bedlam everywhere. The noise was deafening. One of the gunners Miller was asked to aid had been struck down. But the young messman who was not supposed to know how to use a machine gun took over. Dorie Miller is credited with bringing down four Japanese dive bombers before his gun was rendered useless. Amazingly enough, Dorie himself was not wounded, in spite of the strafing of enemy tailguns in the swift little planes that followed the bombers.

When the smoke of that initial battle cleared and all America knew that we were at war with the Japanese, Dorie Miller went back to being a messman again. He served aboard the aircraft carrier *Liscome Bay* where he was given an advancement to Mess Attendant Third Class. Secretary of the Navy Frank Knox had personally commended Miller for his bravery at the moment of attack. And Admiral Chester W. Nimitz, Commander-in-Chief of the Pacific Fleet, presided at the ceremonies aboard ship when Dorie Miller was awarded the Navy Cross. The Admiral personally pinned the ribbon of this medallion on the chest of the tall, dark hero, citing him for "distinguished devotion to duty, extraordinary courage and disregard for his own personal safety during the attack on Pearl Harbor."

In December 1943, Dorie Miller was killed in action in the South Pacific. Now, every year in Chicago, the Dorie Miller Memorial Foundation holds a service in his honor and in New York City a group of cooperative houses bears his name.

Benjamin O. Davis, Jr.
General of the Air Force

1912–

Upon his completion of fifty years' service in the United States Army, Brigadier General Benjamin O. Davis, Sr., received a scroll from the Commander in Chief of the Armed Forces, President Franklin D. Roosevelt. General Davis was an army career man, devoting his life to the service. His son, Benjamin O. Davis, Jr., followed in his father's footsteps and, like his father, eventually became a Brigadier General. But the elder Davis worked himself up from the ranks; the younger Davis began at West Point.

Both Davises were born in Washington, the father in 1877, the son in 1912. Benjamin Oliver Davis, Sr., attended Howard University at the capital. When the Spanish-American War broke out, Davis enlisted and saw service in Cuba. He had attained the rank of First Lieutenant when he was mustered out. And by then the army was in his blood. After three months of civilian life, he enlisted again, starting over as a buck private in a cavalry unit, but he was soon promoted to Sergeant. After five years of service he became a First Lieutenant; in 1915 a Captain; in 1917 a Major; and during World War I, a Lieutenant Colonel of the Ninth Cavalry, and one of the four top ranking Negro officers in the armed services. In 1930 he became a full Colonel, and in 1940 a Brigadier General, the highest rank yet attained by a man of color in the United States Army.

During his long military career the elder Davis saw service in three wars as well as serving in periods of peace in the Philippine Islands, as Military Attaché to the American Legation at Monrovia, Liberia, and instructor in the science of soldiering at Wilberforce University in Ohio, at Alabama's famed Tuskegee Institute, and as commanding officer of the 369th Infantry of the New York National Guard. Among other duties in 1929 Davis escorted a large group of Gold Star mothers to Europe to visit the graves of their sons killed in World War I. During World War II he was appointed special advisor to the commander of the European Theatre of Operations. At the close of the war he became an assistant to the Inspector General of the Army, and later an advisor of the Secretary of War. In 1948 Brigadier General Davis was retired from active duty. His medals by then included the Bronze Star, the French Croix de Guerre, and the Distinguished Service Medal.

About the time that his son, Benjamin, was born, the elder Davis was recalled from Liberia and assigned to service in the Mexican Border Patrol. When Ben, Jr., was five years old, his mother died, so for a time he lived with a grandmother. But when he was about seven, his father married again, then young Ben went to live with him and his new mother at Tuskegee. Later the family moved to Cleveland, Ohio. Here Ben finished the grammar grades and was graduated as president of his class at Central High School. For a year he attended Western Reserve University, but transferred to the University of Chicago for the remainder of his college work. He majored in mathematics.

In Chicago the Negro Congressman, Oscar De Priest, took an interest in young Davis and, feeling that he should follow in his father's footsteps, appointed him a candidate for the United States Military Academy at West Point. Young Ben, however, was not sure he wanted to attend West Point, from which no Negro had been graduated in almost fifty years, since Charles Young's graduation. A number of Negroes had been appointed, but rumor had it that prejudice made life so difficult for them at the Academy that they either dropped out or had been flunked out before finishing their studies. And then, if one did graduate, there was in the United States only a strictly segregated army in which Negroes might enroll. All his life Ben's father had seen service only in all-Negro units, and in such units there was room for but a very few colored officers. Young Ben Davis did not approach his examinations for West Point with enthusiasm. And when he took them, he failed.

Perhaps it was the jolt of failure that made Ben decide to defeat his own pessimism, and to prove to himself that he *could* enter West Point— *and remain there.* Reappointed a second time, Ben settled down to several weeks of hard study. He took the examinations again, and this time passed. On the first day of July, 1932, he entered West Point. The news made all the papers, and white Americans and black Americans alike wondered if this young Negro would stick it out. He would be the only colored student at the Point and, like all freshmen, subjected to hazing on the part of upper classmen. But for him, a colored boy, would the hazing be so severe it would cause him to drop out? Would the prejudice of those who still thought of Negroes as an inferior race make life so miserable he could not stay? In his book, *We Have Tomorrow,* Arna Bontemps has written about Ben's experiences at West Point as follows:

"There is no longer any doubt that a significant American drama was acted out during those four tense years—a drama which came close to tragedy at times and which finally had a happy ending only through the heroism of its leading character. Ben started life at West Point in the same way as any boy who has grown up in the cosmopolitan schools of great northern cities like Cleveland and Chicago. Many of the boys of his class were from the same general background. They were like the fellows at the University and at Central High. Ben made acquaintances among them swiftly and seemed on the way to a normal school year, when something happened. It started with whispers in locker rooms and in hallways. Somebody was passing a word around. Ben could feel rather than hear what they were saying, and he was sure that the 'word' concerned him. Within a day or two he knew it, for all the boys stopped speaking to him. Somebody had organized the demonstration and the others, boy-like and easily led, took it up and fell in line. Few could have realized the unfairness, the unworthiness of this behavior. Perhaps some of the boys resisted those who took the lead, but feared to stand out against what they believed to be the majority. In any case, it continued and became more marked as time passed. Nobody did anything which could be described as hostile of itself, yet nobody co-operated with Ben. No one greeted him. If he asked a simple question he was not answered. If he approached a group in which a conversation was in progress, all talking suddenly ceased. He was left alone—completely alone. His classmates were giving him the 'silent treatment.' . . . It is hard to believe that any group of boys could continue a demonstration of this kind for a whole year. It is also hard to believe that a solitary colored boy could last it out—especially when one remembers how easy it is to give up under a strain. The silence, with slight interruptions, lasted through Ben's plebe year, and Ben stood up to it until the end. Taller than most of his fellows, as handsome as anybody who wore the uniform, as fond of companionship and good fun as any boy, Ben took what was dished out to him without a whimper or a complaint. Never once did he let anyone think that he depended on others for his happiness. He simply took the medicine.

"The demonstration ended even more dramatically than it had begun. At the end of the first year at the Military Academy there is always an important gathering at which those plebes who have stood up under the hard conditioning of the testing year are congratulated by their superiors and in turn congratulate each other. Ben Davis came to this annual ceremony congratulating himself silently and thinking that at least he had accomplished something for all those colored people who had kept their fingers crossed as they waited to see what would happen to this second colored boy to face the grim music of West Point in recent years. . . . To his complete surprise, however, a miracle happened. When the preliminaries were over and the boys were free to congratulate each other and to receive the congratulations of upperclassmen, Ben suddenly discovered that he was surrounded. They swarmed around him. They cheered him noisily and shook his hand until his arm was weak. Ben Davis, Jr., had stood the most severe test any boy had stood at West Point in at least fifty years, and he had passed it to the satisfaction of the whole class of his fellows. The wall of silence fell down like the walls of Jericho, and was never raised again."

On June 12, 1936, the graduation ceremonies were held and Benjamin O. Davis, Jr., received his diploma from General John J. Pershing, plus his commission as Second Lieutenant. That same year he married Agatha Scott of New Haven, and was assigned as an officer of infantry at Fort Benning, Georgia, in the heart of the South. A year later he was promoted to First Lieutenant; in 1939 he became a Captain, then a Major, and in 1942 a Lieutenant Colonel. Meanwhile he had served as a Professor of Military Tactics at Tuskegee, and as Aide-de-Camp to his father during his time as Commanding General of the 4th Cavalry Brigade at Fort Riley, Kansas. While young Davis was at Fort Riley in 1940 the Air Force, which had hitherto not admitted Negroes as pilots, changed its policy, and established an Advanced Army Flying School for the training of young colored officers at Tuskegee. Davis was among the first to enroll in the spring of 1941, and the following year he won his wings. Meanwhile, the United States had become embroiled in World War II. Upon graduation from the Army Flying School, Davis was placed in command of the all-Negro 99th Pursuit Squadron then preparing to go overseas to the European battlefronts. The members of this Squadron were the first group of colored pilots to undergo combat service in the American military forces, and their record as bomber escorts and on perilous strafing missions became a gallant one.

So successful was the leadership of young Colonel Davis that in the fall of 1943 he was recalled to the States to direct the training of the 332nd Fighter Group then in formation at Selfridge Field, Michigan. Under his command, the 332nd was assigned to the Mediterranean Theatre as a part of the 12th Fighter Command. This outfit participated in the sinking of an enemy destroyer, protected the 15th Air Force Bombers in their strategic attacks on the Rumanian oil fields, and in the North African and Italian campaigns brought down more than a hundred planes in the air and knocked out a hundred and fifty on the ground. Most of the pilots of the 332nd received the Distinguished Flying Cross.

When the Allied invasion of southern France was planned, to the 332nd Fighter Group under Colonel Davis was given the vital task of destroying the German radar stations on the Mediterranean coast in advance of the Allied landings. The night before the invasion the Negro flyers went into action. They did so thorough a job of knocking out the various enemy bases for air-protection and communications, that when the surprise attack came, the Germans were caught completely off-guard, so among Allied troops there was a minimum of casualties. From destroyers off shore, Prime Minister Winston Churchill and other Allied leaders watched the progress of the highly successful attack, and had only praise for the colored aviators who had prepared the way so well. Many of these men were awarded medals. And Brigadier General Benjamin O. Davis, Sr., proudly pinned on the chest of his son, Colonel Benjamin O. Davis, Jr., the Distinguished Flying Cross. Members of the 332nd participated in the ceremonies. By war's end this intrepid group had flown over Europe more than 3,000 missions and had put out of action some three hundred enemy planes.

As fighters for the Free World, the colored aviators who served under Colonel Davis were also fighting for a greater share of democracy for themselves and their race, not only in the armed forces, but in civilian life on the home front. As to the American military set-up—then undergoing a transition from separate, segregated units of either all white or all-Negro groups—the contributions which the heroism and daring of these colored aviators made to the cause of interracial good will was invaluable. In 1944 the Negro journalist Roi Ottley, reporting from the battlefronts, wrote:

"I have heard more than one Southerner say he hoped, when the war is over, that Negroes would enjoy the social benefits that they are fighting to preserve and extend. The Air Force has perhaps achieved the greatest amount of mutual respect and admiration among its personnel. Negro aviators have been overseas in combat more than nineteen months. They have seen action from Munich to Vienna, from Salerno to Budapest, and from North Africa to Sicily. They have won commendation from General Montgomery for their dive-bombing and strafing of enemy positions both in the Italian and North African campaigns. In the desperate Anzio beachhead assaults, they shot down seventeen enemy fighters and bombers in one day, providing cover for our ground forces. This sort of performance is difficult to refute with nonsense about the 'inferiority' of the Negro, for the facts stand out dramatically and must of necessity make deep inroads into the thinking of every white G.I."

That same year, in addressing the 23rd class of Negro pilots to be graduated from the Tuskegee Army Air Field, their white commanding officer, Colonel Noel Parrish, recalled the exploits of that field's early Negro graduates flying so brilliantly under Colonel Davis. In concluding his speech, he said in part:

"Today the problems of race are still somewhat bewildering. Perhaps we can all find truth earlier if we will take the attitude of mutual respect and understanding, and remember that in all things white people are just as much the victims of their environment and training, or lack of training, as are Negroes. . . . To you the problem of racial adjustment is constant and inescapable. You cannot run away. . . . You must continue to hold up your heads against pity and hatred alike, to do your best and hope for the best. Such advice is easier to give than to follow, but I know of no other way. It is the way you learned to fly. Few of us choose to fight against odds, but perhaps there is some compensation in the fact that to win against them brings a greater glory and a greater personal satisfaction. . . . You will have many disillusionments and embarrassments and perhaps some bewilderment as to just what is desired or expected of you. But men who have the patience and the perseverance to win through the rugged training program you have just finished must have the stamina and courage to achieve even greater things in the future. You now have before you the example of others who have proved it can be done. You can play a mighty part in the greatest battle for all freedom, including your own. See that you are worthy of those who have gone out from this field ahead of you and that you provide an even more inspiring example for those who follow."

The men who had left Tuskegee Air Field before, in 1944 were still in the thick of warfare, and they finished out the conflict with distinction. At the conclusion of hostilities their leader, Colonel Davis, was assigned to the Lockbourne Air Base as commander of the 477th Composite Fighter-Bomber Group. There had been considerable opposition on the part of whites to the stationing of Negro flyers at this major base, but the War Department paid it no heed. Negroes were now being trained as navigators, bombardiers, flight engineers, and in air corps administration, and integration of personnel at various fields was proceeding apace. Colonel Davis remained at Lockbourne until he was assigned for study at the Air War College at Maxwell Base, Montgomery, Alabama, from which he was graduated in 1950. After a period of administrative service at the Air Force Headquarters in Washington, he was appointed by President Eisenhower in 1954 as director of operations and training of the Far Eastern Air Forces in Japan, and in 1955 he was made 2nd in command, and later commander, of the 13th Air Task Force on the Chinese Nationalist island of Formosa, having by now been raised to the rank of Brigadier General. Early in 1957 Davis was appointed a member of the Air Force Board at the Pentagon, and later that year named Deputy Chief of Staff of the 12th Air Force in Germany.

This important assignment made General Davis the third highest ranking officer in the German area of command. Stationed at Ramstein, his work became that of coordinator of the various units of the 12th Air Force, a vital group in the NATO defense plans for Western Europe. From a pessimistic young man who flunked his first examinations for West Point to a flying hero of World War II and now a most valuable officer of the Air Force, Benjamin O. Davis, Jr., well deserves to wear the medals that have been bestowed upon him. Aside from the Distinguished Flying Cross, some are the Air Medal with four Oak Leaf Clusters, the Legion of Merit Award, and the French Croix de Guerre with Palm. For conducting successfully an extremely hazardous mission over Berlin, Davis and his entire 332nd Fighter Group received a Presidential citation—which made his father, a fifty-year veteran, very proud. The two Davises have served their country, militarily speaking, for a long time. And they have served it well.

Index

Note: This index combines the indexes from Hughes's three original volumes. In some
cases, page listings are more extensive than in the original volumes because those
indexes did not always include the same items, even though references to the same
subjects did occur in the books themselves.